The Life & Teachings of Carlos Castaneda

Volume I

William Patrick Patterson

Including Daniel Brinton's 1894 essay
Nagualism: A Study in Native American
Folklore and History

Barbara Allen Patterson, Editor

Arete Communications, Publishers
Fairfax, California

The Life & Teachings of Carlos Castaneda
Including Daniel Brinton's 1894 essay
"Nagualism: A Study in Native American Folklore and History"

Design by Henry Korman
Wordplay Consulting
Korman@wp-consulting.com
Cover: Huichol Indian snakes

Library of Congress Catalog Number is 2007942996
Patterson, William Patrick
The Life & Teachings of Carlos Castaneda
Chronology, Notes, Bibliography, Index, Appendices

1. Carlos Castaneda
2. don Juan Matus
3. G. I. Gurdjieff
4. Sorcery
5. Shamanism
6. Nagualism
7. Fourth Way

First casebound edition 2008
Casebound ISBN: 978-1-879514-97-3
First softcover edition 2009
Softcover ISBN: 978-1-879514-96-6

Printed on Acid-Free Paper ∞
The paper used in this publication meets the minimum requirements of the American National Standard for Information Services—Permanence of Paper for Printed Library Materials, ANSI Z39.48-1984.

Arete Communications
773 Center Boulevard, Box 58
Fairfax, CA 94978-0058
www.Gurdjieff-Legacy.Org
Email: Arete@Gurdjieff-Legacy.Org

www.CarlosNagual.Net

Dedication

To my don Juan

by the same author

Eating The "I"

Struggle of the Magicians

Taking with the Left Hand

Ladies of the Rope

Voices in the Dark

Contents

Chapters

The Writer writes his Letter to the World.
When the World answers it is like
the Sorcerer's Apprentice.
He cannot control what he has summoned.
—Anaïs Nin

Anaïs Nin, from jottings dated 4/1/69 in Folder 1970, UCLA Archives

Prologue

THERE ARE PEOPLE WHOSE LIVES DOMINATE A TIME. We think of them usually as world figures walking the stage of history, reacting to the forces of their time. That is how we have been taught. There are others, however, nowhere near as historically commanding, that either initiate a new perception or reignite an older one, and in so doing create a line of self-questioning whose destination is not so apparent but which issues a direct challenge to what has been the consensus belief. Such a figure for me, and some eight million others who have read his books, is Carlos Castaneda. By the sheer force of his connection with intent, Castaneda brought to life and inseminated into Western culture an age-old sorceric perspective long ago rendered insensible by the modern world's pursuit of rationality.

The brilliance of his early near-archetypal renderings of nonordinary reality clash with his accrued reputation as a manipulator, liar and trickster. And that, no doubt, is the way he would have wanted it. He leaves us in not knowing, in questioning. Like many of those whom he deeply touched, I did not know him or know anyone who did. Yet he excited my imagination and lived in me for a time. The story he told of his apprenticeship to a man of knowledge played its part in leading me to a path of self-transformation. Ultimately, the path was quite different from his, though—as I now see—very much the same, but not in the way one would expect.

I was first introduced to his world and ideas when I was working as a part-time bartender at Remington's, an underground bar in the Village. A noted painter of the time sat at the bar telling a friend in the most astonished tones of a book he was reading, one like no other he had ever read. I went right out and bought *The Teachings of Don Juan: A Yaqui Way of Knowledge.* It enthralled me from the first page. I'd studied philosophy and psychology in college, but the sophistication of the concepts was like nothing I'd ever encountered. What Castaneda was saying was coming from another level entirely. I devoured it. I was right there with him through his second and third books, *A Separate Reality* and *Journey to Ixtlan,* as don Juan brought him deeper and deeper into an experiencing of nonordinary reality.

But his next books seemed forced in some way the others hadn't. The narrative that had been so poetic and incisive suddenly seemed weighted; the dialogue once so dimensional, metaphorical, sometimes mythological, seemed stilted. The information was still there, but the magic was gone. What Castaneda did do for me was nurture the wish that some day I would meet my own "don Juan." And, as happens more often than we realize, I did, though not in the desert of Sonora but a Manhattan skyscraper.

What is the meaning of life? That was the question Castaneda's drug experiences and entry into a nonordinary reality evoked for me. It wasn't an insistent burning question, I was too self-absorbed for that, but his experiences put the question on the table. What was the sense of doing anything if at death it was all taken away from you? With this question still faintly alive in me, one twilight evening, sitting on the stoop of an old brownstone, a friend unexpectedly rolled a joint, offered me a hit and I accepted—though I didn't smoke, didn't much drink, and didn't use drugs of any type, even aspirin. Soon after, though my sense of time had elongated, an old Slavic-looking woman in a babushka hurrying down the street suddenly stopped to talk. At one point she asked me to feel the side of her head. When I put out my hand, she grabbed it and pushed my fingers against her temple. My fingers went right inside her head. It was all mush, no bone! The shock sent a shiver right through my whole body. "I've had a lobotomy," she laughed and still laughing she toddled off. I couldn't know it then, but this prefigured in its way what was going to happen.

Not long after, a fellow named Kevin came to my door to place an ad for his model agency in the small magazine I published and edited, *In New York*. While talking, he told me he was on acid. He seemed "normal." I was surprised. I had thought when you took acid you went off and talked to the devil or thought you could fly. He assured me that wasn't true, or didn't have to be true, and invited me to a party he was throwing that Saturday evening at his penthouse apartment. I soon found myself looking out at an incredible view of the city skyline, as well as an equally incredible assemblage of beautiful women, when Kevin handed me a tiny azure pill which I immediately swallowed.

A half hour or so went by. Nothing happened. Maybe it's a dud, I thought, and asked for another. No sooner had I swallowed the second pill than this queasy feeling hit my stomach and then—*pure perception.* No overlay, no description, no leveling—there was this *seeing.* I saw, or rather, *it* saw, everyone my eyes focused on—in dimension, like folds of an accordion that suddenly stretched full out. People's emotional and psychological states were seen, not only in the present but also as they had been before. Marveling at this, a thought shot into my head: *You are so relaxed. You must be dead.*

You must be dead—like a thought bullet, it hit the mind and lodged there. I tried to get rid of it, think of something else, but the thought stayed; it had implanted itself. In the struggle to get rid of it, the pores of my body opened. All my energy began spilling out. I grew so weak I had to lie on the floor. Kevin came over and knelt down beside me.

"What's happening?" he asked.

I told him about the thought frozen in my head.

"No," he said softly with a knowing smile, "You're not dead, you've just been reborn."

The words clicked. They made coherent what I was feeling but couldn't have formulated. The words were like magic. They reassembled all the parts of me together again.

I stayed throughout the night. Words formed themselves in the immediacy of experiencing. I wrote them down:

We are energy. Energy never dies. It simply passes into new forms, completes old circles. Feelings are energy patterns. Good feelings are harmonious energy patterns. Sex is interacting energy. Bodies are changing covers. Love is the oneness of two consciousnesses that know they are energy.

The next morning, as such experiences sometimes happen, was Easter. There was no thinking about the consciousness that was being experienced—there was no thinking about anything. The assumption, though unformulated, was that this consciousness would never change. But walking home, suddenly there was the sensation of a familiar gait, the slight hunch of the shoulders—not through thought but through the body "Patterson" had returned. Amazing. I went home and crashed. When I woke up I was back in the old consciousness. The only change was that the body felt really "wasted." The difference between the experience of having once been so wide and deep and now so narrow and shallow had left an imprint and created a question:

If I can do this on drugs, how can I do it naturally?

During the summer I read Alan Watts' *The Book: On the Taboo Against Knowing Who You Are.* I could only take in a few pages. The ideas crashed like waves against a lifetime of rock-hard societal belief. Then I read P. D. Ouspensky's *In Search of the Miraculous.* The ideas were clear, precise, practical, of great scale. There was no personalization, no "sorceric twist." The ideas were said to come from a conscious level of humanity. They were even sharper, deeper, of greater scale than don Juan's. The ideas set my mind and feelings on fire. . . . But then the company I had sold *In New York* to went bankrupt. I was just another creditor.

The magazine had been my life. All my dreams destroyed, I was left with nothing. I still walked around, talking and acting like everyone else, but inside I had "died." Only then, at the lowest point in my life, paradoxically but also necessarily, did I meet my "don Juan." He was not a Yaqui Indian but a British businessman, a "Lord" no less, whose office, The American-British Electric Corporation, The Hunting Group of Companies, was in Rockefeller Center. That meeting and my don Juan telling me that drugs "weakened the will and cultivated imagination and fantasy in higher emotional center" ended whatever interest was left in Castaneda and his world. But it had shown me that, looking from our viewpoint, consciousness had many levels. But nothing is free. There is always a payment. Without knowing it, I was looking for a "hit." But consciousness isn't a hit. It took a lot of observation to realize the assumption hidden in my question—*If I can do this on drugs, how can I do it naturally?* It presupposed the idea of my being an indivisible I, that this "Patterson" which I took myself to be was going to do this.

Some twenty-eight years passed and I never gave a thought to Carlos Castaneda. But then he died, and shortly afterward his last major book was published, *The Active Side of Infinity*—such a great title. What did it mean? I wondered what he had come to, our paths apparently being so different. I had heard that Castaneda had spent a weekend with *my* don Juan at a retreat. Then I read that Castaneda had met the Nagual woman, Carol Tiggs, when she was a student of my don Juan. When in Los Angeles, I visited his "compound," as he called it, in Westwood and found it enclosed by twelve-foot hedges. At the site of Ships restaurant, the scene after Castaneda's "jump into the abyss," I found only a towering pole remained with its symbol of a rocket flying into space. My interest piqued, I began rereading his books. And now the hidden correspondences between his ideas and those I had studied and practiced suddenly became apparent. The years were coming full circle. . . .

This book, *The Life & Teachings of Carlos Castaneda,* presumptuous as the title may sound, is my journey back into his world. It is by no means definitive, but it does represent what I have learned of this enigmatic, highly gifted and guilt-ridden man of sorceric mystery whose experiences of nonordinary reality in the deserts of Sonora and streets of Los Angeles so powerfully reinserted the idea of the sorceric-shamanic-warrior into our modern world.

—William Patrick Patterson
San Anselmo, California

1

Paths of Heart

HE SAID THAT HE FOLLOWED THE PATHS OF THE HEART, THE PATHS HIS TEACHER DON JUAN MATUS DESCRIBED:

> For me there is only the traveling on paths that have heart, on any path that may have heart. There I travel, and the only worthwhile challenge is to traverse its full length. And there I travel looking, looking, breathlessly.

This vision, both mythical and magical, ignited a whole generation to renew the search for what a seeker from a much earlier generation had called:

> An entirely new or forgotten road [that lay] beyond the thin film of false reality. . . . The war, in the possibility of which I had not wanted to believe and the reality of which I did not for a long time wish to acknowledge, had become a fact. We were in it and I saw that it must be taken as a great *memento mori* showing that hurry was necessary and that it was impossible to believe in "life" which led nowhere.

The exploration of a separate reality on this "new or forgotten road" was founded on giving up self-importance and membership in the conventional notion of reality. Initially for Carlos Castaneda, entry into the sorcerer's world of seeing, energetic facts, allies, stalking and dreaming was through the use of "power plants" and only later through energetic techniques.

This sorceric world first became publicly known with the publication in April 1968 of *The Teachings of Don Juan: A Yaqui Way of Knowledge*, a thrice rewritten and revised master's thesis by an unknown, quirky UCLA anthropology student. Bearing the academic imprint of a prestigious university press, reviewed enthusiastically by distinguished professors of anthropology, and telling of a nonordinary reality inhabited by mysterious powers and beings, the book quickly sold out on college campuses. It became "a runaway best seller," eventually selling millions of copies in the U.S. and throughout the world.

Three years later, in 1971, Carlos Castaneda published *A Separate Reality: Further Conversations with Don Juan*, and it, too, became a best seller. The following year saw the publication of his doctoral thesis, "Sorcery: A Description of the World," retitled for the mass market as *Journey to Ixtlan: Lessons of Don Juan.* The books gave him financial freedom and made the name Carlos Castaneda famous the world over.

With the trilogy published, one might have thought it would all end there, but the very next year Castaneda published still a fourth book, *Tales of Power.* Stranger than its predecessors, it ends with a great climactic scene.

> Don Juan and don Genaro stepped back and seemed to merge with the darkness. Pablito held my forearm and we said good-bye to each other. Then a strange urge, a force, made me run with him to the northern edge of the mesa. I felt his arm holding me as we jumped and then I was alone.

Certainly, that should have ended the series of books, for "Carlos Castaneda" had died. But of course the author lived to tell us he died—so the "dying" can only have been metaphorical or allegorical. If there was to be another book, we could reasonably expect that Castaneda would tell what actually happened. But when *The Second Ring of Power* was published in 1977, Castaneda seemed as confused about whether or not he actually jumped from the mesa as he was in the very first book about whether or not he flew like a crow.

In the following twenty-one years he would publish seven more books—*The Eagle's Gift, The Fire from Within, The Power of Silence, The Art of Dreaming* and *The Active Side of Infinity*, plus *Magical Passes* and *The Wheel of Time*—each taking the reader deeper and deeper into a nonordinary reality that becomes increasingly bizarre, violent and dangerous, as they serve to break what Castaneda came to call "the human mold." It is a reality predicated on ideas of losing self-importance, recapitulating one's life, erasing personal history, intent, recognizing the "foreign installation," moving the "assemblage point," stopping the world, inner silence, seeing energetic facts, awareness of the Second Attention, the *Tonal* and *Nagual*, dreaming, the "flyers" and "seymours," the Eagle, the Death Defier, becoming a sorceric inorganic being whose awareness lasts as long as the earth exists, entering the definitive journey.

Just who was Carlos César Salvador Aranha Castañeda? He was born on Christmas Day 1925 in Cajamarca, Peru. His father's family came from Italy and had roots in São Paulo, Brazil. His father, César Aranha Burungaray, was an Italian watchmaker and goldsmith. Castaneda's feelings for him were ambiguous—"I despised my father beyond anything I could say, and at the same time I loved him, with a sadness that was unmatched." The sadness was because his father always spoke of living by ideal acts but never actually did so. Margaret Runyan, Carlos Castaneda's wife, remembers him "disparaging his father, calling him an intellectual, a teacher, a literary man who had never written a thing. . . . What he really disliked was that his father was average, that everything ran on schedule. 'I never want to be like that,' he said." But she believes Castaneda was not so much talking about his father as himself, the fear that he would be "average." The phrase "the average man" appears again and again in his books. The grandfather, a short, red-haired, craggy-faced Italian immigrant, was the real patriarch of the Castaneda side of the family. Except for the red hair, Castaneda bears a strong resemblance to him.

His relationship with his mother, Susana Castañeda Navoa, was also ambiguous. During a peyote session he said, "I suddenly felt the horrendous burden of my mother's love. When I heard her name I was torn apart; the memory of my mother filled me with anguish and melancholy, but when I examined her I knew that I had never liked her." Castaneda believed his parents had injured him. Don Juan told him, "I believe that your parents did injure you by making you indulgent and soft and given to dwelling."

His mother died in 1949. Castaneda was twenty-four years old. Her death, despite his feelings, left him so grief stricken that he locked himself in his room for three days without eating. When he opened the door he announced he was going to America. During those three days, Runyan says, "Carlos concluded that his attachment to his mother had been too strong and the only way to avoid that in the future was to fight his notions of attachment and dependency."

José Bracamonte, a friend and fellow student at the National Fine Arts School in Lima, Peru—Castaneda wanted to be an artist—remembers that going to America was a desire Castaneda "harbored like an obsession." Bracamonte also said, "We all liked Carlos. He was witty, imaginative, cheerful—a big liar and a real friend."

Two years after his mother's death a new major octave began. At the age of twenty-six he left Peru, and a pregnant fiancée, and came to America. Four years later—four years in which his whereabouts are uncertain—he met Margaret Runyan. It was December 1955. She remembers Castaneda as:

> A short dark man, with black curly hair that gathered in a dangling cluster of tiny curls at the forehead. His eyes were large and brown and the left iris floated out a bit, giving [the impression] that one eye was always looking beyond you. It was a flaw that he sought to hide

> by squinting quizzically or looking away, which made him seem painfully shy. He had the look of a high countryman, short but slim with an ample chest, thin eyebrows, a broad, and ingratiating smile, and the aquiline nose of one with more than a random share of Indian genes.

He said nothing but she was intrigued. Her friend warned her that he had power, that "he can charm your soul, he is a *curandero*, a shaman, a magician." So even before he met don Juan, Castaneda evinced power. There were many *curanderos* at herb stands in the market at Cajamarca buying and selling magic plants. Perhaps he had learned something from them or was simply born with a charismatic power.

Runyan gave him a book, *The Search,* with her name and phone number in it, but Castaneda never called. The book was by Neville Goddard, a local mystic and guru who taught what he called "controlled imagination" (which Castaneda would later call "controlled dreaming"), a spin-off perhaps of Carl Jung's "active imagination." For six months Runyan concentrated intensely, imagining Castaneda coming to see her. He finally did so in June 1956. A relationship began.

Reading Aldous Huxley's *The Doors of Perception* about the author's experiences with LSD, Andrija Puharich's *The Sacred Mushroom,* Gordon Wasson's *Mushrooms, Russia and History*, and Weston La Barre's *The Peyote Cult*, Castaneda was immediately taken by the idea of using drugs to gain spiritual awareness. According to Runyan, he had experimented with mushrooms, peyote cactus and jimsonweed long before the summer of 1960, when he met don Juan.

Castaneda enrolled in Los Angeles City College and

supported himself with odd jobs. In 1959 he graduated with an Associate of Arts degree in pre-psychology. In January 1960 he and Runyan married in Tijuana. But the marriage didn't last. Six months afterward the two drove back to Tijuana and got a divorce. Later, as he'd had a vasectomy, he convinced a friend to impregnate Runyan and then adopted the boy, Carlton Jeremy Castaneda. Only much later she learned the divorce papers he showed her were a fake. (It wasn't until 1973 that the divorce was final.) "He had a habit of going full-bore into relationships," she said, "and then breaking them off suddenly, sometimes pretending he had never heard of the person."

The next major octave for Castaneda began in 1960. Not only did he marry Runyan but he took an undergraduate class in ethnography at UCLA with the archeologist Clement Meighan, who had helped to develop the university's anthropology department. Meighan required a term paper and anyone who interviewed an Indian automatically aced the course. "Carlos wanted something [a topic] sufficiently deep and scholarly to assure publication," said Meighan, "so he could get into graduate school and yet something kinky enough to sustain his interest." He finally decided on ethnobotany, the classification of psychotropic plants that sorcerers use. Reading his paper on don Juan Matus—Runyan says Mateus was Castaneda's favorite wine, "which he jokingly referred to as his most valuable teacher"—and the use of datura, Meighan was delighted and praised the paper which later would become the template for *The Teachings of Don Juan.* Besides Meighan, the professor who made the biggest impression on Castaneda was UCLA sociology professor Harold Garfinkel, a Jewish scholar in his fifties known for his ponderous discourses on phenomenology, the philosophy developed by Edmund Husserl (1859–1938) whose three-volume work, *Logical Investigations,* was published 1900 to 1903. The term "phenomenology" wasn't new. The philosophers of the 1700s used it to mean the abstraction of consciousness and experience from objects, gross and subtle, within a philosophical matrix. It also meant how self-consciousness developed from primary sensations to rational thought.

For Husserl though, as Castaneda would write,

> Phenomenology was a philosophical method for the study of essences, or the act of putting those essences into the flux of life experience. He thought of it as a transcendental philosophy dealing only with the residue left after a reduction is performed. He called this reduction *epoché*, the bracketing of meaning or the suspension of judgment. . . . Husserl expected to inject into any given philosophical inquiry, as an integral part, a world that exists before reflection begins. He intended Phenomenology to be a method for approaching living experience as it occurs in time and space; it is an attempt to describe directly our experience as it happens, without pausing to consider its origins or its causal explanation.
>
> To achieve this task, Husserl proposed *epoché*: a total change of attitude where the philosopher moves from things themselves to their meanings; that is to say, from the realm of objectified meaning—the core of science—to the realm of meaning as it is experienced in the immediate life-world.

Hence, Husserl's famous dictum—"To the things themselves!"

The approach then was to focus exclusively on the essential structure of perceptual consciousness—all preconceptions about an object were to be erased—so that it, in itself, could be seen. Garfinkel held that socialization depended on the agreement of descriptions defining the real world. Whatever people agree on as true becomes true for them. (As an example, when Captain Cook's ship anchored in the bay, none of the natives could see his ship; it didn't fit their description of the world.) Garfinkel, Castaneda's doctoral supervisor, held Castaneda to a high standard and made him revise and rewrite what became his master's thesis three times.

Garfinkel had applied many of the concepts of phenomenology in the creation of ethno-methodology. Its primary idea is that every kind of reality is subjective, or at least "intersubjective," the result of people talking about things using language that signified their membership in a society or particular category of society. The fundamental practice of ethno-methodology was to question the unquestioned, to make a problem of what hitherto had been unproblematic. Before ethno-methodology, sociology and anthropology had focused on how members of a society interrelated. Garfinkel and his fellow ethnos put the focus on how sociologists and anthropologists *themselves* related to the society they were in the act of describing.

According to Richard de Mille, a Castaneda debunker familiar with what was going on,

> Garfinkel thought up some diabolical schemes for calling assumptions into question, techniques labeled "breaching" procedures because they tore holes in people's shared understand-

> ings and disrupted their social relations. Students went home on vacation with instructions to act like boarders. They were told to conduct conversations as though they suspected the other person were trying to trick or mislead them. They learned to talk with people whose noses their noses were almost touching. They were authorized to mistake people's social roles, like persistently demanding a table in a full restaurant from a person who was only another unseated customer. And, in a technique that was soon dubbed "Garfinkeling" on the UCLA campus, students were taught to pretend they didn't know the meaning of ordinary words. This was to teach the breachers that human interactions, particularly conversations, depended on shared but unstable assumptions.

Garfinkel had seen Castaneda's manuscript of *The Teachings of Don Juan* as early as 1962—six years before it was published. When Castaneda went into a long analysis of his encounters with don Juan, Garfinkel told him:

"Don't *explain* to me. You are a nobody. Just give it to me straight and in detail, the way it happened. The richness of detail is the whole story of membership."

"He didn't like my efforts to explain don Juan Matus's behavior psychologically," said Castaneda.

When Castaneda argued his point of view, Garfinkel shut him off dismissively, saying, "Do you want to be the darling of Esalen?"

It was either rewrite the manuscript as Garfinkel demanded or face an interminable wait for his master's degree. In a sense, then, Garfinkel's views really were the substrate to the published book.

Arnold Mandell, a former student of Garfinkel's, now a psychiatry professor at UC San Diego, thinks that in the end what Castaneda did was to give Garfinkel just what he wanted. Said Richard de Mille:

> Mandell suspected that in making Castaneda rewrite an intended thesis three times Garfinkel had imposed his ethnographic nihilism so ruthlessly that the wily graduate student had determined to go him one better, to "outgarfinkel Garfinkel," to prepare a beautifully wrapped empty package, a bogus thesis, a fake ethnography, which would achieve continuity and a sense of reality, thereby demonstrating the student's capacity to manipulate ethnomethodologic tools without contradicting the master's teaching that all reality in social science was manufactured by social scientists.

But de Mille, psychologist and son of the film producer Cecil B. DeMille, and an embittered former Scientologist—he did the publicity for L. Ron Hubbard in the early 1950s—thinks that Mandell carries it a bit too far. If Castaneda met don Juan, as he says, in the summer of 1960, and he tells his wife about it shortly thereafter when he was still an undergraduate, then the stories began to be embellished long before he met Garfinkel. More likely, contends de Mille, "I suspect the two men found each other perfect partners, whose respective needs, interests, and talents were mutually sustaining. It may have been a beautiful collaboration."

In his last major book, *The Active Side of Infinity*, Castaneda speaks of a "Professor Lorca," a thinly veiled Garfinkel. He writes that he enrolled in his class on cognition (a big word in Castaneda's books), as he was "one of the most brilliant academics in existence." To him the professor's most novel idea was that "every individual of every species on this earth interprets the world around it, using data reported by its specialized senses." That Castaneda dedicated this last book to Meighan and Garfinkel shows his enduring respect for these men. That aside, as a student Castaneda found himself caught in what he speaks of as "a most deadly juxtaposition of ideas that had me mercilessly in its grip: don Juan's wisdom and Professor Lorca's knowledge." It was sorcery versus phenomenology with Castaneda in between. These two cognitions, of two different descriptions of reality, fought within Castaneda's mind. He had to somehow meld them together, or choose between them.

Castaneda often visited Professor Garfinkel at his home in the Pacific Palisades. A rigorous, no-nonsense intellect, still Garfinkel found himself increasingly intrigued by the young Peruvian's research. Once, in the middle of one of their scholarly conversations, Castaneda suddenly announced that the ally, an inorganic being whom he had contacted, was on the professor's porch. Would it be all right if he invited it inside?

"Oh, that's all right, Carlos," Garfinkel said calmly, pulling back in his chair. "That's fine. I believe that the ally's here, so it's all right."

Had Castaneda gone bonkers? Garfinkel had to wonder. That sometimes happened to anthropologists who became too deeply identified with alien cultures. If he allowed the ally to come into his home, Garfinkel could just hear what his colleagues at *Phenomenology Sociological Review* would be saying.

After Castaneda received his Ph.D. and began to teach at UC Irvine (one of his first courses was on "The Phenomenology of Sorcery"), he often repeated this story.

That he did so would indicate that the story might have a deeper subtext. Garfinkel had always preached about "to the things themselves"—that is, to see a thing in its essential structure rather than through the bias of societal membership—but he obviously drew a line when it came to inorganic beings. This refusal of Garfinkel's to explore beyond the organic began to weight Castaneda in favor of the sorceric view of reality. As he would write near the end of his life:

> From my association with don Juan Matus and the other practitioners of his line, I came to the conclusion, by directly experiencing their shamanistic practices, that the bracketing of meaning, or the suspension of judgment that Husserl postulated as the essential reduction of every philosophical inquiry, is impossible to accomplish when it is a mere exercise of the philosopher's intellect. . . . In the sorcerers' world, suspending judgment is not the desired beginning of any philosophical-practical inquiry, but the necessity of every shamanistic practice. Sorcerers expand the parameters of what they can perceive to the point that they systematically perceive the unknown. To realize this feat, they have to suspend the effect of their normal interpretation system. . . . In this sense, the practitioners of don Juan's knowledge go a step beyond the intellectual exercises of philosophers.

Castaneda was a prodigious reader; along with Husserl's phenomenological approach and Garfinkel's "the world as description," the most powerful academic influences on him were the sociologist Talcott Parsons' "glosses" on reality or units of perception, and philosophers Ludwig Wittgenstein's linguistic philosophy, *Tractatus Logico-Philosophicus,* Arthur Schopenhauer's *The World as Will and Idea,* and Martin Heidegger's *Being and Time.*

Passionate, respectful and sly, Castaneda charmed most people he met. Michael Korda, an editor at Simon & Schuster who bought the hardback rights to *The Teachings of Don Juan* and became his editor for several other books, first spoke to Castaneda on the phone and was greeted with a voice that was "rich, modulated, and had a slight Hispanic accent." Korda told him he wanted to meet him. To which Castaneda chuckled and said, "I would be happy to, but first you ought to talk to my agent. You see, I am *a pushover*, but *he* is really fierce and mean, so I have to be careful not to anger him." Castaneda's agent was Ned Brown, an agent known for his tenacity.

"That Castaneda had somehow found his way to Ned Brown," said Korda, "seemed an indication that he was not as unworldly as his book made him out to be."

Brown arranged that Castaneda would meet Korda that evening in the parking lot of his hotel. Castaneda drove up in a Volvo and waved Korda inside. "He was a robust, broad-chested, muscular man, with a swarthy complexion, dark eyes, black, curly hair cut short, and a grin as merry as Friar Tuck's, displaying perfect teeth. His handshake was firm and his hands were broad, strong, with blunt fingers."

Korda asked how he recognized him.

"I'm a sorcerer," he said mischievously. "How could I miss you? Of course, it didn't hurt that Ned described you to me."

Korda would later write of his impressions, saying:

> I have seldom, if ever, liked anybody so much so quickly—a feeling that remains undiminished

> after more than twenty-five years. It wasn't so much what Castaneda had to say as his presence—a kind of charm that was partly subtle intelligence, partly real affection for people, and partly a kind of innocence, not of the naïve kind but of the kind one likes to suppose saints, holy men, prophets, and gurus have. Castaneda's spirit was definitely Rabelaisian and ribald, and he had a wicked sense of humor, but nevertheless he gave off in some way the authentic, potent whiff of otherworldly power, to such a degree that I have never doubted for a moment the truth of his stories about don Juan or of the miracles he says he witnessed and, later, participated in.

They went to dinner at a restaurant he chose, a small, elegant steak house in Santa Monica. Castaneda ordered wine knowledgeably. Instead of steak, he chose lamb and ate with gusto. Korda found:

> Not only was he a good talker in a town where good talkers are a dime a dozen, but, far rarer, a good listener. He transformed listening into a physical act, his dark eyes fixed on me, his mobile, expressive face showing, like a good actor's, a combination of attention, sympathy, and warm amusement. Chunky and solid as he was—he was no beauty—Castaneda had an actor's physical grace and an exact sense of timing, together with the ability to convey, by small gestures and changes of expression, a whole range of emotion.

Korda asked how he had come to choose Ned Brown as his agent.

"Don Juan found him for me," he said, laughing hard. "He told me to pick the meanest little man I could find, and I did."

Castaneda paid the bill and outside he mentioned—"He told me you would come too. Somebody will come along who's interested in power. You'll see."

"Am I interested in power?" Korda asked.

Castaneda gave him a crushing hug, tipped the parking attendant and smiled.

"Do bears shit in the woods?" he asked.

Korda says he ended up getting the hardcover rights, but for about twice what he had wanted to pay.

II

Castaneda's Muse

THE STRONGEST AND MOST ENDURING LITERARY INFLUENCE ON CARLOS CASTANEDA WAS ANAÏS NIN, a femme fatale best known for her voluminous diaries, her many affairs—the most celebrated with Henry Miller—and keeping two adoring and unsuspecting husbands in tow at once. Her many novels, such as *Children of the Albatross*, *A Spy in the House of Love* and *Under a Glass Bell*, are all based on her dreams.

As Nin argued in *The Novel of the Future*: "Why should

we want to penetrate this realm of the dream? Because it contains the key to a knowledge of ourselves. Adventuring into the irrational is frightening in some writers. The realm into which the writer may take us may cause us to lose the self we are familiar with. We fear to be changed, influenced, to be immersed in experience, beyond control of the intellect."

Nin felt that creation and dreaming were very much the same. "The mood I fall into when I am truly possessed by my work," she said, "is one which resembles the trances of the mystics. I shut out the outer world to concentrate on what I see and feel. There is no doubt that the act of creation is very similar to the act of dreaming. The difference is that it includes an activity which has been difficult to analyze. It is not only the power to summon an image, but the power to compose with this image."

Nin believed that "Truth and reality are at the basis of all I write (I can always prove the incident which caused the writing, produce the character, the place), but because I insist on extracting the essence, on giving only a distilled product, it becomes a dream, where all reality appears only in its symbolical form. Everything I write will have to be translated, just as when you read dreams."

To do so, the writer had to use the *mensonge vital,* as she called it, the necessary lie. Lying, she felt, was justified because the truth was "not always creative." Neither was it "worth more or more right than untruth," nor was "loyalty [more right] than disloyalty, sincerity than insincerity." For Nin, "wisdom lies in knowing how and when to justly make use of them all." Furthermore, such lies were not harmful, because "even when I lie, I lie only *mensonges vital,* the lies which give life." They were to "improve the reality" and she exhorted others to "live life as a dream, make the dream real." She believed that "all truth lies in the *relationship* between subjectivity and objectivity, not in one *or* the other."

One of her techniques was what she called "*dédoublement*—the moment when I watch myself live." This double state was induced through imagining "someone else watching me. I play at the someone else who, like god, can see me everywhere and must therefore be the face of my guilt, not in relation to myself but only in relation to the one I am betraying at the moment."

Nin had often spoken of creating a "circle," her word for a salon, where like-minded people would gather to share their ideas. She wanted a literary gathering, not one that mixed politics, history and literature. Discussion was to revolve around the psychological, the personal. A strong anima figure possessed of an ethereal, sculptural beauty, Nin was talented, intelligent, a woman of today who had broken free of the societal conventions of yesterday. She had no trouble creating a literary salon at her home in Los Angeles in the late 1950s.

It was to Nin's salon one evening that the poet Deena Metzger brought Carlos Castaneda. Nin and Castaneda, both strangers to America and both having a love of literature, the occult and the mystical, felt an instant rapport. Her literary ideas of using dreams and *mensonges vital* to open to a deeper experience beyond ordinary life would serve him for a lifetime. Nin's keen interest in psychology had led her to read Freud, Jung and Adler, particularly Jung, whose maxim to "proceed from the dream outward," guided not only how she wrote but how she lived. She interpreted his theory of the collective unconscious to be "the intensification of our personal experiences to the point of overflow into the universal—the impersonal experience. . . . A rich personal intensity breaks its own shell and its own obsessions—and touches the mystic whole." This meant to her "living the dream" or "making the dream real." She was particularly taken with Jung's practice of active imagination. Said Jung:

> You start with any image. . . . Contemplate it and carefully observe how the picture begins to unfold or to change. Don't try to make it into something, just do nothing but observe what its spontaneous changes are. Any mental picture you contemplate in this way will sooner or later change through a spontaneous association that causes a slight alteration of the picture. You must carefully avoid impatient jumping from one subject to another. Hold fast to the one image you have chosen and wait until it changes by itself. Note all these changes and eventually step in to the picture yourself, and if it is a speaking figure at all then say what you have to say to that figure and listen to what he or she has to say.

She must have spoken at her salon about what her therapist of twenty years, Otto Rank, a member of Freud's circle, said may happen to artists like her,

> the artist who departs from affiliation with and expression of the "collective" point of view. He is frequently shunned by society. This happens because the artist's thinking and expression are so far in advance of his cultural surroundings that he either frightened or amazed others who shared them. Thcy were either unable or unwilling to confront the reality, the sur-reality, or

> even the dream that the artist portrayed. They could not grasp the meaning and intention of the work, and thus the artist was consigned to various forms of loneliness, ranging from separation to ostracism.

When Castaneda completed the manuscript he had long been working on, it was Nin who provided the necessary contacts. Nin believed her "interest in *The Teachings of Don Juan* is what worried UCLA into publishing it." In gratitude and because of the debt he believed he owed her—it was a strong feature of his to acknowledge and pay debts—it is quite probable that Castaneda named his Yaqui sorcerer—don Juan is definitely not his name—after Nin's father Joaquín, whom she referred to as "Don Juan." In his last book, too, Castaneda gives the name Joaquín to the little button-nosed boy whose collarbone he broke and whose pain he says he could not bear.

In 1971, six years before she died, Nin introduced Castaneda to the writer Ronald Sukenick, whose novel *Out* was heavily based on his dreams. What struck Sukenick about Castaneda was what he called his "stubborn literal-mindedness." There were a number of similarities in idea and incident between his book and Castaneda's.

> The fact that this [the introduction] happened through Nin is an important part of the story. It was Nin who helped Castaneda publish *The Teachings of Don Juan* when he was having publisher troubles. And it is Nin more than any other writer I can think of who has over the years insisted on the continuity of dream and reality, as don Juan does, and whose theories about fiction as controlled dreaming provide such a

> precise counterpart to don Juan's ideas about learning to control one's dreams. . . . That evening he struck me as a kind of Candide parrying with a schizophrenic episode, and in fact a kind of cultural schizophrenia—parallel to what one might call the controlled pathology induced by don Juan—has been the key to his books since the first one, with its experiential reportage in the body of the book, and its attempt at an abstract objective analysis added on at the end. . . . [Concerning Sukenick's book] Castaneda said that there was a common fund of such knowledge that could be tapped by different people in different ways and that one of the ways was through dreams. He seemed to have in mind something like a lost Jungian race heritage. One of the first things I talked about with Castaneda was the novelistic quality of his books.

In a *Harpers'* interview in 1973 Castaneda said, "I dream my books. In the afternoon I go through the notebooks with all my field notes in them and translate them into English. Then I sleep in the early evening and dream what I want to write. When I wake up, I can work all night. Everything has arranged itself smoothly in my head, and I don't need to rewrite. My regular writing is actually very dry and labored."

While *The Teachings of Don Juan* gave instant fame, it also dogged Castaneda for a lifetime with accusations of fabrication. Wrote Weston La Barre, a distinguished anthropologist and author of *The Peyote Cult*, a classic in the field, in a review of the book for the *New York Times* (which it did not publish). "Everything is smarmy with self-importance and really quite trivial feelings and narcissistic self-preoccupation."

But the equally distinguished anthropologist Edward H. Spicer wrote in his review for the *American Anthropologist*, entitled "Early Praise from an Authority on Yaqui Culture," that "Castaneda's literary skill led me to complete absorption in what seemed almost the direct experience itself."

R. Gordon Wasson, the widely respected ethnobotanist and author, wasn't so sure and, suspecting a hoax, in 1968 wrote Castaneda asking a number of questions. Castaneda made a respectful reply [see Appendices for the full exchange] but adroitly dodged Wasson's parries:

> *Wasson:* Am I right in concluding from your narrative that you never gathered the mushrooms, nor indeed ever saw a whole specimen?
>
> *Castaneda:* I have gathered the mushrooms myself. I have held perhaps hundreds of specimens in my hands. Don Juan and I made yearly trips to collect them in the mountains southwest and northwest of Valle Nacional in the state of Oaxaca. I have deleted in my book all specific details about those trips and all the specific details about the collecting process. Don Juan expressed himself very strongly against my desire to include those descriptions as part of my book. He did not object to my revealing specific details about collecting peyote or jimsonweed on the grounds that the deity in peyote was a protector, therefore accessible to every man, and the power in jimsonweed was not his ally (*aliado*). The power in the mushrooms, however, was his ally and as such it was above everything else. And that entailed a total secrecy about specific processes.

Wasson: Did you satisfy yourself that you were dealing with *Psilocybe mexicana*?

Castaneda: No. My botanical identification was a tentative one, and terribly unsophisticated at that. In my book, it appears as though the mushroom was *Psilocybe mexicana*, that is, I am afraid, an editorial error. I should have carried the assertion that it was a tentative classification all the way through, since I have never been completely convinced that it was. The particular species used by don Juan looked like the *Psilocybe mexicana* pictures I have seen. A member of the Pharmacology Dept. at UCLA also showed me some specimens that he had, and based on that I concluded I was dealing with that species. However, it never turned into powder upon being handled. Don Juan picked it always with his left hand, transferred it to his right hand and then put it inside a small, narrow gourd. The mushroom would then disintegrate into fine shreds, but never into powder, as it was forced gently inside.

Wasson: Do you know where your mushrooms grew?

Castaneda: We found them growing on dead trunks of trees, but more often on decomposed remains of dead shrubs.

Wasson: What is don Juan's cultural provenience?

Castaneda: Don Juan is, in my judgment, a marginal man who has been forged by multiple forces outside the purely Yaqui culture. [*Castaneda, too, is just such a "marginal man."*] His name is really Juan. I tried to find a substitute name to use in my book, but I couldn't conceive him in any other way except as don Juan. He is not a pure Yaqui, that is, his mother was a Yuma Indian, and he was born in Arizona. His mixed origin seemed to have rendered him as a marginal man from the beginning.

He lived in Arizona the first years of his life and then moved to Sonora when he was perhaps six or seven years old. He lived there for a while, I am not sure whether with both parents or just with his father. That was the time of the great Yaqui upheavals and don Juan and his family were picked up by the Mexican armed forces and were deported to the state of Veracruz. Don Juan later moved to the area of "el Valle Nacional" where he lived for over thirty years. It is my belief that he moved there with his teacher, who must have been Mazateco. So far I have not been able to determine who his teacher was, nor where he did learn to be a brujo, yet the mere fact that I have to take him every year to Oaxaca to collect mushrooms should be a serious clue as to where he learned, at least, about mushrooms.

As you can see, it is impossible for me at this point to determine with certainty his cultural provenience, except in a guessing manner. However, the subtitle of my book is "A Yaqui Way of Knowledge." This is another mistake in which I became involved due to my lack of experience in matters of publications. The Editorial Committee of the University of California

> Press suggested upon accepting my manuscript for publication, that the word Yaqui should be included in the title in order to place the book ethnographically. They had not read the manuscript but they concluded that I had said that don Juan was a Yaqui, which was true, but I had never meant that don Juan was a product of the Yaqui culture, as appears to be the case now judging from the title of the book. Don Juan considered himself to be a Yaqui and seemed to have deep ties with the Yaquis of Sonora. However, it has become obvious to me now that those ties were only a surface affiliation.

Castaneda admitted some mistakes and answered his questions in enough detail to defend his integrity and defuse the 70-year-old Wasson's queries as to his knowledge and use of hallucinogenic mushrooms and his knowledge of Yaqui culture. Wasson wrote Castaneda a second letter to which he did not reply, but instead the two met in New York and again in California and, despite his doubts, Wasson's impression of the diminutive, budding anthropologist was as "an honest and serious young man."

III

What Is Real?

WHAT IS REAL AND NOT REAL? That was the question readers came to ask. In October 1972, the *New York Times* published a review of Castaneda's books by the anthropologist Paul Reisman. He took them as being totally factual, writing that they were "among the best that the science of anthropology has produced." A month later, in a letter to the newspaper, the noted novelist Joyce Carol Oates responded to Reisman by praising Castaneda's books' construction and the novelistic momentum, but wondered if the books weren't largely fiction. Two years later, with the publication of *Tales of Power*, Oates published a full essay, "Don Juan's Last Laugh," declaring, "Perhaps it takes a writer of fiction to intuit the work of a fellow artist; at any rate it seems to me beyond a doubt that this series of books is art, not mere reportorial observation."

Michael Murphy, co-founder of Esalen, said he had heard from Castaneda himself as early as 1964 about the stories later published in *The Teachings of Don Juan*. Professor and anthropologist Michael Harner, a friend of Castaneda's and an authority on shamanism, defended him. "Most anthropologists," said Harner, "only give the result. Instead of synthesizing the interviews [with don Juan], Castaneda takes us through the process."

Despite earlier impressions of Castaneda, R. Gordon Wasson came to believe that with *The Teachings of Don Juan* he had rightly "smelled a hoax." Wasson thought Castaneda's second book, *A Separate Reality*, "science fiction," and the third, *Journey to Ixtlan*, for which Castaneda received a doctorate in anthropology, "a romance."

The question of whether don Juan was a real person with whom Castaneda spent thirteen years (he later says fifteen) in apprenticeship, or a person he once met and then dreamed, or whether it was all a dream, was and still is a central question. It was hotly debated among professors in the anthropology and sociology departments of UCLA even before the publication of *The Teachings of Don Juan*. Castaneda has always steadfastly defended the figure of don Juan as real and not a denizen of his imaginary world. One early interviewer put it to him bluntly:

"As I followed don Juan through your three books, I suspected, at times, that he was the creation of Carlos Castaneda. He is almost too good to be true—a wise old

Indian whose knowledge of human nature is superior to almost everybody's."

Castaneda told him: "The idea that I concocted a person like don Juan is inconceivable. He is hardly the kind of figure my European intellectual tradition would have led me to invent. The truth is much stranger. I didn't create anything. I am only a reporter."

What seemed to settle the question in many people's minds was the publication in 1976 of de Mille's *Castaneda's Journey*. Setting the events in a time line, he showed the logical or chronological errors in Castaneda's three books. The dating simply doesn't add up. (Castaneda never again dated the events in his books.)

Among those whom de Mille convinced was Barbara Myerhoff. Castaneda and she, both fledgling UCLA anthropologists, were good friends and saw each other often. Myerhoff introduced him to her contact, the Mexican shaman Ramón Medina. She remembered that when she told him of Medina's shamanic, birdlike balancing atop a high and precarious waterfall, Castaneda exclaimed, "Oh! That's just like don Genaro." (It subsequently became a riveting event in his *Journey to Ixtlan*.) As Margaret Runyan said, he had a proclivity for making others' experiences his own. A year or so after de Mille published his analysis, Myerhoff agreed to an interview. She said:

> I have a hard time reconciling the Carlos I knew, or thought I knew, with the one who is supposed to be a hardboiled, manipulative deceiver. Don Juan may be a sub personality, or a personification of a part of Carlos that was underdeveloped and could be developed and manifested in the stories. That seems much more plausible to me than the swindler theory.... The conscious, care-

> ful, diabolical plan to write fake field notes for eight years, get them published by the University Press, add two best-selling volumes, and get an anthropology Ph.D. for the whole *megillah*. . . . He has a profound ascetic streak. If I had to give you a psychological interpretation, I might say he's a tragically isolated man, struggling for discipline, dominated by his will, animus-possessed, anima-terrified, seeking impeccability, seeking passion with control. Willful asceticism. He was merciless with himself. Though he indulged himself by not giving in to the system, at the same time he sternly made himself give up personal relationships. Maybe he really wanted to give them up, but I felt it was a struggle. Made himself give up the little boy. [He had adopted Margaret Runyan's son, Carlton Jeremy Castaneda, or "C.J."] Made himself be there in the library every single day, perfectly dressed in the dark suit, with the briefcase, everything in order, a narrow, determined quality. I suspect it's getting fiercer and deeper as he gets older.

Castaneda never spoke to the incongruities shown in de Mille's timeline. The basic problem he felt was that in his writing he alternated between two memberships. His first membership was as an anthropologist. Through this membership he perceived the world and its phenomena in terms of the empiric, modern-European, intellectual syntax and interpretation. The second was under don Juan's tutelage in which he was initiated into a sorceric syntax based on an energetic way of experiencing and interpreting the world. The two memberships were in contradiction—the one science, the other magic.

His first book, *The Teachings of Don Juan*, demonstrated the crux of this bifurcation. Yes, he believed he had smoked devil's weed and had the experience of flying like a crow. Then he wanted to know whether or not he *actually* flew like a crow.

"Did I really fly, don Juan?" Castaneda asked.

"That is what you told me. Didn't you?" said don Juan.

"I know, don Juan. I mean did my body fly? Did I take off like a bird?"

Like an expert fencer, don Juan parried each of Castaneda's theoretical thrusts.

Because don Juan was speaking from another membership, another way of seeing, Castaneda couldn't get the definitive rational answer he wanted, one that would integrate the two memberships.

Finally, thinking he had cornered don Juan, Castaneda declared:

"Let's put it another way, don Juan. What I meant to say is that if I had tied myself to a rock with a heavy chain I would have flown just the same, because my body had nothing to do with my flying."

"If you tie yourself to a rock," answered don Juan, "I'm afraid you will have to fly holding the rock with its heavy chain."

Fearful of losing his sanity, his European intellectual membership, Castaneda left don Juan. In a radio interview in 1968, just after his first book was published, there was this exchange:

> *Castaneda:* Why did I leave? I got too frightened. There is this assumption in all of us that the distortion you suffer under a psychedelic

> substance is accountable, by saying I'm seeing such and such, and that is because I have taken this drug; that's in the back of our mind—always. So, anything could be accounted for. But, whenever you begin to lose that security, I think that's time to quit.
>
> *Interviewer:* But you haven't really quit.
>
> *Castaneda:* That's the problem. . . . Don Juan flipped me intellectually. He completely destroyed, dislodged, my affiliate to the intellectual man.

In his books Castaneda makes no differentiation between the two memberships or interpretations. He constantly jumps back and forth between the two, that of ordinary physical reality and sorceric reality composed, as he says, of "energetic facts" and awakened dreaming. It is all presented as one. Thus, the reader, unknowingly, is introduced (much as Castaneda was) to sorceric membership, believing all that he reads to have actually happened in the sense of the ordinary reality, the membership, he unconsciously assumes. He is baffled and wonder-struck and kept in question: *Is it real or not?*

When Castaneda says he invented nothing, he is taking all phenomena as an invention, that is, a perception, a description of the perceiver. He admitted:

> The way the books present it, the event seems to heighten some dramatic sequences, which is, I'm afraid, not true [to] real life. There are enormous gaps in between in which ordinary things took place, that are not included. I didn't include [them] in the book because they did not pertain to the system I wanted to portray, so I just simply took them away, you see. And

> that means that the gaps between those very heightened states, you know, whatever, says that I remove things that are continuous crescendos, in a kind of sequence leading to a very dramatic solution. But in real life it was a very simple matter because it took years in between, months pass in between them, and in the meantime we did all kinds of things.

Before writing, Castaneda said in the afternoon he would usually first go through all his field notes and translate them into English. Then in the evening he would sleep and dream what he wanted to write. He would awaken "in the quiet hours of the night, drawing upon what has arranged itself coherently in my head." Don Juan had told him that instead of using a tape recorder it was "better to learn with your whole body so you'll remember with your whole body. By the end of my time with don Juan, I learned to listen and watch and sense and recall in all the cells of my body."

In *The Eagle's Gift*, his sixth book, published in 1981, Castaneda said his work had been "transformed into autobiography [because] the belief system I wanted to study swallowed me." And he emphasized, "I must first of all reiterate that this is not a work of fiction. What I am describing is alien to us; therefore, it seems unreal." In *The Power of Silence*, his eighth book, published in 1987, he wrote:

> My books are a true account of a teaching method that don Juan Matus, a Mexican Indian sorcerer, used in order to help me understand the sorcerers' world. In this sense, my books are the account of an on-going process which becomes more clear to me as time goes by.

When asked about his reaction to critics who accused him of perpetrating a hoax, Castaneda insisted:

> The work that I have to do is free from all that the critics can say. My task consists of presenting that knowledge in the best possible way. Nothing they can say matters to me because I no longer am Carlos Castaneda, the writer. I am neither the writer, nor a thinker, nor a philosopher . . . in consequence, their attacks don't reach me. Now, I know that I am nothing.

Whether or not don Juan was real was one question. The other question was whether or not Castaneda really jumped off the mesa into "an abyss." It wasn't until 1998, the year of his death, in *The Active Side of Infinity*, that he gave an explanation, saying that after he jumped, "An exchange had taken place at the moment of my jump. I was someone else." He then relates that he entered

> . . . a passageway that had a force of its own. It pulled me in. It was a silent passageway. Don Juan was that passageway, quiet and immense. That was the first time ever that I felt that don Juan was void of physicality. There was no room for sentimentality or longing. I couldn't possibly have missed him because he was there as a depersonalized emotion that lured me in.

Afterward, at 3:15 a.m., he found himself at Ships restaurant on Wilshire Boulevard, near his Westwood home in Los Angeles, ordering "steak and eggs, and hash browned potatoes, and buttered white toast." (Castaneda loved symbolism, a different syntax, but there is an actual Ships restaurant. One wonders if he picked the time because of the theosophical addition of the time [3 + 1 + 5 = 9] and the significance of the numbers: 3, the three forces and triad; 1, the One; 5, the pentagram, and so forth.)

Into the restaurant came an obsessive and disheveled street person. He was obviously mentally unbalanced. Castaneda had heard that he was an outpatient at the local VA hospital. The man sat at his favorite stool—he had waited outside until it was vacant—and ordered a cup of coffee. Suddenly, Castaneda's eyes met his. The man gave a bone-chilling scream and ran out. Castaneda ran after him, asking why he had screamed. The man covered his eyes and screamed even louder. Castaneda said, "He was like a child, frightened by a nightmare, screaming at the top of his lungs." When he returned to the restaurant, the waitress asked if that guy was his friend. Castaneda told her—

" 'The only friend I have in the world,' I said, and that was the truth, if I could define 'friend' as someone who sees through the veneer that covers you and knows where you really come from."

Presumably Castaneda, having broken "the human mold"—his identification with himself as a person—has traded his humanity for a sorceric existence, and now has an emptiness that is a reflection of infinity.

Castaneda had been drawn into the sorceric world by the personage of don Juan, now—after his jump into the abyss—he felt don Juan was "void of physicality." Previously, then, he had taken don Juan—whether once a human being, or predicated on and developed from a meeting with a shaman, or a figment of Castaneda's imagination—to have a physicality, a body of some sort, or a dream body.

Earlier, in *The Active Side of Infinity*, in the chapter

"Who Was Juan Matus, Really?" Castaneda writes about two Naguals he had known.

Castaneda is saying a Nagual is a sorcerer, either man or woman, whose attention has been strong enough to break the human mold, and who is composed of not one luminous ball of energy, as all people are, but two. Not only are they double beings, but they are also empty. There is nothing inside them. Only the Nagual has the energetic capacity to be responsible for the fate of those in his party.

Despite the differences of the Naguals "both of them were astoundingly alike in that there was nothing inside them. They were empty." This was an emptiness "that reflected not the world, but infinity." Don Juan then goes on to say:

> The moment one crosses a peculiar threshold in infinity, either deliberately or, as in my case, unwittingly, everything that happens to one from then on is no longer exclusively in one's own domain, but enters into the realm of infinity. . . . The sorcerers of my lineage call it infinity, the spirit, the dark sea of awareness, and say that it is something that exists out there and rules our lives.

All the great esoteric traditions and the great religions speak of dying before one dies physically and being reborn. What one dies into and is reborn into differs. A contemporary Christian dies into the mystical body of Christ Jesus and is reborn in Christ. A Moslem—"Die before you die," uttered the Prophet—dies in Allah and is reborn in Allah. An Advaitic dies into the Self and is reborn in the Self. A Buddhist dies into Sunyata and is reborn into Sunyata, a conscious Nothingness, a full-solid emptiness. A sorcerer dies into infinity and is reborn in infinity. In each case, the "dying" is mental and emotional. What dies is their relationship to ordinary life, their self-importance, dreams, goals, friends, family, the human mold.

Life as it is expressed and manifested on the physical, material plane continues to be what it was, but one's relationship to it is entirely different. Their dream is gone. And in the sense that everyone is dreaming they are someone, then that notion of being someone dies. In the conventional sense, there is nobody there. They are empty. They will still eat, drink and defecate. And, depending on their proclivities, they may still tell stories, make love—whatever. While they will look and talk and act like a person . . . they are *not* a person. At least a person they believe in.

At the moment that he jumped from the mesa and the exchange took place, Castaneda said—"I was someone else." All the books afterward tell in some measure who it was that took his place.

How to understand this? First, what is an abyss? It is defined as "a bottomless pit or the chaos of the old cosmogonies." A secondary meaning is "intellectual or moral depths." If the jump into the abyss was physical, he had to actually die. That he did not can only mean it was not physical but psychological in the deepest meaning of the term. That is, he fully and wholeheartedly *believed* he was jumping. He had so internalized don Juan and don Juan's world that there was no longer "the dual membership" he speaks about in his Garfinkel days. He had now been fully initiated into the sorceric world. So he did "jump" and break the human mold, his identification with himself as a human being. It was such a shock to his psychological being that between the jump and Ships restaurant he wasn't there, had no memory. Through habit he ends up at the restaurant. When his eyes meet those of the street person, who is half-crazed, eaten out, without soul, the two recognize each other as being, in this sense, one and the same, so Castaneda can tell the waitress, "He is the only friend I have in the world."

The next major octave for Castaneda began in 1973. Ironically, though he had "died" with don Juan and his party, Castaneda found himself swathed in the shimmering glow of iconic success. His three books had single-handedly ignited an interest in sorcery. He was well on his way to becoming a millionaire. Magazines pestered him for interviews; Shirley MacLaine invited him to dinner; he hung out with Clint Eastwood, Sean Connery and Michael Caine; hobnobbed with writer Irving Wallace. Topping it off, a drawing of his face—one half of which he'd erased—appeared on the cover of *Time* magazine. This was also the year in which he was awarded a Ph.D. in anthropology from UCLA and his divorce from Margaret Runyan was finalized. And then, inexplicably—Carlos Castaneda disappeared....

IV

The Nagual & His Witches

When the male ejaculates, not only do we women get the semen, but in that moment of energetic outburst, what really happens is that they are what don Juan calls "energetic worms," filaments. And those filaments stay in the body. From a biological point of view, those filaments ensure that the male returns to the same female and takes care of the offspring. The male will recognize that it is his offspring by the filaments

> at a total energetic level. . . . For women to be liberated sexually means that in a way they are more enslaved than before, because suddenly they are feeding energetically not just one male but many males. . . . The womb ensures that the woman is the one that's closest to the spirit in this process of approaching knowledge as being-in-dreaming. The man cones upward, and by sheer definition of the cone, it comes to a finite end. It's an energetic force. He strives because he is not close to the spirit, or whatever we want to call that great energetic force out there. According to sorcerers, the woman is exactly the opposite. The cone is upside down. They have a direct link with it, because the womb for the sorcerer is not just an organ of reproduction; it is an organ for dreams, a second brain.

The speaker was a small-boned, charming but aggressive blonde, blue-eyed woman with spiked hair, just a shade over 5'1". Castaneda described her as being "like a jockey with a shiv, the type of person who takes no prisoners." Her name was Regine Margarita Thal. An anthropology student, she had met Castaneda in the fall of 1971 when he was lecturing in a UCLA classroom on "The Phenomenology of Shamanism." She was then twenty-seven years old. Born in Venezuela to German émigrés and brought up in Caracas, Thal had been married for five years to a much older petroleum engineer. Less than a year after meeting Castaneda, she divorced. As was the custom, she received a new name, Florinda Donner, and she became a member of his sorceric party.

Having "jumped into the abyss," Castaneda was now a Nagual, one who has realized his essential emptiness and has the requisite energy and ability to lead. His party of witches also included Carol Tiggs, Taisha Abelar and Nury Alexander.

Carol Tiggs was born Kathleen "Chickie" Pohlman in 1947 in Pasadena, California. She was nineteen years old, tall, slender and attractive when she went to Mexico to study art. There she met don Juan and Castaneda and became a member of don Juan's party. (Castaneda, however, writes in *The Eagle's Gift* that don Juan first met her at a government office in Arizona where she was working as a clerk.) She was "very young," according to Castaneda, and had a slight lisp. But he adds, "I thought she was beautiful." (Apparently, she and Castaneda had known each other in other dimensions, but in ordinary reality he had forgotten.) Just before the jump, she and Castaneda dreamed together in a Mexican hotel. Carol Tiggs then disappeared in 1973, only to rejoin Castaneda twelve years later.

Taisha Abelar, aka Maryann Simko and Anne-Marie Carter, was a fair, fine-featured nineteen-year-old anthropology student, with long brown hair falling to her waist; she, like Florinda, had met Castaneda at UCLA. Taisha claimed to have been an apprentice of don Juan, though sometimes she denied this and said she was Castaneda's apprentice. Much taller than Florinda, Taisha was more gentle and soft-spoken. She had an interest in karate which Florinda soon shared.

How Castaneda met Nury Alexander, aka Claude, the Blue Scout, whose real name was Patricia Partin, is unclear. "She was a sentient being from another dimension," Castaneda said. He and the witches claimed they found her in rural Mexico in a universe of inorganic beings where she had been imprisoned because of her curiosity. Castaneda claimed to have saved her and brought her back to Los Angeles.

She was born in Southern California in 1957, and never finished high school. At the age of twenty, she married Mark Silliphant, son of the Hollywood writer and producer Sterling Silliphant, who later planned to make a film version of *The Teachings of Don Juan*, the rights to which were subsequently withdrawn. Tall, angular and very tense with a wolf-like pointy face, pouty lips and blue eyes, Nury was so thin as to approach anorexia. She was also "violently jealous" yet an "egoless being," the most difficult of Castaneda's witches. Castaneda supported Nury in a lavish and somewhat infantile lifestyle—she was given to playing with dolls—but she nevertheless wielded great power in that she had the say-so as to who could be a member of Castaneda's inner circle.

Both Taisha and Florinda received bachelor's and master's degrees in anthropology from UCLA and both were enrolled in the doctoral program, though only Taisha completed it. Florinda wrote several books, including *Shabono: A Visit to a Remote and Magical World in the South American Rain Forest* (1982), *The Witch's Dream* (1985), and *Being-in-Dreaming* (1991); while Taisha wrote just one, *The Sorcerers' Crossing* (1992). Meanwhile, Castaneda was as busy as ever publishing *The Eagle's Gift* (1981), *The Fire from Within* (1984), and *The Power of Silence* (1987). Florinda's book, *Shabono*, ran into the same criticism as had Castaneda's. Venezuela-based anthropologist Rebecca B. De Holmes pointed out in "*Shabono:* Scandal or Superb Social Science," an article published in the journal *American Anthropology*, that there were extensive similarities between Florinda's book, its language and events, and that of Ettor Biocca's *Yanoama: The Story of Helena Valero, a Girl Kidnapped by Amazonian Indians*, which had been published seventeen years earlier. A number of other experts in the field agreed. Despite this, the *Los Angeles Times* published a front-page review in its book section and a lengthy interview with Florinda; *Shabono* became a Book-of-the-Month Club alternate selection.

Although Castaneda was the Nagual, don Juan had left behind a longtime member of his own party, Florinda Matus, or Old Florinda as she was known, to "fine-tune" Castaneda's party. Tall, elegant, and described by Florinda Donner as "packing an incredible wallop," Old Florinda (it was she who gave her the name "Florinda") was presented as Donner's mentor and guide in her book *The Witch's Dream.*

Sometime in the fall of 1985 Carol Tiggs, the Nagual woman, suddenly reappeared. As mentioned, she, too, had "jumped into the abyss" with don Juan and his party in 1973 but had gotten stuck there in what is called the Second Attention, a much expanded concept since Castaneda first spoke of it, as it now was defined as not a dreaming-while-awake state in the ordinary world, but a realm totally beyond ordinary human conception.

A Nagual woman, like a man, Castaneda says, is someone whose luminous egg—the aura or energy body that everyone radiates, though it varies in robustness—has a number of compartments. Most people only have a right and a left side, but the Nagual's right and left sides are divided into two. Castaneda said that when Carol Tiggs and don Juan met, "They found completeness and silence in each other's company. Don Juan said that the feeling they had for each other had nothing to do with affection or need; it was rather a shared physical sense that an ominous barrier had been broken within them, and they were one and the same being."

Tiggs described what happened a bit differently. One evening she was walking in Alameda Park in Mexico City when she saw two "coarse Mexicans," an old man and a short, stocky man staring at her. The short fellow came up close to her and the old man said, "Don't let her get away. Grab her by the leg if you can." Instead, the short fellow involved her in conversation, asking her name and how old she was and if she had a boyfriend. She began to panic and just then the old man made a huge belch that both paralyzed her and caused her to answer the questions. She said his eyes let her know she was a "double woman." By the time she returned to Los Angeles "a fog had closed in around the memory of these men," and she was unable to remember what happened.

In *The Art of Dreaming*, Castaneda writes that later he and don Juan were in Mexico City when the Nagual woman flew in from Los Angeles to help Castaneda to intend a dreaming journey while in full consciousness. Though they experienced many adventures together, the journey was not successful and don Juan recommended that they "see as little of each other as possible."

Afterward, don Juan took Castaneda to a church in Tula where Castaneda met a woman who don Juan claimed was the Death Defier or, as don Juan and his friends say, "the Tenant." The Death Defier is a mythical old sorcerer of ageless renown who, because of her great age, "knew now how to reach and hold hundreds, if not thousands, of positions of the assemblage point." This is the point at which the flux of an immense mass of energy, which he metaphorically called "the dark sea of awareness," is processed as sensory data and then interpreted in terms of our conditioning. This point is between the shoulder blades physically but is located in the energy body about an arm's length behind. Later, don Juan elaborated, saying that the Death Defier knew "particular ways of treating the energy body in order to maintain the assemblage point fixed on specific positions."

Castaneda entered the Death Defier's dream and visited a small town she had conjured. In return she spoke to him about the art of dreaming. Nine days later Castaneda awoke from the dream and found himself in the arms of a woman who told him she was Carol Tiggs, the Nagual woman. The first thing Castaneda noticed was that she had lost her lisp, a defining characteristic of hers. His remark "caught her totally by surprise. She peered at me and broke into a hearty laugh. 'I've been working on it for a long time,' she confessed." Castaneda's suspicion was further aroused when the woman wanted to know if he liked the clothes she was wearing. This seemed odd as Carol Tiggs, according to Castaneda, was known for "her expertise at buying beautiful clothes and wearing them with grace and style." Finally, after much prodding, Castaneda told her she looked "Divinely beautiful. In fact, you're downright stunning."

"Then this must be the right appearance," she said.

None of this seemed relevant until later when Castaneda spoke with don Juan.

"Carol Tiggs hasn't been with us at all," don Juan told him, explaining that the Death Defier made use of Carol Tiggs energy body and created the "Carol Tiggs" Castaneda becamc involved with at the hotel. Castaneda's observation that she had lost her lisp shocked the Death Defier as she hadn't noticed that. Her interest in how Castaneda saw her was because if she looked to him like the Carol Tiggs he knew, then it signaled he accepted her. Castaneda asked what happened to the real Carol Tiggs.

"'Carol Tiggs is gone,' don Juan replied. 'But someday you will find the new Carol Tiggs, the one in the dream hotel room.'

"'What do you mean she's gone?'

"'She's gone from this world,' he said."

Twelve years later, as mentioned earlier, Carol Tiggs showed up.

Though said to have been lost in the Second Attention, on the physical plane it was later discovered that Carol Tiggs had married a Marc LeBel, a Santa Monica acupuncturist. In 1981 she received a degree in acupuncture under the name of "Elizabeth Austin." The question for stalwarts, then: *Is this the real Carol Tiggs who has reappeared, or is it the Death Defier, who has taken over Carol's body?* Castaneda doesn't comment, but from what don Juan said, if we are to believe him, then it must be the latter.

Though Tiggs is said to have returned in 1983, she wandered around disoriented for two years until in 1985 she walked into a Los Angeles bookstore and saw Castaneda. She said her disappearance had been like a dream that seemed like only ten hours. She had found herself in Tucson, Arizona, looking for her old house, which was no longer there. After some ten years she realized something was wrong. "I'm sure that don Juan knew beforehand that this was going to happen because he made me hide plastic packs of money in different parts of Tucson and other towns." So she went and found the packets of money and went to Los Angeles. She said, "I lurked there for awhile in a zombie state until I found Castaneda." And so began another octave.

Her reappearance, Castaneda said, "opened an enormous door—energetically—through which we come and go. Her return gave us a new ring of power; she brought with her a tremendous mass of energy that allows us to come out."

Said Florinda:

> Carlos, Taisha, and I almost *died* when Carol left—we teetered on the edge of evaporation!

> *She*, the *Nagual woman*, is Carlos' energetic sister. She was supposed to be a glowing beacon, shining her light to lead us to the other side. But we couldn't find her, not even in our dreams. We were devastated, struggling to survive. . . . She had total amnesia about her experience! *Gone from the world for ten years! Disappeared!* All she remembers is waking up in Arizona, wandering around. . . . Well, this is an omen! It meant we could go public, after twenty years of hiding! Castaneda could speak to his readers, and could tell the world about *the three of us*—we have been his biggest secret for twenty years!

Tiggs, rather remote and mysterious with a moody cast to her dark blue eyes, was now thirty-eight years old, Castaneda fifty-nine. Why it took another nine years before Castaneda went public with his ideas isn't clear. It's not clear either why the group needed Tiggs' energy, as energy was one thing none of them lacked. Castaneda's explanation was that Tiggs had to persuade him and the other witches that they, being the last of their lineage, should adopt a radically new approach to their work—present the teachings of don Juan openly so that this ancient knowledge might live on after them. As Castaneda would explain later, "With her return, we are no longer an insular group. We're without a guide. We're not going Juan Matus's way. We were insular. She's the one who made it possible to talk to people."

He said later, "What compels us to disseminate don Juan's ideas is a need to clarify [for ourselves] what he taught us."

The witches went even further. "The return of Carol Tiggs marked a total change in our goals and aspirations.

. . . Traditionally, Carol Tiggs' role was to guide us to make that [sorceric] crossing. When she returned, she automatically transformed the insular goal of our private journey into something more far-reaching. That's why we decided to end our anonymity."

And so in 1992 Florinda and Taisha began giving interviews to magazines and speaking at bookstores, talking in detail about their lives and their sorceric experience that offered a uniquely feminine perspective of the teaching.

Public interest was so great that Castaneda—renaming Carol Tiggs as Muni Alexander—gave his blessing to three of his four witches to teach, leaving out Nury Alexander, who was too unstable. The renaming presumably constituted the psychic death of the person's former self and an initiation into a new self, thus cultivating the prized "formlessness" and "fluidity." Castaneda, himself, was also known as Charley Spider, Joe Cortéz, Joe Cordoba and Isidoro Baltazar.

A year later, in 1993, at Rim Institute in Arizona, the three witches gave a weekend seminar, the first of its kind. The seminar was a sort of "sorcery lite," featuring a lot of anecdotal stories about the witches' experiences with don Juan and his party, and the "recapitulation" of the story of their lives, plus a series of body movements called "Tensegrity," which don Juan and his fellow sorcerers practiced but had been kept secret up until then.

Castaneda claimed Tensegrity was brought by the Chinese Nagual Luhan. However, it seems more likely that it was an eclectic mix of karate and tai chi, as well as the kung fu taught by Castaneda's martial arts teacher, Howard Y. Lee. For fifteen years, from 1974 to 1989, Castaneda had studied with Lee. He dedicated *The Fire from Within* to Lee: "I want to express my admiration and gratitude to a masterful teacher, H.Y.L., for helping me restore my energy, and for teaching me an alternate way to plenitude and well-being."

Tensegrity consisted of an ever-expanding series of movements created by Castaneda called "magical passes" that stretch the body's meridians, its energy channels. As many have noted, there are numerous similarities between the Tensegrity movements and karate's katas, Qigong, and various movements taught by the Taoist master Mantak Chia. Castaneda explained the similarities by saying that "Don Juan himself urged us to become versed in the practice of Oriental martial arts." Castaneda was inspired, no doubt, by one of his cohorts, Clara Boehm, Taisha Abelar's teacher, who had studied martial arts in China. At one workshop Taisha was asked about the relationship of Tensegrity to martial arts. She said their intents were completely different.

> Tensegrity's intent is to move the assemblage point, to call back the energy body, and to make us unpalatable to the flyers [inorganic beings that eat the thoughts of the formatory mind, what Castaneda calls the foreign installation, reminiscent of G. I. Gurdjieff's implantation of the organ Kundabuffer]. The intent of the martial arts depends on which one we are talking about; they have a self defense or combat intent. While the martial arts practices began as meditation techniques, they were quickly turned into martial practice. Since the intents are very different, it is important not to mix the two.

Another source in terms of inspiration might be the Gurdjieff movements. It is known that Castaneda did attend Gurdjieff movements classes that were open to the public. Richard Jennings, aka Corey Donovan, a longtime follower of Castaneda, though not a member of his inner circle, says that while the Gurdjieff movements and Tensegrity are quite different, the idea of teaching people to break their habitual worldview by working with the body may have been inspired by what he saw with the Gurdjieff movements. Whatever its origin, Tensegrity became a staple of the seminars that would be given first by the witches and later by Castaneda himself.

Although Castaneda's later books never approached the popularity of his first three, all were still in print. But with each becoming more abstract, or as Castaneda might say, "formless," sales became more and more concentrated. A new readership came with the publication of Florinda's and Taisha's books, which spoke of sorcery from a woman's point of view, and also presented a number of startling ideas.

Florinda, ironic, fanciful and incredibly charismatic, spoke a mile a minute in a way that literally pulverized audiences. The editor of her books had cut out what she said was "the real language of don Juan." For example she said:

> Men have this *pincho* that gets hard and points skyward, so they come upwards toward the heavens—that's how they receive their knowledge—by *coming* with their genitals. Women have a hole that is always open, pointing downwards toward the Earth—we receive our awareness from the Earth itself. Sexual organs *perceive*. We women are always learning without noticing, it's so natural for us. But men have to travel upwards, step by step, as if ascending a ladder. They are meticulous, and more sober

> minded—which we are not. This is because they have to struggle in a way that we don't.

The witches' workshops and seminars hit a nerve and all quickly filled; for example, in Mexico one workshop drew one thousand people. All were strong speakers, especially Florinda and Muni Alexander, who spilled out endless anecdotes of sorceric life and their views on phenomenology, recapitulating one's life, "bored fucks," "poor baby syndrome," "not-doings," luminous and inorganic beings, dreaming, stalking, flyers, and sex.

Muni, the Nagual woman, when asked about her relationship with Castaneda, the Nagual man, at a workshop, said that while "we are energetically the same we don't necessarily get along with each other." He always seems to come out better in the stories, she said. "People who are compulsive always come out looking better in description. There's nothing like compulsion to make you look good." She said, "When Castaneda cooks he has everything arranged, everything wrapped up in neat little bundles, all the pieces he needs, and he knows exactly how many seconds each thing takes." And he was always tense. She wanted things to be calmer, more moderate. "With him," she said, "it's always intense—'We're going to die!' or 'This is complete shit!' And he has all these little rituals, like his 'power walking.' I call it 'jogging' which irritated him." For his part, when Castaneda was asked what it was like to manage three witches he said, "It's as difficult as changing the chain on a chain saw while it's still running."

The expansive insider talk and spirited question-and-answer sessions, together with the practice of Tensegrity movements, brought hundreds, if not thousands, of people from all over the world to the workshops and seminars, each costing between two hundred and a thousand dollars. Participants could also purchase Castaneda's, Florinda's and Taisha's books and two Tensegrity videos, as well as T-shirts emblazoned with "The magic is in the movement," "Self-importance kills . . . do Tensegrity." Castaneda set up a corporation, Cleargreen, Inc., to manage the workshops and seminars and to sell the books and merchandise. It soon grossed upwards of a half-million dollars a year.

Beneath the buzz was the power and electricity that the women, all of them charismatic and versed in mass hypnotism, were able to generate. One longtime Gurdjieff student who attended a number of seminars recounted that at one seminar he accidentally looked into Muni's left eye (*mal ochio*, the evil eye, in Italian) at close quarters. "I was struck speechless, inner and outer," he said. "She was merely trying to correct me at a particular position and I got quite a shock. I'd like to think of myself as being a little less suggestible. I've studied hypnotism a little bit as well. It seemed to me that there might be something else here."

At one seminar, someone told Muni—attractive and witty—she looked so normal. She responded, "What did you expect? Lightning coming out of my tits!" Then she brought seven people up on stage and seated them side by side; she walked down the line and said, while gently pushing each one to recline, "Look into my left eye." This maneuver (which Gurdjieff talked about in his *All and Everything*) apparently stopped their internal dialogue.

V

Castaneda Reappears

TWENTY YEARS PASSED BEFORE CARLOS CASTANEDA REAPPEARED. Ostensibly, his talk in 1993 at the Phoenix Bookstore in Santa Monica was to promote his newest book, his ninth, *The Art of Dreaming*. But, as everyone would learn, there was more to it than the promotion of a book. A lot more.

Though he looked more fit and trim than the pudgy Castaneda of before, his dark hair, close-cropped, was heavily streaked with gray. The eyes were still large, sharp and direct, but the serious, academic-looking dark suit and tie he had worn so often that it was taken to be his uniform was now replaced by a silk shirt, jeans, brown leather vest and cowboy boots. He spoke and answered questions for about three hours. It became clear that time certainly hadn't dimmed his intensity, charm, humor and ability to mesmerize a crowd, which took in his every word about stopping the internal dialogue, recapitulating one's life story and entering into sorceric dreaming—the conscious intent to wake up in one's dreams and to travel to other worlds.

Suddenly, without pause, he intentionally stopped talking, left the stage, and quickly exited through the rear door. He was already in his van when C.J., his adopted son, who had attended the talk with his mother Margaret Runyan, knocked urgently on the window.

"Oh," cried Castaneda, opening the door and getting out of the van, "there's my Chocho."

Castaneda chatted with the young man for a while and then, promising to see him soon, approached Margaret, greeting her with a kiss and a hug. Castaneda seemed delighted to see her as well, yet when she showed him the copy of *The Art of Dreaming* she had just bought and asked him to sign it, he demurred.

He held out his hands in a weary gesture and told her, "My hands are too tired."

Margaret, not to be one-upped, replied—"Oh, don't worry, it's all right, I've ordered the leather-bound edition from Easton Press, and I know you signed those."

With that, Castaneda climbed back into his van and sped off into the night with his entourage. It was the last time Margaret and C.J. would ever see him.

As he had done in 1968, Castaneda caught the upsurge in interest among seekers in the 1990s. And now he had his witches as a supporting cast, ballsy and attractive women who could not only buttress his story but add their own feminine slant to the sorceric teaching.

He was a Nagual now, one who was in the lineage of don Juan, the last of a sorceric line that he claimed extended back through twenty-seven generations. He claimed, too, to have lost the human form, broke the "human mold," as he called it. He had become fluid, formless. "The sorcerer's idea," said Castaneda, "is to venture to a place where socialization and syntax no longer rule. To dream, for a sorcerer, isn't to be the hero—that's the 'lucid dreamer,' obsessed with self to the end. To dream oneself someplace else takes tremendous discipline. One dreams when there's nothing left: no desires or debts, anger or happiness—only silence. Then, boom! When you stop the system of interpretation, that's what you hear: Boom. At that moment, all of you goes to that other place—hair, pocket money, shoes."

That September, wanting to acknowledge the women's success, or, more likely, to keep them tied to himself, Castaneda, as Carlos Aranha, married Florinda in Las Vegas and within two days also married Muni. It's not known whether the women knew about each other's marriages, but the likelihood is they did. To further complicate things, but then Castaneda loved complications, he and Muni adopted Nury, who was in her thirties at the time.

The witches had been igniting interest with magazine interviews and workshops, and now Castaneda himself stepped out of the shadows giving interviews to *Details, Magical Blend* and *New Age Journal.* And then in January 1994 a new octave emerged: the 5' 2" Nagual mounted the stage in Sunnyvale, California, and announced to a large audience in a strong clear voice—"I am . . . Carlos Castaneda!"

The crowd roared with delight, and the voluble, energy-packed sorcerer launched into a nonstop, riveting exposition articulating with precision the subtle points and ideas founding his sorceric world of nonordinary reality.

At one point someone interrupted—

"What happens at death?"

"I've spent my whole life preparing for that moment," answered Castaneda. "Everything you and I can talk about [concerning death] is conjecture. No one has experienced it and is able to talk about it."

He went on to speak about internal silence: "Once we stop the internal dialogue we are not bound by syntax. Our awareness is open to the perceptions of infinity." Then about self-importance: "Don Juan especially tore down my self-importance, pointing out how short and homely I was." Inorganic beings, "flyers," as he called them, were another subject: "They feed on our awareness, leaving only enough for maintaining our self-importance." Tensegrity (an architectural term lifted from Buckminster Fuller, for which Castaneda was sued) he defined as "a system of exercises related to the glandular system which will strengthen and awaken that system." The term, as used in architectural and structural design, is defined in the dictionary as: "The property of skeleton structures that employ continuous tension members and discontinuous compression members in such a way that each member operates with a maximum efficiency and economy."

Castaneda spoke for over two hours, which to many seemed like only minutes. Then he abruptly stopped and casually mentioned he had to use the restroom. Before anyone could clap, Carlos Castaneda disappeared out the back door, his entourage in tow.

Muni Alexander had brought three young women to Castaneda who became his students—Kylie Lundahl, Nyei Murez and Reni Murez. He called them "Chacmools" because don Juan had explained that the Chacmools, those gigantic, reclining figures found at the pyramids of Mexico, were the representations of guardians. There was a look of emptiness in their eyes and faces because they were dream-guards, guarding dreams and dreaming sites. Now at workshops and seminars the Chacmools, dressed in striking black workout clothes, demonstrated the Tensegrity movements. For reasons unexplained, Castaneda would soon eliminate the Chacmools, the rumor being there was too much infighting among them. Later, he would combine them with three others to form a group of six known as the Pathfinders, later changed to the Energy Trackers.

With the number of workshops and seminars steadily increasing, Castaneda himself led a three-week Tensegrity seminar in 1995 in Culver City, California, not far from his Westwood compound. That September he introduced Sunday Tensegrity sessions in Santa Monica. A core group of about two dozen people attended. The two-hour sessions consisted of Tensegrity instruction by Castaneda and others, often preceded or followed by Castaneda's reminiscences of people he had met: Shirley MacLaine—"This big lady with red hair, big boobs. She kept talking about how she lived in China until she was twenty and was always being complimented on how beautiful she was." Alan Watts—"He asked me to go upstairs and he made a pass at my *culo*! He was crude, cynical about spirituality, even sneering at his own books, books I had practically memorized! But worst of all was hearing Watts, my hero, declare: 'Of course we can never live up to the behavior we admire—that's the beauty of it!' " Timothy Leary—"He's senile. Has no attention." Baba Ram Das—"Timothy Leary referred to him as a faggot and would make fun of his name, calling him 'Baba Ram De-Ass.'" Professor

Garfinkel—"There was on the UCLA campus an old professor who when I was a young man was already famous. At that time, he was at the peak of his physical strength and intellectual creativity. Now, he's chewing his tongue of cork. Now I can see him as he is, as a senile old man."

And more than a few times he would refer to G. I. Gurdjieff and his esoteric teaching of The Fourth Way. His friend Claudio Naranjo introduced Castaneda to E. J. Gold who went about pretending to be Gurdjieff and passing himself off as a Fourth Way teacher, writing books on the teaching and leading groups, though he had no direct experience of it. Said Castaneda:

> Once I met a disciple of Gurdjieff who modeled himself completely after the master. He had shaven his head and sported this huge mustache. I invited him to come over. As soon as he came into my house, he grabbed me by the throat energetically. He told me I had to leave my teacher because I was wasting my time! According to him, he could teach me everything I needed to know in six or seven lessons. Can you imagine? In a few classes he can teach someone everything.

The seminars attracted thousands of people and brought in a great deal of money. Seminars were held throughout the United States, Europe and Mexico. Given Castaneda's Latin American background, his experiences with don Juan, and his idea of promoting the Toltecs as the source of the teaching, he was drawn more than ever to Mexico, and particularly to the ancient Toltec town of Tula, some fifty miles north of Mexico City.

Near the end of May 1995, having given several seminars in Mexico City, Castaneda invited a number of his students, along with the witches, to accompany him to Tula, where Castaneda had first encountered the Death Defier, or Tenant, an ageless being and consummate dreamer. It was here in Tula years before that Carol Tiggs had met the Death Defier and entered into a "transcendental agreement." So Castaneda, always secretive, had now decided to pull back the mystical curtains a bit.

The group boarded a bus in Mexico City on a Saturday morning and headed for Tula. The first stop was a small local museum on the outskirts which contained statues and minor artifacts. Here Muni Alexander, the former Carol Tiggs, told the group that "Sorcerers perceive that there are cyclic beings [but] 'cyclic' is not reincarnation. Human beings exist in strands held together by energy links—think of a bead curtain." (Castaneda had earlier explained that the belief in past lives was really a "generation memory" in which memory of another life is based on a memory of our ancestors. The terms "cyclic beings" and "energy links" sound very much like string theory, a view just then becoming popular with physicists, whose idea was that the universe and human beings were held together by currents, or strings, of homogeneous energy.)

The bus parked near an antiquated church with a small chapel, which was said to be where the then Carol Tiggs had made her agreement with the Death Defier. Once inside the chapel, Muni Alexander told Castaneda's students the story of what had happened in 1973. It was what came to be called a "top secret speech," a bizarre tale even by Castanedan standards.

"I am going to reveal things that no one has ever known," Muni Alexander began, "so it is very important that you pay attention. This is not the time for your linear mind. I am no longer linear. Your best efforts of linear thinking should be used in academic pursuits. Not here in Tula. Mine is not a linear world."

Muni then delivered the sorceric bombshell: she and the Death Defier were a bead on the same string.

"The mystery here," she said, "is not how I could be cyclic with the Death Defier, but how I could be sane and talking to you right now." In this very chapel she had met the Death Defier, that strange creature who spoke in "the most terrifying raspy voice."

"I have watched you for a long time, Carol Tiggs," the Death Defier said. [Though the Death Defier was dressed as a woman, Carol could not be sure of the creature's gender.] Sensing what she was thinking, the creature said, "There is nothing male left in me. My assemblage point is totally twisted. As a woman you can't see but you can certainly feel my assemblage point or my pussy." Without warning, the Death Defier grabbed Carol Tiggs's hand and stuck it up her skirt. She was wearing no underwear. The scene described in which the two women have sex together becomes very graphic.

Confused, feeling used and dirty, fearful of becoming a lesbian, Tiggs said she had been embarrassed and worried about what others in the church might think. "You are dreaming inside a dream," the Death Defier told her:

> This church doesn't exist. We are in a vacuum. The church seems to be here but it is not. I want you to lend me a hand and free me from my chains. I don't know what I can do for you in payment for this turn. It's up to you to use me partially or fully. I will catch a ride and will go piggy-back with you and you could do the same thing with me but it will be up to you. I

> have no more decisions. My life ends with your line but it turns out that we are cyclic. I will give all the power I have. If you want to be a man, I'll make you a man. If you want to be a superpussy, I'll make you a superpussy.

Tiggs wanted to know what "superpussy" meant. "Well you could just take any man or woman you want. You could have orgasms through your *nariz*, you could rub against the wall of the church and go. A superpussy means that all of you is a pussy." Tiggs was excited. She asked if she agreed what should she do first. "You could begin by seducing Isidoro Baltazar," the Death Defier suggested.

Looking back on Tigg's experience, Muni Alexander said, "It was such a pitiful exchange between such an awesome creature and the petty concerns of Carol Tiggs worrying about being a superpussy. But that's the way we are, make no bones about it." Muni then said it was time to change dreams. "The next thing I knew I was sitting on this bench. And Carlos was on my lap. I was possessed by extravagant seriousness. I couldn't lisp even if my life depended on it. Never before had I felt such sureness and at the same time awe. I was me, but not the me I know today. The rest of the story you know."

Muni then walked the group of Castaneda's students from the chapel to the Cathedral Hotel where she had taken Carlos. "In spite of the fact he was my brother," she said, "I seduced him as if there was no tomorrow." When she fell asleep, she and Isidoro Baltazar merged totally together. "It was then that he became my true brother. We twirled together in the sea of awareness for nine days until there was no more energetic difference. You see, the mystery of mysteries is that Carlos and I are cyclic to one another and to the Death Defier. That was why I hated and loved him at the same time. I saw him as a man. The Death Defier explained to me that a man and a woman who are cyclic to one another can't see eye to eye in a million years. The only thing Carlos and I could do was to merge together."

When she left the hotel after being with Castaneda, she went back to the chapel and met the Death Defier:

> She took me by the hand through that chapel and a second later I was facing again the sea of awareness. It's not a sea. It's an inconceivable surge of energy, a peculiar energy that is aware and talks to you. Perhaps the mystics of ancient times experienced this. Carlos thinks that at best they only reach the mold of man, a clump of energy fields, like luminous strings. Something like a cosmic mold that stamps energy in the form of man, just like a machine that makes crackers. But I think that perhaps they went beyond it. The sea of awareness is the closest thing to the concept of God; it is an all-inclusive force. In front of it, you're not even a spark, a speck, a virus. Yet it is aware of you. In that sea of awareness my cyclic being, the Death Defier, turned into that something not foreign to me, not disgusting at all. She was me filled to capacity with indifference. Every one of my concerns shut off like one turns off an electric bulb. . . . There were powerful organic sensations, flashy images like in a dream. Finally I was in a concise dream which gained precision until it was the real world.

Returning to the ordinary world, Carol Tiggs searched

for Carlos until one day she heard he was giving a lecture. "Of course I nearly gave him a heart attack. He thought I had gone as the rule dictated. The rest you know."

Muni then offered a last thought. "When the Death Defier and I were in front of the sea of awareness, she told me my name was Muni. She said that some day when I had succeeded to integrate myself, or when nothing matters anymore and my eyes were aligned with hers I would be herself, *Xoxopanxoco*, which means 'fruit of eternal spring.'"

The Death Defier, she said, told her that she had been alive for thousands of years. The reason was not because she was greedy for life but that she loved life and mankind. Her one dream, which had nothing to do with survival, was to help mankind reach a new level of reason and intelligence. She said that to invoke her name in Tula would be like a cue to wake her. And that there could be some daring beings who would do so in my presence.

> By invoking her name in my presence which is her presence, their internal dialogue would stop and they may even catch a glimpse of dreams upon dreams that were woven in this marvelous locale, now occupied by this absurd crummy little town. She told me to say this:
>
> *Can a nicuicanitl huiya*
> *Xochitl in noyollo ya*
> *nicmana nocuic a ohuaya ohuaya*
> *o xoxpanxoco o xoxopanxoco.*
>
> *I am the work of the only God, his creation . . .*
> *He created you,*
> *He uttered you like a flower,*
> *He painted you like a song:*

a Toltec artist.
The book has come to the end:
Your heart is complete . . .

I cry as I speak and discourse with my heart,
Let me see the root of song,
Let me implant it here on earth
so it may be realized . . .
My song is hard and flourishes.
My implanted word is sprouting,
Our flowers stand up in the rain.

VI

Ideas & Sources

CASTANEDA'S SORCERIC IDEAS WHAT ARE THEY AND WHAT ARE THEIR SOURCES? In the end, Castaneda's significance and value rests on his ideas and sources, not the strangeness of his story. Instead of building his ideas from the perspective of the apprentice, let's begin from how he perceives the universe and organic life and only then consider the highest form of the organic, the human being.

The universe is energy. Everything is an expression of the emanations of energy. Energy exists in both animate and inanimate form. The difference between animate and inanimate energy can be seen in the difference between a boulder, an inanimate form, and a bird, an organic being. Within space and time, the vibration of these energetic forces is either increasing or decreasing in scale, their density and frequency of vibration accordingly rising or falling, becoming more alive or less. Organic beings—from plants to invertebrates to vertebrates to human beings—differ in their degree of awareness according to the scale of vibration. Human beings have the *potential* to live at the highest level of organic awareness, so high that they can cross the threshold into inorganic awareness.

The universe is composed not only of energy but will, intent. Everything has a will to sustain itself, to grow, not to die. The intent of the universe has created a ray of descending creation of various levels of cosmoses, worlds within worlds, making possible all the various organic mutations and variations. Only human beings have the ability to align attention—which is defined as "the action of hooking and channeling perception"—with the intent of the universe. This is called "intending." In intending, the will of the universe is recognized as conscious.

All organic beings receive and transmit energy. The reception and transmission of this energy is mechanical, from the highest ordinary level of organic life to the lowest. This energy is converted into impressions. Castaneda speaks of impressions as "sensory data," but this is a second processing not a first, as the sensory impressions directly received only become "data" once the impressions are cognized. For human beings this cognizing is overlaid with societal and personal conditioning. Where impressions are transformed into data and processed into cognitive units is called the assemblage point. Data is rendered here in a series of symbols within a given language syntax as interpretations, descriptions. Cognition, then, instead of being pure and direct, is instantly enframed in perception, language and memory, a descriptive gloss. The assemblage point can be moved by shocks, hypnotism, sleep, illness and so forth, but otherwise it is stationary. Because the assemblage point is stationary there is a basic agreement as to the composition and components of the world humans experience. However, because cognition is subjective—not pure and direct—and because it occurs within a particular societal gloss, there is ongoing disagreement about descriptions and interpretations.

Every human being is caught within the gloss, or consensual belief system, into which they are born. Each is enframed within a wall of description. The description, societal and personal, is taken for reality. The mind is swamped in description, self-reflection, self-narrative and random associations continually processed in inner talking or internal dialogue. Everything experienced is immediately rationalized and reduced to the inherent and unchallenged assumptions of the ruling self-belief system. Therefore, one's attention remains identified and fragmented, not only within the various interpretations of data but, more importantly, fragmented between the direct seeing of impressions in contrast to data interpreted through societal glosses.

This "human mold" is the conditioned matrix of self-belief in which all humanity is born, lives and dies, except for the few who have the power to break the mold. To do so, one must be able to "stop the world." That is, shut off the internal dialogue so that the "world" one is always telling oneself about stops. What is then cognized is the substrate of inner silence that has been hidden by the incessant self-talk. To stop the world means to redirect the attention from the self-talk by intentionally moving the assemblage point, that which is determining how the world is seen. To be able to move the assemblage point, or the specific gravity of attention, a dissonance has to be created by first experiencing the mechanicality of functioning and perceiving because of the assemblage point's fixity. Dissonance is created by "not-doing," that is, by disrupting routines and habits; by gazing rather than looking, noticing the shadows, not the objects, and so forth. One also examines the story of one's life, recapitulating the major and memorable events and the people associated with them. Societal beliefs and relationships are thus weakened and in so doing one begins to lose their self-importance and the self-love and vanity upon which it is based. Moreover, one strives to be impeccable, that is, to give full attention to whatever and whomever we are engaged with, no matter how insignificant. We thus assume full responsibility for our lives. And because our organic life is only a temporary manifestation, we use our death as an advisor in how we live our life. To access these various levels or worlds, as mentioned, the organic being has to intend the movement of the assemblage point. The universe is constantly testing one's awareness by exerting pressure of movement and the resultant shocks; if these are absorbed and assimilated consciously they will enrich and enlarge organic awareness, with the result that the *universe* also becomes more self-aware.

In intentionally acting, our attention and will strengthen, the physical body becomes enlivened, the energy is refined and one's personal power increases. The physical body, saturated with intention, becomes the energy body. Our level of being in the world—our energetic vibration—and our self-knowledge develop as well. With this as a foundation, we now have the internal strength and knowledge to move the assemblage point, or specific gravity of attention, to a new location within and beyond the body. There are levels or qualities of attention. Each is an independent domain of knowledge and complete in itself. The first or ordinary attention is the experiencing and knowledge of the physical world. The second is the attention of the energy body, a more refined and sensitive attention. The two attentions evolve and unify into a third attention, based in and about the totality of the body. The inner silence of mind, the real mind, is directly experienced. It has always been present but has been hidden by all the inner talking and self-concern. Now the world we perceive is no longer static but dynamic and alive with energy. It has always been so, it is just that our gloss covered it over.

To stop the world, stop the inner dialogue, there must be intent. Intent is the pervasive force that connects everything and causes us to perceive. There must be, as Castaneda insists, "the purposeful guiding of will. . . . We do not become aware because we perceive; rather, we perceive as a result of the pressure and intrusion of intent." This seems to suggest that if we are not consciously intending then our interpretations and judgments are predicated on another's intent, mechanical or conscious, or on one's own mechanical functioning. As intent is a force that is immeasurable and indescribable, the only way to know it is through the direct connection existing between intent and all sentient beings and other life forms.

There are other ways of stopping the world. A common one is the use of power plants, which was how Castaneda began his apprenticeship. Power plants flood the ordinary mind, the Tonal, the describable world, with so much information that internal dialogue stops. The chemistry is also changed. Castaneda never mentions this directly, though he does say:

> Power plants cause untold damage to the body. This is their drawback, especially with the devil's weed. . . . Those plants lead the apprentice directly to the Nagual, and the ally is an aspect of it. . . . Here is where I varied from the tradition. After a lifelong struggle I know that what matters is not to learn a new description but to arrive at the totality of oneself. One should get to the Nagual without maligning the Tonal, and above all, without injuring one's body.

Drugs not only harm the body, but they harm the psyche as well. Because one does nothing more than smoke some weed or take some hallucinogenic, no will is involved. And so the will is weakened and will-lessness can result. Then, too, because they lessen the gradient between the everyday mind and the subconscious—that which houses a lot of unprocessed and unintegrated material—what surfaces can create imagination in the deeper recesses of the mind. It can also inflame one's self-importance.

In stopping the world one comes to the totality of oneself and experiences inner silence and so may hear what Castaneda calls a buzzing or a high frequency. Though he speaks of listening to "the holes between sounds," Castaneda only mentions this inaudible sound current three times, in the first book, second book and the last major book. He speaks of it as reminding him of a "gigantic bee." He later says he "divided his attention" between the buzzing and the external world. Lastly, he notices a "peculiar buzzing, a mixture of the sound of flapping wings and the buzzing of a radio whose dial has not picked up the frequency of a radio station."

"We are luminous beings," said Castaneda. "We are perceivers. We are awareness; we are not objects; we have no solidity. We are boundless. The world of objects and solidity is a way of making our passage on earth convenient. It is only a description that was created to help us. We, or rather our reason, forget that the description is only a description and thus we entrap the totality of ourselves in a vicious circle from which we rarely emerge in our lifetime."

Our rational mind cannot bring us to this experiencing, as the mind is trapped in the consensual societal view. We must change the location of the assemblage point. The physical connection with the assemblage point is located at the spine between the shoulder blades and at an arm's length behind. (Castaneda's description of the exact location has changed over the years.) What keeps this point fixed is the internal dialogue. This incessant self-talk occurs in ordinary mind which absorbs human beings in self-reflection. It is not our real mind but a "foreign installation," an implantation of the predator which has come "from the depths of the cosmos and took over the rule of our lives" and given us "our systems of beliefs, our ideas of good and evil, our social mores." The predator eats our energy by keeping our attention trapped in inner talking of the implanted mind. When inner talking stops, the quality of attention is refined, and the ordinary attention that belongs to the physical body becomes the second attention, which belongs to the luminous body. It is situated in front of the body at the level of the navel. When the two attentions merge into a totality of attention inner silence reigns. "Inner silence," said Castaneda, "is the stand from which everything stems in sorcery." By learning how to move the assemblage point, we experience a dynamic world of what Castaneda calls "energetic facts," impressions that are not static and labeled by conditioned societal descriptions. The ability to move this point allows other worlds to be cognized, the worlds beyond the thin film of false reality in which practically everyone lives, suffers and dies. "Man's battlefield is not in the strife of the world around him. His battlefield is over the horizon, in an area which is unthinkable for an average man, the area *where man ceases to be a man . . . the only thing that matters is the encounter with infinity.*" Then the unity of organic attention passes into the inorganic and one becomes "the active side of infinity." At the death of the body, if our attention is not unified, we are emptied of our life experience and extinguished, or we survive as inorganic beings, "clumps of cohesive energy" that are self-aware and invisible to the human eye.

We have two minds. One is the true mind that is, as Castaneda says, "the product of all our life experiences, the one that rarely speaks because it has been defeated and relegated to obscurity. The other, the formatory mind we use daily for everything we do, is a foreign installation." As mentioned, the recapitulation of one's life can weaken the grip of the ordinary mind. Recapitulation has a number of stages, the first is a simple recounting of the incidents of our life. The second is taking our life as it is in the present moment and moving backward, making as detailed a recollection as we can. The events of one's life are to be relived, thus freeing one's energy from the event and recapturing it for one's individual power, which unfortunately Castaneda calls "personal power," thus still unconsciously propagating the aegis of the "person." This process weakens the allegiance to the person by subjecting his or her story, their life, to direct observation and so, in time, disintegrates the foreign installation, the perpetuator of the story.

Our story is the story of ourselves in the ordinary world, which Castaneda calls the Tonal [this and its corollary the Nagual are capitalized to differentiate them from definitions other than Castaneda's]. This is where attention is trapped, the locus of description. The Tonal encompasses the rules and behaviors and perceptions of ordinary life. It is how we comprehend and apprehend the world. It makes two sides of everything. If there is a right way, there is a wrong; if there is good, there is evil, and so forth. When the perception of the Tonal is shocked one contracts. If we amp up the power of the Tonal through recapitulation and not-doing, we amp up our personal power. We are then positioned to embrace the Nagual, which is neither experience nor intuition of consciousness but what cannot be named. Castaneda gives a beautiful image of this. He describes the Tonal as being what is on the table—forks, knives, spoons, and so forth—all known within the context of the table; and the Nagual being all of that which is *off the table,* invisible to the ordinary eye and beyond description.

Don Juan speaks of the Tonal as both personal and collective, or societal. Our personal Tonal is our distinct personality and its perception of the world. Before we can experience the Nagual we must strengthen the Tonal in terms of holding our own in the world, paying our bills, living in a way so that we have emotional stability and physical health. In a word, becoming impeccable.

Through observation, we begin to discriminate between the Nagual and the Tonal. Our eyes belong to the Tonal because of conditioning. They keep reducing the world, leveling it to the accepted societal description of the Tonal. When we blink, stare, gaze, do otherwise with our eyes, we break the hypnotic self-referential overlay of the Tonal. Through reason we observe the effects of the Tonal; through will we observe the effect of the Nagual, which is in essence a reflection of that indescribable void which contains all and everything and nothing and no-thing.

What most differentiates Castaneda's approach is his emphasis on dreaming. It plays a significant part in Castaneda's teaching, beginning with *The Second Ring of Power*. He says there are four gates to dreaming. We must first set up dreaming by becoming aware before deep sleep of a sensation similar to a "pleasant heaviness that doesn't let us open our eyes." We reach the first gate the moment we realize we're falling asleep. We gaze in the dream and then move to "the attention of the Nagual" by finding and focusing our attention on our hands (Castaneda said in one interview he wanted to say penis, but his publisher insisted on hands). Once established in the dream one becomes aware of the specific features of the dream—streets, buildings, things—not looking directly at them but being aware of them. Dreaming is real only when everything comes into focus. But this vividness can be an obstacle if our attention becomes trapped in it. Our intent is to contact the energy body. We must wish without wishing, do without doing. This means it must be an objective wish and doing, not that of the person. While dreaming, he says to press the tip of the tongue to the roof of the mouth (which is also a meditation technique of spiritual ways).

The second gate is reached when one wakes up from one dream into a second one. To do this we have to learn to pick out and follow the "foreign energy scouts." Only in changing dreams, by allowing ourselves to be pulled by the energy of these "sentient beings from another dimension," do we learn about these scouts. "Scouts are always aggressive and extremely daring," says Castaneda. "Sustaining our dreaming attention on them is like soliciting their awareness to focus on us. Once they do so, we are compelled to go with them. And that, of course, is the danger. We may end up in worlds beyond our energetic possibilities." We contact the third gate only when we, the dreamer, discover a person who is asleep who turns out to be us. This "breakage is a division of sorts in the otherwise unified personality." Here one intentionally merges one's dreaming reality with the reality of the ordinary world. This completes the energy body. With the fourth and final gate, the energy body travels to specific places in this world or those of another; or, travels to places existing only in the intent of others—dreaming together. In this way, "a double" is created in which one can perceive "the here and the there at once." As the dreaming body develops, so does the strength of one's gaze and the capability to absorb the Eagle's emanations, the energy field. (The Eagle is a metaphoric name Castaneda gives for the Source of all and everything.) Like looking directly at the sun and losing one's eyesight, if one gazes too long the dreaming body may lose itself, disintegrate, in the Eagle. By its emanations organic beings are created. At their death the Eagle reabsorbs their emanations. (Compare this with Robert Monroe's *Journeys Out of the Body* published in 1971, twelve years before the appearance of *The Art of Dreaming*.)

What needs to be clear, and Castaneda does make it clear, though unfortunately not until *The Art of Dreaming*, is that the relationship between the old sorcerers and inorganic beings was very much like the idea of selling one's soul to the devil in exchange for immortality. Inorganic beings, he says, are female and are attracted to emotions, animal fear being most attractive. Inorganic beings want our awareness, as theirs is slow in comparison. "They will give us knowledge," he says, "but they'll extract a payment: our total being." By dreaming, we compel them to interact with us. Once a connection is made they become allies. We can't be forced to stay with them, yet they can imprison us by indulging us. "Beware of awareness that is immobile," says Castaneda. "Awareness like that has to seek movement, and it does this by creating projections."

A difficulty Castaneda faced in bringing these ideas into ordinary life is the association of sorcery with evil. Castaneda dealt with this semantically by adopting the word *shamanism* and using it interchangeably with *sorcery*. But the two words, while having some similarity, are quite different. The dictionary defines sorcery as "the use of power gained from the assistance or control of evil spirits." Shamanism is defined as "a religion practiced by indigenous peoples of a far northern Europe and Siberia that is characterized by belief in an unseen world of gods, demons and ancestral spirits." The word *shaman* is thought to derive from the Tungus language of Central Siberia. Some think the genesis of the word comes from the Manchu word *saman,* meaning "one who is excited, moved, raised." *Saman* is pronounced *shaman*. Shamans, who can be male or female, exist within families and within communities and serve them as priests, medicine men, prophets. Shamans are called to their role and often have "Arctic hysteria." A shaman will possess many unusual qualities but the chief one is power. There are white shamans and black; the black are not necessarily bad, but they do deal with evil powers. They foretell the future, call up spirits, and wander into the spirit-land, giving accounts of their journeys. Whereas Northern European and Siberian shamans use drums and generally do not use hallucinogens, the indigenous people in Central and South America usually do not use a drum, but in religious rituals they ingest psychotropic plants, such as the *Psilocybe* mushroom, jimsonweed (*Datura*), peyote cactus, and tobacco taken as snuff or its smoke quickly inhaled to produce a hallucinatory experience.

With the publication in English of Mircea Eliade's *Shamanism: Archaic Techniques of Ecstasy* in 1964 (the French edition appeared in 1951), the definition of shamanism was broadened. While acknowledging that "Shamanism in the strict sense is pre-eminently a religious phenomenon of Siberia and Central Asia," Eliade defined the shaman as "the great master of ecstasy" and said, "a first definition of this complex phenomenon, and perhaps the least hazardous, will be: shamanism=*technique of ecstasy*." So defined, Eliade was able then to expand shamanism from its roots to the world at large. He did however make this distinction:

> If the word "shaman" is taken to mean any magician, sorcerer, medicine man, or ecstatic found throughout the history of religions and religious ethnology, we arrive at a notion at once extremely complex and extremely vague; it seems, furthermore, to serve no purpose, for we already have the terms "magician" or "sorcerer" to express notions as unlike and as

> ill-defined as "primitive magic" or "primitive mysticism."

Though Eliade broadened the term, he also sought to limit it. If the ecstatic experience is interpreted within a religious context, then it is clearly shamanic, given the origin of the word. But if it is *not* religiously interpreted, as with Castaneda—religion, for him, being simply another gloss—then what is it? Castaneda does not put himself or don Juan forward as a priest, medicine man or prophet, the terms anthropologists use to define different categories of shamans. Instead, he speaks of being a "warrior." Other anthropologists began to use the word *shaman* in the 1960s when seeing South American ritual leaders enter an ecstatic state, thus blurring the line between sorcery and shamanism.

To further distinguish the ideas he was presenting, Castaneda began to speak of them as *Toltec.* Castaneda had never liked the negative associations ascribed to sorcery, and so he began to reposition it as a shamanic teaching derived from the ancient Toltecs. The Toltecs belonged to an Indian culture in southern Mexico that was already extinct at the time of the Spanish conquest and colonization of Mexico. They lived in Tula between 1150 and 900 BCE. He said he used *Toltec* not in its anthropological meaning, but as one who knows the mysteries of watching and dreaming. The objective of the Toltec, Castaneda said, is "to leave the living world with all that one is but with nothing more than what one is. The goal is not to take anything or leave anything." In his last major book, Castaneda switches to a new term, "warrior-travelers." He also has don Juan saying:

> To be a sorcerer doesn't mean to practice witchcraft, or to work to affect people, or to be possessed by demons. To be a sorcerer means

> to reach a level of awareness that makes inconceivable things happen. The term "sorcery" is inadequate to express what sorcerers do, and so is the term "shamanism." The actions of sorcerers are exclusively in the realm of the abstract, the impersonal. Sorcerers struggle to reach a goal that has nothing to do with the quests of the average man. Sorcerers' aspirations are to reach infinity, and to be conscious of it.

Sorceric or shamanic, the source of Castaneda's ideas has long been debated. Some hold that there are possible published sources for almost everything he wrote. Certainly Castaneda was an omnivorous reader of occult, mystical and anthropological texts. For example, with Daniel Brinton's 1894 paper "Nagualism: A Study in Native American Folklore and History" (see Appendices) Castaneda may very likely have encountered the concept of the *nagual* and *tonal*, two Aztec words. In the Nahuatl language the word *tonalli* is translated as meaning a person's unique individuality; it is the individuality with which a person is born. It can be made stronger or weaker depending on how a person lives. The word *tonalli* is derived from the radical *tona*, which means to warm or be warm and is related to *tonatiuh*, the sun. The belief is that the guardian spirit of the tonal can be represented by an animal, and it can be lost or stolen and so result in misfortune or sickness, depression or other disorders.

To strengthen the tonal, shamans would perform ceremonies to reenergize the tonal, in doing so the shaman, or the teacher, plays the part of the *tetonaltiani*, "he who concerns himself with the tonal." The man of knowledge is one who reconnects one to the nagual. Brinton says that Spanish missionaries talk of the *naualli* as "masters of wisdom." In the Nahuatl language the root *na* contains the idea to know or knowledge.

Was Western thought also a source? An interviewer asked Castaneda directly: "There seem to be many parallels between existential philosophy and don Juan's teachings. What you have said about decision and gesture suggests that don Juan, like Nietzsche or Sartre, believes that will rather than reason is the most fundamental faculty of man."

"I think that's right," Castaneda said, and instead of speaking to what was asked—existential philosophy as a source and therefore legitimizing "mind" and "reason," as they are commonly thought of—he immediately shifted the discussion, saying, "Let me speak for myself." He then brings up his mind's control over his life and says, "it would rather kill me rather than to relinquish control." He speaks of a period of futility and depression, with thoughts of suicide. "He [don Juan] said my reason was making my body feel that there was no meaning in life. Once my mind waged this battle and lost, *reason began to assume its proper place as a tool of the body.*" [Italics added.]

Earlier in the interview, he is asked:

"There is an ordinary reality that we Western people are certain is the only world, and then there is the separate reality of the sorcerer. What are the essential differences between them?"

Castaneda replied:

> In European membership the world is built largely from what the eyes report to the mind. In sorcery the total body is used as a preceptor. As Europeans we see a world out there and talk to ourselves about it. We are here and the world is there. Our eyes feed our reason and we have

> no direct knowledge of things. According to sorcery this burden on the eyes is unnecessary. *We know with the total body.* [Italics added.]

Awareness of the total body—this is the foundation to everything Castaneda is saying. He does not amplify this, but without an inhabited body, without being consciously embodied, we are simply an idea, feeling, impulse, reaction. We are so addicted to ideas, systems and all things mental that we do not realize it is only a mental way of looking at and describing the world. Modern science was quite useful in challenging superstition and ordering life on a rational basis, but its very success has entombed us in the mind. The body is taken for granted. It has been forgotten. Not entirely forgotten, of course, since we are concerned about how the body appears to others. We are ultrasensitive to that and constantly dress it for the best effect possible. But in terms of giving the body attention, we only do so when it reacts to the demands of hunger, lust, fear and illness. Then we do all we can to assuage its organic needs or rid it of disease so we can return to our primary occupation—our heads. That is, our thoughts, ideas, judgments, dreams and fantasies. And so it could be said we only know with the head.

Head and body. Castaneda and don Juan. This was the essential struggle—whether to perceive from the mind alone, or to perceive from the body-mind. Castaneda came to realize that the intellectual world of which he was a member had exhausted itself with the sophistication of its concepts. These had brought it to a nihilism of the mind in which, like the Ouroboros, the mind turned on itself. The snake of wisdom with all its glosses and logical investigations of the world had arrived at a standstill. The body was the undiscovered country.

The interviewer said to Castaneda: "Western man begins with the assumption that subject and object are separated. We're isolated from the world and have to cross some gap to get to it. For don Juan and the tradition of sorcery, the body is already in the world. We are united with the world, not alienated from it."

Answered Castaneda:

> That's right. Sorcery has a different theory of embodiment. The problem in sorcery is to tune and trim your body to make it a good receptor. Europeans deal with bodies as if they were objects. We fill them with alcohol, bad food, and anxiety. When something goes wrong we think germs have invaded the body from outside and so we import some medicine to cure it. The disease is not part of us. Don Juan doesn't believe that. For him disease is a disharmony between man and his world. The body is an awareness and it must be treated impeccably.

Earlier, Castaneda said that after his mind lost the battle for dominance, the reason of the mind alone became the reason of the body-mind, or, better stated, the reason of the body-feelings-mind. So it isn't that Castaneda is doing away with reason. It's simply that if reason is not body-feeling based, then it has walled itself off in the tower of the head. So, accepting that, how to become embodied?

Few, if any, have recognized a major source of Castaneda's ideas as being derived from the ancient esoteric teaching that G. I. Gurdjieff rediscovered and reformulated for modern mentality that he called The Fourth Way. Born in 1872 in Alexandropol and raised in Kars in the Caucasus, at an early age George Ivanovitch Gurdjieff came to "the whole sensation of himself." Seeing the suffering, misery and illusion with which people lived, the question arose in him—"What is the sense and significance of life on Earth, and human life, in particular?" The answers of the religion and science of his day did not satisfy, and so he with some like-minded friends, they called themselves the "Seekers of Truth," believing that the ancient wisdom societies had found the answer, set out to discover it. Their search took them to many remote and dangerous areas. In time, Gurdjieff realized the origin of the fundamental ideas and principles of this ancient teaching lay in Egypt, "only not from the Egypt that we know but from one which we do not know. This Egypt was in the same place as the other but it existed much earlier. Only small bits of it survived in historical times, and these bits have been preserved in secret." Realizing that over time elements of it had migrated northward, he made a second journey to the Hindu Kush and elsewhere, reassembling and reformulating the teaching. Understanding that the world needed a major shock—"*Unless the 'wisdom' of the East and the 'energy' of the West are harnessed and used harmoniously, the world will destroy itself*"—he brought the teaching of The Fourth Way to St. Petersburg, Russia, in 1912. He said, "The teaching here being set out is completely self-supporting and independent of other lines and it has been *completely unknown* up to the present time." [Italics added.]

Many of the fundamental ideas Castaneda puts forth can be seen to have a correspondence with Gurdjieff's teaching. It is not in the province of this book to summarize it, but the following are some examples of the cross-referencing:

> *Guardian spirit* of Tonal is the inner animal.
> *Assemblage point* is the specific gravity of the

attention, where the attention is active, whether in thought, feelings or instinct, the head, solar plexus or spine. Castaneda speaks of not being in the physical body but in the luminous shell, or cocoon, but in terms of physical connection it is "over or around the right shoulder blade."

Shifting the assemblage point is moving the specific gravity of attention so that one is in a higher state of self-consciousness or self-remembering.

Stopping the world is what happens with the initial shift of the assemblage point into a state of self-consciousness.

Second attention is the attention of self-consciousness.

Third attention is the shift of attention to self-remembering of the emotional center and/or the higher intellectual center.

Buzzing is an initial inaudible frequency which prepares for reception of the Nirioonossian-World-Sound.

Inner silence is the point at which the practices of self-consciousness, self-remembering and self-observation converge and one is delivered beyond the mind full of inner dialogue to the higher intellectual center.

Seeing energy is not seeing outside oneself but seeing the energy inside the body as it flows, which is experiencing self-sensing.

Real mind is the higher intellectual center connected with the higher emotional center.

Reason is the reason of knowledge, that of the foreign installation. When reason is connected with the awareness of the totality of the body it is the reason of understanding.

Stalking is "following a way that involved becoming invisible." It was not a new idea. Gurdjieff had often said that those in the Work should know how to become invisible. The secret lay in not engaging the attention of those around one. "One should be able to move though a crowd without being noticed, without making any impression on anyone, " said Robert de Ropp, author of *The Master Game* and a student of Ouspensky's. One also stalks oneself in self-observation.

Foreign installation is the formatory mind. Castaneda speaks of this as an implantation. Gurdjieff speaks of Kundabuffer as an implantation.

Human mold is founded in self-love and vanity, i.e., Kundabuffer.

The Eagle is the moon in its aspect of eating, and mechanical people are food for the moon.

Predatorial universe is reciprocal maintenance in which man is used to unconsciously or intentionally receive and transmit energies.

Predator eating our attention is reminiscent of the 1967 novel *The Mind Parasites* by Colin Wilson, who has written many books on Gurdjieff.

Ape is what Gurdjieff calls "A male who is a Passive-Active, instead of an Active-Passive, a monstrosity, an 'ape.' A female who is an Active-Passive instead of a Passive-Active, as she should be, is also a monstrosity, an 'ape.'"

Self-importance is the result of the implantation of the organ Kundabuffer, later removed, but whose specific properties of egotism remain, which cause the seeing of reality topsy-turvy.

Foreign implantation is the implantation of Kundabuffer.

Losing self-importance is self-observation combined with self-remembering.

Recapitulation is sincerely telling the story of one's life.

Intent is the development of real will that connects with a greater will.

Energy body is the Kesdjan body developed through practices of self-sensing and the impartial observation of the functioning of the physical body.

Inorganic being is having a soul that is immortal within the solar system. Castaneda believes there is no soul, yet inorganic beings, who were once organic, continue to exist as awareness after the body dies.

Dreaming and infinity, see Appendices, "On the Study of Dreams" and "Experimental Mysticism" in P. D. Ouspensky's *A New Model of the Universe.*

Eight-pointed diagram is the enneagram. (See Notes.)

Man of knowledge is man without quotation marks.

Soul is that which, Gurdjieff holds, has to be made. Man is not born with a soul. Castaneda believes man does not have one.

Sorcerer's aspiration is to see Infinity, and to be conscious of it is to become a Sacred Individual and a help for God.

In considering Castaneda's ideas, one can only marvel at his ingenuity in using language to not only suggest a metaphorical reality, but more importantly, if one is trying to understand what the words point to, to misdirect one's attention. For example, he speaks again and again of seeing the energy of the universe as it flows into the world, so his words would naturally lead one to look outside oneself. Certainly, if the mind is quiet, there is a shimmer in space, and with some people an aura can be seen, but is that what Castaneda is really talking about? Two years before his death he gave a new or added formulation. "What you are feeling is the flow of energy," he recounts don Juan telling him. "It is like a very mild electric charge, or a weird itching on your solar plexus, or above your kidneys. *It is not a visual effect, yet every sorcerer I know speaks of it as seeing energy. I'll tell you a secret. I have never seen energy. I only feel it.* My advantage is that I have never tried to explain what I feel. I just feel whatever I feel, end of the story." [Italics added.] This flow of energy, then, is not outside but inside. It is the self-sensation that is boosted and elaborated when one directs their attention to the physical body itself. This, in time, rightly conducted and with repeated effort, develops the energy body. Seeing, then, is really a self-sensing, a self-remembering.

Turning from the ideas to a more incisive consideration of Castaneda's language, we see that where Gurdjieff's use of language stressed the impersonal, Castaneda gives the ideas a sorceric twist and gloss. Is this intentional? If so, it could only be to hide their origin. As with all things Castaneda, one can't be sure. But the correspondences between the ideas he presents (and often enlarges and changes) and those of The Fourth Way often taste like fruit from the same tree. To be fair, the sorceric ideas rooted in a pre-scientific world would, of course, be stated in metaphoric language indigenous to that period. So it could be argued that similar does not mean the same. Nevertheless, the similarities to Gurdjieff's Fourth Way are striking enough to legitimately consider whether this is the primary source of Castaneda's ideas.

Not only ideas, but even some of Castaneda's stories clearly have a Gurdjieffian parallel. Castaneda constantly proclaimed, for example, that all of humanity was just food, nothing more. "Think of the owners of a chicken coop," Castaneda would declare in the hyperbolic way of speaking he often used. "They really don't care for the well-being of the chickens! They just raise them and eat them—and that's how the flyers are with us. If one chicken escapes they don't waste all their time chasing it down to bring it back. A few of us might escape, by doing the magical movements and the recapitulation. I can't save you! But without me, you don't even have a chance."

In Ouspensky's *In Search of the Miraculous*, Gurdjieff tells of the rich magician who hypnotized his sheep into imagining that they were eagles and lions so they could be slaughtered when the time was right. Gurdjieff held that unawakened people were simply machines, food for the moon; that long ago an organ was implanted in us so that we see life topsy-turvy, and do not recognize our situation and in despair commit suicide. Though the organ was later removed, its specific properties of self-love and vanity (the human mold) continue to exist.

Gurdjieff says that only when one has come to a true recognition of their nothingness is there the first true taste of understanding. Castaneda speaks of becoming nothing, of breaking the human mold, so that one can see the world as it is. Gurdjieff says the higher intellectual center is obscured by the formatory mind; Castaneda speaks of two minds, a higher mind obscured by a lower. Gurdjieff talks of doing otherwise, Castaneda of not-doings. Gurdjieff speaks of moving the specific gravity of one's attention; Castaneda of moving the assemblage point. And so forth.

Castaneda did have an actual, as opposed to simply a theoretical, connection with the Work, as it is sometimes called. His first direct encounter was in 1970 when he attended Movements demonstrations in Los Angeles. Later, he accepted an invitation from Lord John Pentland, the man Gurdjieff appointed to lead the Work in America, to spend a weekend at St. Elmo, the home of the Gurdjieff Foundation in San Francisco. There Castaneda met Kathleen Pohlman, aka Carol Tiggs, a student of Pentland's. He is said to have also attended meetings at the Los Angeles Foundation for a time.

Given what Castaneda says about his "eight-pointed diagram"—which represents how the will connects to feeling, dreaming and seeing, and reason and talking—he certainly did know of the enneagram, the primary symbol of the Work. An alchemical symbol, the enneagram was unknown until Gurdjieff introduced it to his students during his Russian period, 1912–1918. It first appeared in the public domain in 1949 with Ouspensky's *In Search of the Miraculous.* Researchers ever since have made many attempts to find earlier sources for the symbol. (The closest they have come is the Jesuit Athanasius Kircher's (1602–1680) symbol, but it is not the same. The Sufis, of course, claim it, but then they claim everything.) Castaneda certainly knew of the enneagram. As a close friend of his reported:

> Carlos, I knew, was acquainted with pupils from Gurdjieff's lineage . . . Kathleen Speeth, a

> therapist [whose parents brought her up in the Work] who had popularized Enneagram studies in America, knew Carlos and cited him on the first page of her book, *The Gurdjieff Work*. When I introduced the subject, Carol [Tiggs] blew up.
>
> "Didn't you understand anything tonight? It's all a big mystery, a question mark—that was the *whole* point! And now you're making categories."
>
> Years later Carol told me that Carlos forbade her to take a class or otherwise pursue her deep interest in the Enneagram.

So Castaneda had to know about the enneagram not only from Speeth but also from her lover Claudio Naranjo, who Castaneda calls "a good friend." It was Naranjo who induced her to leave the Work she had been born into and then to give public classes in the enneagram, thus gaining the knowledge he coveted. But Naranjo's heavy drug use finally broke the relationship and he left for Spain. The group he founded, SAT, Seekers After Truth, an eclectic mix of Gurdjieff, Sufism and psychology, later adopted by A. H. Almaas, the millionaire Kuwaiti and self-made teacher who founded the "Diamond Approach," was passed to a teacher in New York, who like Naranjo and Almaas had never been a student in an authentic Gurdjieff group. Why was Castaneda so adamant about not studying the symbol? Was this part of his private knowledge that he didn't want known?

As striking as the similarities are, so, thankfully, are the differences. The teaching Gurdjieff brought is based on sacred science; what Castaneda brought is based on sorcery. Both aim to awaken one from the dream of ordinary life, but while Gurdjieff rejects working with the dream state and insists on grounding consciousness in ordinary life in order to come to real life, dreaming for Castaneda is the basis of sorceric exploration.

What one finds missing—is that the right word?—with Castaneda is a spiritual appreciation and valuation of the scale of Being and the duty to serve and offer "help for God," as Gurdjieff says. The genuine experiencing of the reason of understanding and unity that lead to conscience and divine love, which are at the core of Gurdjieff's teaching, seems to be missing. Certainly it is never mentioned.

VII

Castaneda's Lover

WHO KNOWS A MAN BETTER THAN HIS MISTRESS? However that is argued certainly such intimacy gives a perspective of its own. Amy Wallace, Castaneda's lover and his student of seven years, was in and out of his inner circle. She relates the experience in her *Sorcerer's Apprentice: My Life with Carlos Castaneda.* Her father, the writer Irving Wallace, introduced her to Castaneda. It was 1973. She was seventeen at the time. Thereafter, she and Castaneda only met casually and infrequently until 1991, when at the age of thirty-six, married nine years and recently divorced, Amy Wallace entered his sorceric world.

Wallace, a mature woman, an accomplished writer, having authored and coauthored a number of nonfiction books and one novel, *Desire*, had a wide circle of cultural and countercultural friends, and considered herself "steeped" in Eastern philosophy and religion and martial arts. So what drew her into Castaneda's circle? "He had one of the most charismatic personalities I've ever known," she said.

Like the three witches, Wallace's name was changed, in her case to "Ellis Laura Finnegan." He demanded she break off all contact with friends and tell her parents "I send you to hell!" He had an obsession with body odor, so at all times she and the witches had to be well-bathed and had to use identical bath products. All body hair had to be removed and pubic hair shaved in prescribed ways. As former lovers had left "energetic worms" in their wombs, the women had to take frequent five-minute baths in rosemary cuttings. No one but Castaneda was allowed to give them haircuts. (But they weren't allowed to ask for a haircut.) He hated body fat, and so the women did hours of daily exercise. They could own no jewelry—all was to be given to him—and their best clothes were to be shredded. The aim was to destroy their self-importance.

All students were to constantly recapitulate their lives so as to erase all personal history. Words like love, friendship, family and need—and other "human words"—were forbidden. The aim, presumably, was to destroy the "human mold," their identification with the human world and themselves as human beings. No longer identified, the incessant inner monologue would stop, and the self-love and vanity caused by the "foreign installation" would be destroyed.

In breaking their human identification, their awareness would no longer be "food" for "the flyers," and at a deeper level, "seymours," both inorganic beings, who fed on awareness. With this, inner silence would emerge and the true seeing of energetic facts—what the philosopher Edmund Husserl had called "the things themselves," but they would take this concept to its sorceric limit. As one witch said, "Husserl didn't live his theories. Only we do that." What she meant was that Husserl confined his investigations to the ordinary organic world, whereas Castaneda and his party dreamed their way into inorganic worlds. They did this by losing the "human mold" so that their awareness would be so honed and freed from all human constraints that they could travel through dreaming to unimaginable worlds. The aim was freedom. Castaneda said he was "the Nagual of freedom."

The sorceric picture of the world Castaneda fed his students was antithetical to conventional worldviews. Whatever seemed obtuse, students had to accept. There was no means of verification. Asking "Why?" was forbidden. The world Castaneda set up was one in which he exerted total control and those who would be his students had to accept that. They also had to accept that while he constantly proclaimed his celibacy at seminars, he was a sexaholic. "Carlos had this urge to have sex with as many women as possible. It was so strong. It meant so much to him," said Amy. "He was so obsessed with his height that it probably stemmed from that." Like the womanizing French philosopher Jean Paul Sartre (both were 5' 2"), Castaneda was intent on bedding every woman he met. As his grandfather told him, "You can't fuck all the women in the world, but you can try!" His female students, however, were not allowed to have sex with anyone but him. Women students lived together in pairs. A call would come for one of them to come to him: the chosen one would quickly bathe and run to Castaneda leaving her roommate in tears. The men were to live entirely celibate lives. "What kind of real man would accept these conditions," Florinda would sneer. "*Coño!* No balls. These guys are *castrati!*"

Early on, Florinda, pimping for Castaneda, told Amy, "You really should sleep with Carlos. You'd love it—he's great! He can go on forever. Consider having sex with the Nagual, sometime."

When Amy agreed, he took her to a run-down motel in Hollywood. She found him unaccountably nervous. Signing in at the desk he whispered in her ear, "Tonight Amy Wallace dies." And later in the motel room where he insisted they both keep their clothes on during sex, he told her, "When you're dead, nothing can hurt you. What can they do to a corpse?"

In subsequent liaisons, the clothes came off and she found he was capable of repeated ejaculations, often as many as three or four in quick succession. But, with diabetes setting in, he was not able to get a full erection. While he enjoyed various positions, only he could initiate them, thus maintaining total authority in the bedroom as he did in every other part of his life. The experience varied with his moods, which were erratic at best.

Sex between Castaneda and Amy, though torrid—"Carlos and I," she says, "had great chemistry"—was always at his instigation and with him always in control. She never knew what to expect, as he could by turns be sweet and tender or verbally abusive. He continually shocked, sometimes talking on the phone while they made love, even talking about her. She came to see it as "bust-the-ego between the sheets."

After having sex, Castaneda would frequently call her, often in the early morning hours, and begin a tirade, presumably to lessen her self-importance. He would yell—"I piss on you. You're shit. You think you're so wonderful, so important, such problems! *Carajo!* What makes you special?"

Nevertheless, he bedded Amy once a week and more, along with others. She consoled herself with believing it wasn't as often with the others. "He insisted it was magically critical that I shave my pubic hair in certain ways," she said. "This is the utmost sorceric importance—you must shave the lower half of your *conchitga*; it will allow the energy to flow smoothly, and make you less human," he told her. Now she could heal men energetically with her "powerful *poto*," though he made her vow never to allow "a poisonous human male" to enter her body.

As he had with the other witches, when he grew tired of having sex with her, he insisted she be celibate but also pimp for him. "You're my wife now," Castaneda declared, "you're a lioness. Go out and hunt for your husband, bring him magical gifts, energetic gifts—you must do it—this is your task. Hunting as a lioness for her husband means bringing him women." Castaneda did not mind the women enjoying one another sexually—"He was pro-lesbian," said Amy—but he was definitely against homosexuality.

Amy happened to tell him she took Prozac to lessen the effect of the migraines she got during her monthly period. Castaneda flew into a rage. She was trying to kill him, he told her, "by having sex with him with the poisonous Prozac in her body." So once again he kicked her out of his inner circle, this time for good.

Deeply depressed, Amy thought of suicide. She spoke to Florinda about it.

"You think you can get our attention? . . . Do you think

we care what a poor baby like you does to get attention? . . . Well, let me tell you, it won't work here."

When she called Taisha, she heard a sarcastic laugh, and then—"Oh, everyone tries that!"

Muni told her there are two kinds of suicide. "One is the warrior's suicide, when you're prepared to face your death. The other is a 'poor baby' suicide—that's what I think is going on here."

Why did Amy stay?

> There was the power of my passion for Carlos. Additionally, there was the adventure, there were exotic magic rituals, there was the elated sense of being on the vanguard of evolution. There was the group pride in being "amoral"—morality was part of "the social order," and we were beyond that. Morality was for bored fucks. And though I didn't admit it to myself for years, there was a dark side to my upbringing, which led me to expect bad treatment from a man.

She speaks of Castaneda's huge, luminous brown eyes; how he gave his whole attention to what he did or the person he was with; of his ability to totally listen and his great storytelling; how he could be very generous, compassionate, as well as wild and cruel. In being with him there was always excitement, a danger. And so like all the others she stayed until the very end, an end that would be no less bizarre than his life had been.

A deeper reason why she and others stayed on—these were strong and intelligent people—is demonstrated with the level of conversation which Castaneda had in the mid-1970s when he went to see Swami Muktananda, a very powerful siddha yogi.

VIII

The Nagual's Star

AGUAL'S STAR NEVER SHONE BRIGHTER OR MORE
JS THAN IN THE EARLY 1990S. In the U.S., Mexico
ope the seminars he and his witches gave drew
ds. Would-be students clamored to speak with
ny desperately hoping to be among the favored
en or so seminar attendees who would be invited
nday class, an amalgamation of Tensegrity exer-
l sorceric discourse.

e end of 1995, however, Castaneda hit a descending octave. His moods, always ominous and unpredictable, began to worsen and increase. His once black hair turned silver and the luminous eyes—his most outstanding physical feature—developed glaucoma. His diabetes became worse and full erections became impossible, though he still was able to have multiple orgasms. Tests revealed liver cancer, though he'd always claimed he would never get "the big C," as he called it. So having come out of the sorceric closet, Carlos Castaneda found himself increasingly confined to his "compound," the military term he called his home.

The compound was in Westwood, at the corner of Pandora Avenue and Eastborne—the name *Pandora*, as in all things with Castaneda's magical mind set, must have been an attraction. A 2,827-square foot, four-unit, Spanish-style complex, it was built in 1938 and bought by Castaneda in 1973 for a half million dollars plus. Hidden from view by twelve-foot hedges, it was entered by a heavy wrought-iron gate. The grounds were covered by orange, grapefruit, lime, lemon, and fig trees with rosemary climbing the walls. Inside, the white walls were bare except for framed jackets of each of his books. The floors were hardwood, the furnishings spare—a couch, chair, TV and CD player. A series of rooms, each more minimal than the preceding, and each exuding a Zen-like feeling, led to his bedroom, where he now spent much of his time. A large, long room, it had a queen-sized bed, night table and a plain desk covered with stacks of paper, a voluminous Spanish/English dictionary and a book of Spanish love songs. There was no computer, not even a typewriter. In the corner was a stand holding his collection of antique canes and walking sticks which Castaneda claimed belonged to don Juan. He also had a knife collection. On the night table were a large-faced clock, strands of amber, moonstones and opals, and a two-pronged rubber dildo with eyeglasses propped between the rubber penises. What light there was came from two spacious skylights.

Gaby Geuter, a former member of the Sunday Class, had spent every weekend for two years stalking Castaneda, hiding outside the compound and videotaping his and his witches comings and goings. Said Geuter:

> He had the sickly look of a hospital stay, the balding skull of chemotherapy treatment. He shuffles along the street as if on a hospital hallway in house slippers, wearing an unbecoming cap that only partially hides his emaciated head and thin hair. . . . Hundreds of heart-wrenching forlorn steps he schleps himself to the gate without determination, clarity or certainty, a seemingly endless walk caught in the fog of pain, until my heart and eye break in sadness.

Castaneda slept a great deal, dictated a novel, *Assassin*, about what he said was his time as an assassin for the CIA in Spain. He ate what he could, goat broth gradually becoming all he could stomach. He constantly demanded attention. Said Florinda, exasperated, "He can't stand it when I leave, he's driving me crazy with his neediness. He won't ever be alone." That Castaneda was needy was a shock because after the word "Why" one of the most forbidden words in the sorcerer's vocabulary besides "love," "friendship" and "family" was human "need."

Nevertheless, the day began with the witches assembling by his bed and Florinda reading the headlines from the *Los Angeles Times* and *New York Times*. Then, came a scathing critique of each one's self-importance, so harsh that, despite their many years of like poundings, it left his witches in tears. This verbal abuse, and Castaneda's sexual treatment of the witches and his students, could be seen as sadism but from his point of view he was trying to break their identification with themselves as persons, so they might break the human mold.

Castaneda's one entertainment—he continued to see life as a battlefield—was watching war movies. He had seen so many it was difficult to find videos he hadn't seen. The novel he was writing, *Assassin*, was supposed to be a sorceric love story, but because of his medications it became so garbled it was barely readable.

As the disease progressed, he would talk of the "Trigger event," his death. A castrati kept asking, "Is it black Nike time yet?" alluding to the Heaven's Gate cult who videotaped its thirty-nine members, wearing matching sneakers, as they committed suicide the year before when the comet Hale-Bopp passed by the planet. Said one former member of the Sunday Class, "The outward appearance of the men and women, in short haircuts and asexual clothing, mirrors a close similarity to the androgynous look of Carlos' inner group."

As Castaneda grew thinner and weaker, in his last days he had to be carried. The women spent the days burning Castaneda's records and tax documents. Taisha, still looking despite the years of abuse, according to Amy, "like a Renaissance beauty, her delicate features carved in ivory," told her: "This is not the death of a Nagual! He's not supposed to die this way! It isn't right, something has gone wrong. It must be . . . his karma. He's paying for the bad things he did." Taisha then closed all her bank accounts. Later, in the trash outside the compound a note was found listing the Wilshire Coin exchange and the current rate of Maple Leaf, American Eagle and Krugerand gold coins.

Taisha called a few days later telling Amy how much she truly loved her and saying she had put some things out for her to have, including a necklace that reminded her of Amy, and asking if she would call her the next day to pick up a window for her at the hardware store.

When Amy called the next day both phone lines were dead. She called Florinda. Both her lines were dead. Her cell phone was "out of range." Muni's phone was off the hook.

Later she learned that at three o'clock the morning of April 27, 1998, the Nagual had left the world permanently. He had said that he would die in a burst of energy, but he died a very human death, horribly jaundiced by liver cancer. (Interestingly, in 1983 he had said of his early drug taking, "That's why my liver's in shreds.") Castaneda was cremated the same day at a Culver City mortuary. Characteristically, it wasn't until nearly two months later, on June 19, that his death was announced in the *Los Angeles Times*. The headline, "A Hushed Death for Mystic Author Carlos Castaneda," appeared in the lower right-hand corner of the front page. In an irony that certainly would have made Castaneda smile, the *New York Times*, the paper of record, ran his obituary not with a photo of the Nagual, but another Carlos Castaneda, a historian.

Of his death Amy Wallace said:

> Carlos had begun as a genuine seeker, a true philosopher, he had ended as a tyrant watching over a cult of terrified followers. Power had wielded its legendary seductions, illness had weakened him terribly. But nothing, I believe, can subtract from the sincerity and beauty of his early works. To take their wisdom and leave

> the rest would be to take the best of Castaneda. . . . I do not believe that Carlos was a con man who callously sought money and women. I think that he believed in his dream to the last, and did his best to make it come true; that he made terrible mistakes as the years went by, due to poor judgment, narcissism, and illness; and in his last decade he did create an abusive cult. This is no black and white tale, for Carlos was not a shifty huckster but a misguided philosopher whose experience of power was corrupting. Thus he damaged many lives, at the same time exalting many others. . . . I sometimes find it remarkable that my deep feeling for Carlos persists so strongly. Despite what I've learned about the perversity of a sexual guru/disciple relationship, I love him still, and I continue to grieve for him.

Before his death, the witches and the apprentices often spoke about Castaneda's death and their intention of committing suicide. Soon after his cremation, two of the witches, Florinda and Taisha, disappeared, as did Nury Alexander and Kylie Lundahl. Nury's car was later found abandoned in Death Valley. In 2004, seven years later, bones were found near the site of the abandoned car. In 2006 DNA identification showed the bones to be Nury's. It's generally assumed that the others committed suicide.

Given Castaneda's rapid decline, his death could not have been a surprise. Three days before he died, he signed a will leaving assets of just over one million dollars—"expressly and intentionally omitted" are his son C.J. and his natural Peruvian daughter Maria del Rosario Peters,

"Charo"—and giving all other assets, estimated as high as twenty million, to the Eagle's Trust, which is to be administered by Cleargreen, Inc. So he clearly was thinking ahead. Though Castaneda had always maintained that he was the last Nagual of his lineage, the creation of the Eagle's Trust shows that he certainly wanted the sorceric work he had established to continue. If true, might the witches' disappearance—"Usually the Nagual and all the members of his party leave the world together," Castaneda had claimed—have been a maneuver to leave their departure in question and mystery? That would provide the necessary seclusion for the witches to work on themselves until such time as they were ready, and when the moment was right, to give a shock by reappearing. As with practically everything concerning Castaneda—who knows? So much of his life and actions can only be reasoned conjecture.

Of the witches, only Muni Alexander, the Nagual woman, aka Carol Tiggs, remains alive. She lives in Los Angeles. Why didn't she disappear with the other witches? From her comments about Castaneda's drama-acring, she certainly saw "the person" in him. That she met don Juan and jumped with him and spoke of herself as being a member of his party, though she would also confound the issue by saying she was a member of Castaneda's party, would suggest that he did not have the primal influence over her that he had over the other witches. He did say she "was famous among us for her speed in adapting to any situation." There apparently was some disagreement between her and Castaneda, too, for a chapter he was naming after her in *The Active Side of Infinity* was left out. It must have also bothered him that she talked about him in workshops, exposing a human side of him that he had spent years hiding. Could the fact that the Nagual woman stayed on indicate her intention to start a "new line"? Said Amy, "The idea of Muni leading a group is absurd . . . she's not a leader type. Muni kept saying [after Castaneda's death], 'It's like the whole group of them are sucking on my tits, like I'm a big sow or something. I just want to be left alone.'" Of course she said she's not really Muni but the Death Defier so she couldn't die. Or maybe it's as simple as this—the person in her just didn't want to become inorganic.

IX

The Summing Up

The life of the Nagual cannot be summed up, for, by definition, it is not of this world. But what of the life of Carlos Castaneda himself? Though filled with lies, obfuscations, the deliberate attempt to erase all personal history, to not "pay taxes to the world," as he said, his books cast a spell on his readers that approached the mythological, the archetypal. How his life as a Nagual and a person will be seen and what its ultimate value and effect will be are questions for another generation.

That he lost his way, that the new or forgotten road he believed he found, what he took to be (or led his readers to believe) a path of heart, became a path of isolation, acute psychic narcissism, paranoia and violence—this is how many now see him and for good reason.

Many former students, their egos eaten out, went into therapy trying to free themselves of the cruelty they had experienced. Amy Wallace wrote a book. Richard Jennings created a Castaneda website, sustainedaction.org, and used his training as a lawyer to build a case and track down documents. Ralph Torjan made a documentary, *Carlos Castaneda: Enigma of a Sorcerer*. Unfortunately, though earnest, it was neither well-done nor well-received. A San Francisco critic called it "an infomercial posing as an expose . . . the talking heads against backdrops of psychedelic computer screensavers—is cheesy and distracting." A *New York Times* critic agreed, but said, "Mr. Torjan makes no secret of having been deeply affected by his time with Castaneda. He tries to reclaim what he can from his former guru, offering testimony from several ex-members of the cult about the profound, positive effect Castaneda's teachings had on their lives."

Unexpectedly, Douglas Price-Williams, Professor Emeritus of Anthropology and Psychiatry at UCLA, offered a more positive view:

> I had intense experiences with Carlos that are difficult to explain. You see, you can't say his work is factual, but you can't say it's false either. It's so much more complex than that. He did have profound experiences of his own. And he had a great deal of ethnographic knowledge. He also engaged in elaborate role playing that he took to the point that I think he could no

> longer tell the difference. But the thing that set Carlos apart was his genius for taking all this and communicating it in a way that really moved people.

Yes, so many have written about sorcerers, shamans and nonordinary reality, but Castaneda alone of his time had the unique poetic genius for absorbing and internalizing the world of which he wrote with an immediacy and dimension that in his early work approaches the archetypal. But the weight of time, the world's judgment, and the driving need in book after book to make real the ideas of nonordinary reality took its toll. Yet from first book to last his consuming interest in the warrior's adventure—the quest for knowledge in realms of the inorganic and the *seeing* of infinity—never changed. To Carlos Castaneda it was all real. What does that mean? What does it mean to be *real*? Perhaps that will be the essential question of the life of the Nagual as lived by Carlos Castaneda.

That said, one is left wondering if he was running from this world from some deep sense of guilt? Was he just exchanging one war movie for another? Without undue psychologizing, could it be that Castaneda really did assassinate someone for the CIA, as a way to get citizenship? Castaneda's cousin, Lucy Chavez, who was quite close to him, kept the letters he wrote home until 1969 which indicate he served in the U.S. Army and left after suffering a wound or "nervous shock." However, the Defense Department has no record of his service. Still, Castaneda kept this idea brewing all his adult life. Bruce Bebb, who lived with Castaneda in a rooming house in 1957, remembers Castaneda telling him stories of his missions for the U.S. Army Intelligence, claiming that after three missions he'd had a breakdown and had to be hospitalized.

Margaret Runyan, who married Castaneda in 1960, remembered that not long after she first met him:

> Carlos told me about the time he was in the Army and was wounded and got the scar on his lower abdomen and groin. It was a serious wound and as he tottered there on the edge of death, every existential question crashed through his skull. That's when he became so serious. It was dark when the enemy came, he said, in pitch black night, and he was in bed. He was serving in the Intelligence division in Spain or Korea or someplace.
>
> It was never really clear. Suddenly, he was rousted from sleep by the cries of his buddies. By the time he realized what had happened, everyone in his squad either had escaped or was dead, and only he was left in camp. Somehow, they had missed him. Carlos sat up perfectly still, squinting into the darkness and listening for any sound. For a long time there wasn't anything. And then, suddenly they were there, looming in front of him, looming spectral figures which he knew absolutely had brought his death. They grabbed him, maybe a half-dozen of them, and they jerked him up off the ground and wrapped his ankles with rope and then strung him to a tree. Dangling there upside down, his mind flashed pure panic. He barely saw the bayonet that somebody slammed into his abdomen, slicing into the groin. Blood gushed out and down, covering his stomach and chest and shoulders and hair and the pain exploded in his chest. When he woke up he was spread-eagled on a

> stainless steel bed with doctors talking solemnly over him. The doctors weren't aware that Carlos was conscious enough to hear the conversation. They concluded among themselves that he would not live.
>
> Carlos told me that at that moment he decided that, if allowed to live, he would be a different person. Given the opportunity, he'd make every minute count. Everything, he knew in that electric transcendent moment, everything is very important.

Amy Wallace remembers that when he first slept with her he told her the scar on his abdomen was from a hernia operation but also that he had a secret. He would often nap and then "wake up and start telling me some bizarre tale about how he murdered people—he was really into telling me about how he murdered people. That was one of his favorite stories." He told her he had "killed a man with a garrote while in the employ of an unnamed government agency." It happened, he said, before he met don Juan. Finally, he confessed it to don Juan.

"I killed people, don Juan. Lots of people."

"That's it?" said don Juan surprised. "You killed people. *Carajo,* Carlos, you killed apes. And you're making yourself sick with this Great Big Secret? *Qué coño*?"

At first Castaneda was horrified by don Juan's "coldness, this terrible inhumanity." But then he felt this burden lifting from him. "Don Juan," he told Amy Wallace, "forced me to see my insignificance. I was so important in my own eyes, my guilt was so all-important. In reality my actions meant nothing. Apes, that's what we are, unless we leap and become the magical creatures we are truly meant to be."

Don Juan had also admitted that he had killed a man. Is guilt then what drew don Juan and Castaneda to explore other worlds, to become powerful enough to elude the grasp of the Eagle? Was this the motive behind all the exploits, the drugs, drama, lies, the erasing of personal history, the breaking of "the human mold"?

Could another be his guilt concerning homosexuality? He was, as Wallace says, "ravingly homophobic." That he was brought up Catholic certainly could have influenced his attitude, but to be *ravingly* so? He said about his mother that her love was a "horrendous burden." He admits to "never liking her." He completely dominated the lives of his witches and inner circle, demanding they have no body hair or fat, cutting their hair short, making them look like little boys, making sex functional and circus-like with any expression of love being a weakness. If Castaneda wasn't sublimating a homosexual desire, why all the fuss? He thought as the Nagual he had no person left . . . but the person, some kind of person, hid behind the Nagual's supposed emptiness. Had the arch-trickster tricked himself?

Interestingly, too, Castaneda allowed no homosexuals into his talks, much less his students or inner circle. Robert Burton, the founder of the Fellowship of Friends, a faux Fourth Way teaching, also denied membership to homosexuals. Burton, like Castaneda, was never in an authentic Fourth Way group, and was in a faux group for only a year or so. Like many such New Age types, Burton arrogated Gurdjieff's ideas and practices that he gleaned from books, mixing in some other-worldly stuff of his own. Under mounting pressure of lawsuits settled out of court in favor of his male students, adults and young, married and single, Burton finally publicly owned up to his homosexuality.

And, finally, in writing about Harold Garfinkel, the UCLA professor who was a seminal influence for him, Castaneda calls him "Professor Lorca." Names were very important to Castaneda. So why "Lorca"? Certainly Castaneda was thinking of Federico García Lorca, a gifted Spanish poet executed in the early days of the Spanish Civil War. A homosexual, his body has never been found.

And so, again, to the seminal question:

Is don Juan real or a fiction?

Jay Courtney Fikes, who decided to become an anthropologist after reading Castaneda's first four books, says, "I suspect that most of Carlos Castaneda's model for don Juan was originally built on exchanges with sorcerers Ramón Medina Silva and don José Matsuwa." Phil Weigand, another anthropologist, speculates Castaneda used don José Matsuwa's initials, DJM, to refer to don Juan Matus.

For Amy Wallace, don Juan was a composite figure made up of Gurdjieff, Oscar Ichazo, Claudio Naranjo and others.

Margaret Runyan believes

> "Don Juan" was real. He was a real Indian, somebody Carlos actually was making trips to see. It's just that once Castaneda got to the point of putting it all down in a readable form, the don Juan of his books became a different creature, a broad and omniscient construction made up of equal parts real Indian, pure Castaneda imagination, library research and dozens of conversations and experiences with people like C.J., myself, Mike Harner, colleagues at UCLA, his grandfather and others.

It seems unlikely that such a compelling and archetypal figure as don Juan could have simply been invented from thin air, though it would be well to remember that Castaneda's muse, Anaïs Nin, said, "The mood I fall into when I am truly possessed by my work is one which resembles the trances of mystics. . . . There is no doubt that the act of creation is very similar to the act of dreaming. . . . It is not only the power to summon an image, but the power to compose with this image." But, pondering all that is known, it seems more likely, at least to this writer, that Castaneda did meet and study sorcery with a sorcerer he calls don Juan. The first three books, and certainly the first, have a quality and substance that only much later reappears. Did Castaneda internalize, become one with, the being and force of don Juan and the sorceric knowledge to which he was initiated? In effect, did Carlos Castaneda "become" don Juan in heart and mind, if not in body?

In his "dreaming"—leaving his person—could Castaneda project his "don Juan" into a story, real, semi-fictive and fictive; one that both did and did not happen in physical life, but happened all the same? That is, stories and events that Castaneda actually lived in his dreaming? If we erase the line between physical reality and dreaming, then how to say what is true? If all life, as Professor Garfinkel contended, is interpretation, then what is the difference between ordinary and nonordinary reality? Between physical life and dreams? For Castaneda, then, don Juan and "don Juan" are real. As real, from Castaneda's point of view, as you or I. It is up to the reader to discover how, when and from what perspective he means the word *real.*

But isn't this being a bit too slippery? There were a good many people he hurt, and that isn't a description. Said Amy Wallace:

> If I had observed Carlos' methods working successfully, and we'd all been broken of our struggles for domination and position, I would have applauded his Theatre of Cruelty, the Carlos Castaneda University of Tough Love, as a supreme accomplishment. Instead I saw spirits crushed, particularly by public humiliation; I saw malevolence, breakdowns, illness and anguish.

Anthony Quinn as don Juan and a tall guy as himself—that's what Castaneda feared Hollywood would do with his books if he allowed them to be made into films. During his life Castaneda refused all offers, saying don Juan had told him that no film could be made while he lived. Now, with the New Age dying and organized religion on the wane, and Wicca on the rise, and fantasy blockbusters like *Lord of the Rings* and *Harry Potter* ruling the minds of the impressionable, it seems likely movie moguls will make their move. Cleargreen, knowing a major shock is needed if Castaneda's sorceric life is to continue as an influence, could accept their offer, and so movie screens around the world would be filled with a series of films exploring *The Teachings of Don Juan*, and probably a line of action figures, certainly video games.

The Italian director Federico Fellini was interested in bringing *The Teachings of Don Juan* to the screen. He met with Castaneda in Rome.

> Castaneda's personality is quite different from what you might imagine. He seemed like a Sicilian—a cordial, easygoing, smiling Sicilian. This likeable gentleman, who had seen all my films, told me that one day with don Juan, thirty or

> forty years ago, he had seen my film, *La Strada*—which was made in 1952 [some thirteen years or so *before* Castaneda says he met don Juan]. Don Juan had told him, "You will have to meet the director of this film." He said that don Juan had prophesied this meeting. That's what Castaneda told me. The one thing that fascinated and almost alienated me was Castaneda's and don Juan's particular vision of the world. I saw something inhuman there. I couldn't help being invaded at times by a feeling of strangeness. As if I were confronted with a vision of a world dictated by a quartz! Or a green lizard! In don Juan's vision of the world, there was no comfort, nothing of what so many other texts can give.... This was what made them terrible and fascinating for me.... Maybe madness can resemble this kind of astral, icy cold, solitary silence.

Finally, what is the sorceric life? According to Castaneda, the sorceric aim is to have the freedom to explore inorganic worlds through dreaming, the creation of a "double." Are Castaneda's sorceric life and the spiritual life different, or do these two traditions come from "the same university," as Swami Muktananda said? Only one who has traveled both paths, or found the one path in the other, can speak. One thing is certain: if we remain enthralled by the ordinary world, well . . . welcome to the Eagle or the moon. The universe eats its own. It gives humans the gift of freedom to grow and hone awareness, so that at physical death, emptied of all memory and ordinary desire, the entity that this awareness is will not disintegrate. If this indeed sounds much like what Gurdjieff has said—we will "die like dogs" unless we grow a Kesdjan body—it would not seem to be a coincidence.

According to Castaneda, the death of the average human being is a termination of their awareness and the end of the body. They are jolted into the "dark sea of awareness" in which their individual awareness and life experience are eaten and they are extinguished. For sorcerers, however, their awareness is such that they take advantage of "death's hidden option." Only the individual moods in the body, activated by the body's different organs, are terminated. Awareness remains. Death for sorcerers is an "act of unification." Their physical body through sorceric practices has developed into an energy body, one that could withstand infinity without losing its sense of self. Its cognitive boundaries, which are deleted by ordinary death, still function because awareness is whole, not fragmented.

Wrote Castaneda:

> What happens to sorcerers when they pick up that hidden option of death, is that they turn into inorganic beings, very specialized, high-speed *inorganic beings*, beings capable of stupendous maneuvers of perception. Sorcerers enter then into what the shamans of ancient Mexico called their *definitive journey. Infinity* becomes their realm of action. . . . The old sorcerers believed that the awareness of this type of *inorganic being* would last as long as the earth is alive. The earth is their matrix. As long as it prevails, their awareness continues.

Don Juan said:

> You will find yourself alive in an unknown land. Then, as is natural to all of us, the first

> thing you will want to do is to start on your way back to Los Angeles. But there is no way to go back to Los Angeles. What you left there is lost forever. By then, of course, you will be a sorcerer, but that's no help; at a time like that what's important to all of us is the fact that everything we love and hate or wish for has been left behind. Yet the feelings in a man do not die or change, and the sorcerer starts on his way back home knowing that he will never reach it, knowing that no power on earth, not even death, will deliver him to the place, the things, the people he loved.

For the thirtieth anniversary of *The Teachings of Don Juan,* in 1998, Castaneda wrote a commentary for its reissue, along with his two newer books, *The Active Side of Infinity* and *The Wheel of Time* (a compilation of quotations from his books with short introductions by the author). In neither the commentary nor the books is the path of heart mentioned with which he had begun his search. Instead of heart, Castaneda now speaks of man's battlefield. Quoting don Juan he writes:

> The world of everyday life cannot ever be taken as something personal that has power over us, something that could make us, or destroy us, because man's battlefield is not in his strife with the world around him. His battlefield is over the horizon, in an area which is unthinkable for an average man, the area where man ceases to be a man.

Perhaps from the beginning we have all misunderstood what don Juan meant by "heart." In the second book, *A Separate Reality*, there are two references:

> A man of knowledge chooses a path with heart and follows it; and then he looks and rejoices and laughs; and then he *sees* and knows. He knows that his life will be over altogether too soon; he knows that he, as well as everybody else, is not going anywhere; he knows, because he sees, that nothing is more important than anything else. In other words, a man of knowledge has no honor, no dignity, no family, no name, no country, but only life to be lived, and under these circumstances, his only tie to his fellow men is his controlled folly.

> In his day-to-day life a warrior chooses to follow the path with heart. It is the consistent choice of the path with heart which makes a warrior different from the average man. He knows that a path has heart when he is one with it, when he experiences a great peace and pleasure in traversing its length. The things a warrior selects to make his shields are the items of a path with heart.

We see now that a man of knowledge has become a warrior and that, in words Castaneda will later use, he has broken the "human mold." His only connection with other human beings is his controlled folly, which is "that our acts are useless and yet we must proceed as if we didn't know it."

To say that the path don Juan and Castaneda and their parties have traveled is a path of heart means what?

Certainly not a path of deep consideration for others, feeling, warmth, and, yes, compassion. Instead, *heart* must refer to the warrior's heart; one of courage and fearlessness and resoluteness in face of all obstacles. That Castaneda is taken by the sorceric path into a deadly psychic battlefield, an inorganic world, that is at once so sinister yet insubstantial that it is beyond all definition, all critique, has been expressed from the start, only all the sorceric bells and whistles and manipulative use of language has created another image entirely.

What drove Carlos Castaneda to this path? What was the presiding and unconscious idea? The sense and intuition here is that he really did kill someone or did something he judged to be equivalent. It filled him with the fear of dying and the retribution that awaited him. That is what hooked him to his don Juan, to the sorceric life. It offered a way past the Eagle. So, as much as Carlos Castaneda dies, he is afraid of dying. That's what his guilt has given him, done to him. That's why all the tension, drama, disappearances, appearances, life on the psychic edge. So for all his power—and Carlos Castaneda is powerful, he is . . .

An Advaitic sage of nondualism spoke of leaving the body, which he had done only once. What was the point? he asked. It was simply a *siddhi*, a power, something not to get caught in. He said it didn't bring one closer to spiritual truth but took one further away.

Perhaps that is the seminal question—*For what are we searching*?

As don Juan said in *The Teachings of Don Juan*:

> Look at every path closely and deliberately. Try it as many times as you think necessary. This question is one that only a very old man asks. My benefactor told me about it once when I

was young, and my blood was too vigorous for me to understand it. Now I do understand it. I will tell you what it is: does this path have a heart? All paths are the same. They lead nowhere. They are paths going through the bush, or into the bush. In my own life I could say I have traversed long, long paths, but I am not anywhere. My benefactor's question has meaning now. Does this path have a heart? If it does, the path is good; if it doesn't, it is of no use. Both paths lead nowhere; but one has a heart, the other doesn't. One makes for a joyful journey; as long as you follow it, you are one with it. The other will make you curse your life. One makes you strong; the other weakens you.

Finis

Castaneda Chronology

1925

December 25 Carlos César Aranha Castañeda born in Cajamara, Peru, a historic Andean town. His father is César Aranha Burungaray, an Italian goldsmith and watchmaker. His mother, an Indian, is Susana Castañeda Novoa.

1932

Attends elementary school.

1948

Family moves to Lima. Castañeda graduates from Colegio Nacional de Nuestra Senora de Guadalupe and enters

Bellas Artes, the national fine arts school.

1949

Mother dies. Castañeda, grief stricken, stays in room for three days.

1951

Meets Dolores, young Chinese-Peruvian girl. Proposes marriage. She becomes pregnant. He leaves.

September 23 Castaneda arrives in San Francisco. Resides in Los Angeles.

1955

Summer Enrolls in Los Angeles Community College.

December Meets Margaret Runyan.

1956

June Contacts Margaret Runyan.

1957

April 26 Petitions for naturalization.

June 21 Petition granted.

1958

Poem wins first place in contest and is published in the school paper, *The Collegian.*

1959

June 19 Graduates from LACC with an Associate of Arts in psychology.

September Enrolls at UCLA. Takes U.S. citizenship.

1960

January 27 Marries Margaret Runyan in Mexico.

July They separate. Castaneda gets a false divorce in Mexico.

Summer Meets don Juan Matus.

December Castaneda, having had a vasectomy, convinces his friend Adrian Gerritsen to father a child with Runyan.

1961

June Castaneda begins apprenticeship with don Juan.
August Runyan gives birth to Carlton Jeremy Castaneda. He later changes name to Adrian Vashon.

1962

September Receives B.A. in anthropology. Enrolls for a Ph.D. at UCLA.

1968

September Castaneda signs contract with University of California Press.
The Teachings of Don Juan published.
Radio interview "Don Juan: The Sorcerer."
Interview "Don Juan's Teachings" in *ElectroPrint Graphics.*
Castaneda meets Kathleen Pohlman. Renames her "Carol Tiggs." Later changed to "Muni Alexander."

1969

April Edward H. Spicer, distinguished professor of anthropology at the University of Arizona, gives a glowing review of Castaneda's book in the *American Anthropologist.*
June Edmund Leach, cultural anthropologist at Cambridge University, rebuts Spicer's review.
Radio interview.

1970

September Regine Margarita Thal enrolls at UCLA. Meets Castaneda.

1971

A Separate Reality published.

Spends a weekend at the Gurdjieff Foundation, San Francisco. Meets Lord John Pentland.

1972

November Joyce Carol Oates writes letter to the *New York Times.*

Castaneda teaches at University of California, Irvine.

Journey to Ixtlan published.

December Sam Keen interview with Castaneda in *Psychology Today.*

Florinda Donner-Grau divorces husband. She receives B.A. from UCLA.

1973

January Novelist Ronald Sukenick presents case for Castaneda's credibility in the *Village Voice.*

February Gwyneth Cravens interview with Castaneda in *Harper's* magazine.

March 8 *Time* magazine cover story.

March Castaneda receives Ph.D. in anthropology from UCLA.

December Castaneda and Runyan divorce.

Meets Amy Wallace, daughter of writer Irving Wallace.

1974

Begins study of kung fu with Howard Y. Lee. Stops practice fifteen years later in 1989.

Tales of Power published.

June Florinda Donner receives M.A. in anthropology from UCLA.

November "Gina" Thal and Anne-Marie Carter co-write article for *Samurai,* official publication of the All

American Karate Federation.

1975

Castaneda makes will leaving equal shares in his estate to Anne-Marie Carter (Taisha Abelar), Regine Thal (Florinda Donner), Mary Joan Baker and Beverly Evans. Abelar and Donner live in the "compound" with Castaneda; Mary Joan Baker, over the garage. She was with him from very early on until the end, but nothing is known about her.

June Taisha Abelar receives Ph.D. in anthropology from UCLA.

Meets Swami Muktananda (this year or next).

Abelar and Donner live in Castaneda's Westwood "compound," with Baker living over the garage.

1976

Florinda Donner advanced to doctoral candidacy at UCLA.

Richard de Mille's *Castaneda's Journey* published.

Daniel Noel's *Seeing Castaneda* published.

1977

The Second Ring of Power published.

December Florinda Donner leaves UCLA graduate program.

1980

Richard de Mille's *The Don Juan Papers* published.

Elizabeth Austin, aka Carol Tiggs, graduates from California Acupuncture College.

October 24 Carol Tiggs marries Marc Benoit, aka LeBel.

1981

The Eagle's Gift published.

Elizabeth Austin's acupuncture license issued.

1982

Florinda Donner's *Shabono* published.

May Review of *Shabono* in *Los Angeles Times* calling it an "anthro-romance."

1983

American Anthropology prints article "*Shabono*: Scandal or Superb Social Science." Notes extensive similarities to Ettor Biocca's *Yanoama*.

1984

The Fire from Within published. Dedication to Howard Y. Lee.

Marc LeBel files for divorce from Elizabeth Austin.

Spring "Carlos Castaneda: Further Conversations, Part 2," in *Seeds of Unfolding*.

1985

"Carlos Castaneda—Evasive Mysteries," in *Magical Blend*.

Castaneda executes new will leaving his estate in equal shares to Mary Joan Baker, Regine Thal (Florinda Donner), Anne-Marie Carter (Taisha Abelar), and Nury Alexander (Patricia Partin). Intentionally omits Adrian Vashon, aka C.J. Castaneda, and Maria del Rosario "Charo" Peters, Castaneda's natural daughter.

Florinda Donner's *The Witch's Dream* published.

"Carlos Castaneda—Evasive Mysteries, Part 2," in *Magical Blend*.

July La Gorda said to die of brain aneurysm at Castaneda's Westwood compound.

Fall Carol Tiggs reunites with Castaneda.

1987

The Power of Silence published.

1988

Elizabeth Austin, aka Carol Tiggs, files change of name to Muni Alexander.

1991

Castaneda contacts Amy Wallace.

Florinda Donner's *Being-in-Dreaming* published.

1992

February Florinda Donner interview, "A Conversation with Florinda Donner," in *Dimensions.*

Florinda Donner interview, Brian S. Cohen, "Being-in-Dreaming: An Introduction to Toltec Sorcery," in *Magical Blend.*

Taisha Abelar's *The Sorcerers' Crossing* published.

October 10 Taisha Abelar gives talk at Alexandria II bookstore, Pasadena.

October Florinda Donner lectures at Jewish Cultural Center, Berkeley.

November Interview with Florinda Donner in *Body, Mind & Spirit.*

1993

The Art of Dreaming published.

Castaneda gives Phoenix Bookstore talk.

July 23–25 First Tensegrity seminar at Rim Institute, Arizona. Led by Florinda, Taisha and Muni. Chacmools' first workshop.

July Muni Alexander lectures at East West Bookstore, Menlo Park, CA.

September 27 Castaneda, using the last name "Aranha," marries Florinda Donner in Las Vegas.

September 29 Castaneda, again using "Aranha," marries Carol Muni Tiggs Alexander in Las Vegas. Marriage license C 472425.

October 14–17 Witches give workshop at Akahi Farms, Maui.

November 19 Taisha Abelar gives talk at Gaia Bookstore, Berkeley.

November Witches give Esalen workshop.

1994

January 7 Taisha Abelar gives talk at Menlo Park bookstore. Last lecture until Castaneda's appearance in Sunnyvale in December.

Taisha Abelar interview, "A Conversation with Taisha Abelar," Alexander Blair-Ewart, in *Dimensions*.

Tensegrity video released.

March "The Secret Life of Carlos Castaneda: You Only Live Twice," in *Details*.

March "Carlos Castaneda Speaks," in *New Age Journal*.

April "Castaneda's Clan," in *Magical Blend*.

April Florinda Donner marries Castaneda's agent and student Rick Fosterman, aka Simon McKrindle.

Amy Wallace, aka Ellis Laura Finnegan, moves from Berkeley to Los Angeles to be closer to Castaneda.

June The Nagualist newsletter published by Dan Lawton. Four more issues published through March 1995. Cleargreen requested publication cease.

Fall Muni Alexander thought to take Cleargreen members to Tula, Mexico.

Magical Blend and *Details* magazines publish interviews with Castaneda.

1995

Files suit against Victor Sanchez, former friend, claiming

the jacket of Sanchez's book, *The Teachings of Don Carlo*, infringed Castaneda's copyright.

March 14–16 Workshop, Silverlake, CA.

March 24–26 Workshop, Maui.

March *Details* article.

April "Carlos Castaneda Speaks," *New Age Journal*, March, 1994.

April 21–23 Workshop, Longmont, CO.

May 19–21 Workshop, Mexico City.

May 22 Muni Alexander gives "top secret speech" at Tula.

May 26–29 Omega workshop, Rhinebeck, NY.

June 16 Cleargreen incorporated. Talia Bey named president.

August 1–20 Castaneda leads three-week Tensegrity workshop, Culver City, CA.

August 25–27 Workshop, Scottsdale, AZ.

September 11 Sunday sessions begin, West L.A.

October "War of the Wizards," in *Magical Blend*. Merilyn Tunneshende castigates Castaneda. She describes a "battle of the sorcerers in 1980" over one of the immortality practices. Tunneshende claims to have met don Juan in Yuma, Arizona, in 1978 and studied with him until his death in 1991. Says he was a Yuma Indian, not Yaqui.

October 13–14 Workshop, Culver City.

November 10–12 Intersubjectivity workshop, Culver City.

Thanksgiving Castaneda admits having diabetes.

December "Carlos Castaneda's Tensegrity," in *Yoga Journal*.

December 9–10 Review workshop, Anaheim.

December 26 *Los Angeles Times* interview.

1996

January Cleargreen begins publishing Castaneda's *The Warrior's Way: A Journal of Applied Hermeneutics*.

Name changed to *Readers of Infinity*. Discontinued in spring after four issues.

January 26–28 Mexico City workshop.

March 1–3 Women-only workshop, UCLA.

April Castaneda interview, "My Lunch with Carlos Castaneda," in *Psychology Today*.

April 19–21 Oakland workshop.

May "Interview with Carlos Castaneda, Part 2," in *Los Angeles* magazine.

July 20–25 Tensegrity workshop, UCLA.

September 27–29 Workshop, Mexico City.

October Castaneda interview, "Journeys with Carlos Castaneda," in *Sedona Journal*.

November 29–December 1 Pasadena workshop.

Castaneda becomes seriously ill.

1997

January Margaret Runyan's *A Magical Journey with Carlos Castaneda* published.

Castaneda sues Runyan and her publisher claiming damage to reputation and infringement of privacy. Seeks $100,000 punitive damages and ban on book's distribution.

February Castaneda interview, "An Interview with Carlos Castaneda," in *Uno Miso*.

February 15–16 Intensive review workshop, Long Beach.

April 1 "Interview with the Witches," in *Mas Alla*, Spain.

April 18–20 Workshop, Mexico City.

June 20–22 Workshop, Barcelona, Spain.

July Castaneda diagnosed with hepatocellular cancer. Glaucoma grows worse.

July 19 Workshop, Seattle, WA.

July 27–29 Workshop, Berlin, Germany.

August 23–27 Intensive workshop, Los Angeles.

Late summer Sunday meetings end.

September "Of Sorcery and Dreams: An Encounter with Carlos Castaneda," in *The Sun* magazine.

October 11–12 Workshop, Omega Institute, Rhinebeck, NY.

October 22 Signs new will. Adopts Nury Alexander as his daughter. Omits son C.J., aka Adrian Vashon.

December 13–14 Workshop, Mexico City.

1998

January Magical Passes published.

January "Castaneda's Magical Passes," in *Yoga Journal.*

February 7–8 Not-Doing workshop, Pomona.

April 4 Workshop, Santa Monica.

April 23 Castaneda signs six-page will.

April 27 Carlos dies at 3 a.m. Immediate cause of death is metabolic encephalopathy preceded by liver failure due to ten previous months of hepatocellular cancer. Body cremated at Spalding Mortuary, Culver City.

Late April Florinda, Taisha, Nury, as well as Kylie Lundahl and Talia Bey, disappear. Phone numbers disconnected the same day.

May 2 Workshop, Santa Monica, led by Muni Alexander.

May 8 Castaneda's will filed with L.A. Superior Court.

June 19 Obituary, *Los Angeles Times.*

June 20 Obituary, *New York Times*, shows photo of another Castaneda, no relation.

June 6 Workshop, Los Altos, CA.

July 31–August 2 Workshop, Ontario, CA, conducted by Muni Alexander. This marks her last public appearance.

August "Shaman or Sham," in *Electronic Telegraph.*

The Active Side of Infinity published.

The Wheel of Time published.

Notes

Prologue

1. *We are energy.* Scott Jones, aka William Patrick Patterson, "The Outlaw Christs," *In New York*, vol. 4, no. 2 (1969).
2. *Alan Watts. The Book: On the Taboo Against Knowing Who You Are* (New York: Collier Books, 1966).
3. *P. D. Ouspensky's. In Search of the Miraculous* (New York: Harcourt, Brace, World, 1949).
4. *A weekend with* my *don Juan.* Conversation with Don Hoyt, president of the Gurdjieff Foundation of San Francisco, 1984–1987.
5. *The Nagual woman, Carol Tiggs.* James Moore, *Gurdjieffian Confessions* (London: Gurdjieff Studies Ltd., 2005), p. 134.

Chapter I
Paths of Heart

1. *Paths of heart.* Carlos Castaneda, dedication to *The Teachings of Don Juan* (New York: Simon & Schuster, 1968).
2. *Entirely new or forgotten road.* Ouspensky, p. 3.
3. *I despised my father.* Castaneda, *The Active Side of*

Infinity (New York: HarperCollins, 1998), p. 207.

4. *Ideal acts.* Carlos Castaneda, *Journey to Ixtlan* (New York: Simon & Schuster, 1972), pp. 62–63. See also Castaneda, *A Separate Reality* (New York: Simon & Schuster, 1971), p. 5. "Whenever he [his father] said he 'was only a man' he implicitly meant he was weak and helpless and was filled with an ultimate sense of despair."
5. *Disparaging his father.* Margaret Runyan, *A Magical Journey with Carlos Castaneda* (Victoria, BC: Millenia Press, 1997), p. 26.
6. *Carlos' grandfather.* Runyan, p. 16.
7. *I suddenly felt.* Castaneda, *A Separate Reality*, p. 57.
8. *Carlos concluded.* Runyan, pp. 29–30.
9. *Harbored like an obsession.* Runyan, p. 31.
10. *A short dark man.* Runyan, p. 33.
11. *He can charm your soul.* Runyan, p. x.
12. *Experimented with mushrooms, peyote cactus and jimsonweed.* Runyan, p. 78.
13. *He had a habit.* Runyan, p. 34.
14. *Matus.* Runyan, p. 38. In *The Active Side of Infinity*, p. 58, Castaneda changes don Juan's last name to "Flores."
15. *Phenomenology.* Carlos Castaneda, *A Journal of Applied Hermeneutics*, vol. 1, no. 3.
16. *Garfinkel thought up.* Richard de Mille, ed., *The Don Juan Papers: Further Castaneda Controversies* (Santa Barbara, CA: Ross-Erikson, 1980), pp. 68–71, 75.
17. *Do you want to be the darling of Esalen?* Daniel Noel, ed., *Seeing Castaneda* (New York: G. P. Putnam's Sons, 1976), pp. 105–06.
18. *Mandell suspected.* Richard de Mille, *Castaneda's Journey: The Power and the Allegory* (Santa Barbara, CA: Capra Press, 1976), pp. 80–81.

19. *I suspect.* De Mille, *Castaneda's Journey,* p. 81.
20. *One of the most brilliant.* Castaneda, *The Active Side of Infinity,* pp. 118–27.
21. *Oh, that's all right, Carlos.* Runyan, p. 154.
22. *Ally.* Castaneda, *The Teachings of Don Juan,* p. 23.
23. *I would be happy to.* Michael Korda, *Another Life: A Memoir of Other People* (New York: Random House, 1999), pp. 276–83.

Chapter II
Castaneda's Muse

1. *Why should we want.* Anaïs Nin, *The Novel of the Future* (New York: Collier Books, 1968), p. 12.
2. *The mood I fall into.* Nin, p. 11.
3. *Truth and reality.* Deirdre Bair, *Anaïs Nin: A Biography* (New York: G.P. Putnam's Sons, 1995), p. 304.
4. *Mensonge vital.* Bair, p. 102.
5. *Lies were not harmful.* Bair, p. 135.
6. *Dédoublement.* Bair, pp. 228–29.
7. *A literary gathering.* Bair, p. 315.
8. *Nin met Castaneda for the first time.* De Mille, *Castaneda's Journey,* pp. 188, 196.
9. *Proceed from the dream outward.* Bair, p. 157.
10. *The intensification of personal experiences.* Bair, p. 111.
11. *You start with any image.* Carl Jung, *Letters, Vol. 1* (Princeton, NJ: Princeton University Press, 1973), p. 460.
12. *The artist who departs.* Bair, pp. 187–88. Dream interpretation was a hallmark of psychoanalytic investigation. Among Rank's books that Nin said influenced her was his *Don Juan et son double,* pp. 228–29. For a time during her therapy Nin and Rank were lovers.
13. *Don Juan.* Bair, p. 185.
14. *It was Nin who helped Castaneda.* Ronald Sukenick,

"Upward and Juanward: The Possible Dream" in Noel, pp. 110–11.
15. *The fact.* Sukenick, p. 115.
16. *I dream my books.* Gwyneth Cravens, "Talking to Power and Spinning with the Ally," *Harpers* magazine, February, 1973.
17. *Everything is smarmy.* Weston La Barre, "Stinging Criticism from the Author of *The Peyote Cult*," in Noel, p. 42.
18. *Early praise.* Edward Spicer, "Early Praise from an Authority on Yaqui Culture," in Noel, p. 31.
19. *Honest and serious young man.* De Mille, *The Don Juan Papers*, p. 328.

Chapter III
What Is Real?

1. *Among the best.* Paul Reisman, "A Comprehensive Anthropological Assessment," in Noel, pp. 46–53.
2. *Perhaps it takes a writer of fiction.* Joyce Carol Oates, in Noel, p. 68.
3. *"Don Juan's Last Laugh."* Joyce Carol Oates, in Noel, pp. 122–28.
4. *Michael Murphy.* Jeffrey J. Kripal, *Esalen: America and the Religion of No Religion* (Chicago: University of Chicago Press, 2007), p. 272.
5. *Most anthropologists.* Michael Harner, in Noel, p. 107.
6. *Smelled a hoax.* De Mille, *The Don Juan Papers,* p. 120.
7. *As I followed don Juan.* Sam Keen, "Sorcerer's Apprentice," *Psychology Today,* December, 1972.
8. *Oh, that's just like don Genaro.* De Mille, *The Don Juan Papers,* p. 340.
9. *I have a hard time reconciling the Carlos I knew.* De Mille, *The Don Juan Papers,* pp. 347, 353.
10. *Did I fly?* Castaneda, *The Teachings of Don Juan*, p. 132.

Runyan, p. 98, says, "Just a few hundred miles from Carlos Castaneda's hometown, in the Ucayali region of eastern Peru, the Conibo-Shipbo Indians say it's common after taking ayahuasca for the shaman's soul to leave the body in the form of a bird. The Amahuasca to the east in the Peruvian Montana say the same thing, as do dozens of other tribes."

11. *Why did I leave?* Jane Hellisoe, University of California Press interview, *ElectroPrint Graphics,* 1968.
12. *The way the books present.* 1968 radio interview with Carlos Castaneda: "Don Juan: The Sorcerer."
13. *Learn with your whole body.* Keith Thompson, "Carlos Castaneda Speaks," *New Age Journal,* March 1994.
14. *My books are a true account.* Castaneda, foreword to *The Power of Silence.*
15. *The work that I have to do.* Graciela Corvalan, "Carlos Castaneda, Further Conversations, Part 2," *Magical Blend,* no. 15 (1985).
16. *Ships restaurant.* This event is first mentioned in *The Eagle's Gift* (New York: Simon & Schuster, 1981), pp. 57–58: "In my dreaming," Castaneda wrote, "I saw the usual waitresses who worked the graveyard shift; I saw a row of people eating at the counter, and right at the very end of the counter I saw a peculiar character, a man I saw nearly every day walking aimlessly around the UCLA campus. He was the only person who actually looked at me. The instant I came in he seemed to sense me. He turned around and stared at me.

    "I found the same man in my waking hours a few days later in the same coffee shop in the early hours of the morning. He took one look at me and seemed to recognize me. He looked horrified and ran away without giving me a chance to talk to him." Contrasting what is written here with what Castaneda wrote in *The Active Side of Infinity*, some seventeen years later, gives an example of how he works the material (as most writers do) to use the "surface" of experience to get at its deeper import.

Chapter IV
The Nagual & His Witches

1. *When the male ejaculates.* Alexander Blair-Ewaret, "Interview with Florinda Donner," *Dimensions* magazine, February, 1992.
2. *Like a jockey with a shiv.* Bruce Wagner, "The Secret Life of Carlos Castaneda: You Only Live Twice," *Details* magazine, March 1994. Wagner, aka Lorenzo Drake, was an apprentice of Castaneda's.
3. *Phenomenology of Shamanism.* Runyan, p. 145.
4. *Violently jealous.* Amy Wallace, *Sorcerer's Apprentice: My Life with Carlos Castaneda* (Berkeley, CA: Frog, Ltd., 2003), p. 67.
5. *The Nagual's right and left sides are divided into two.* Castaneda, *The Eagle's Gift*, p. 178.
6. *They found completeness.* Castaneda, *The Eagle's Gift,* p. 221.
7. *Tiggs described it a bit differently.* Colorado workshop, April 21–23, 1995, and at the Mexico City workshop, May 19–21, 1995.
8. *Particular ways of treating the energy body.* Castaneda, *The Art of Dreaming* (New York: HarperCollins, 1993), p. 217.
9. *Carol Tiggs is gone.* Bruce Wagner, *Details.* March, 1994.
10. *I lurked there.* Mexico City workshop, May 19–21, 1995.
11. *Opened an enormous door.* Bruce Wagner, *Details,* March, 1994.
12. *Present teachings openly.* Michael Brennan, "Of Sorcery

and Dreams: An Encounter with Carlos Castaneda," *The Sun* magazine, September, 1997.

13. *What compels us.* Daniel Trujillo Rivas, "An Interview with Carlos Castaneda," *Uno Mismo* magazine, February, 1997.
14. *The return of Carol Tiggs.* Concha Labarta, "Interview with the Witches," *Más Allá* magazine, April, 1997.
15. *I want to express my admiration.* Castaneda, dedication in *The Fire from Within* (New York: Simon & Schuster, 1984).
16. *Tensegrity's intent.* Bruce Wagner, "Carlos Castaneda's Tensegrity," *Body, Mind & Spirit* magazine, April, 1995.
17. *Working with the body.* Corey Donovan, "Letters," www.sustainedaction.org.
18. *Men have this pincho.* Wallace, p. 40.
19. *We are energetically the same.* Muni Alexander, Pasadena workshop, November 29–December 1, 1996.
20. *When Castaneda cooks.* Muni Alexander, Oakland workshop, April 19–21, 1996.
21. *It's as difficult as changing the chain on a chain saw.* Graciela Corvalan, "Carlos Castaneda—Evasive Mysteries, Part 2," *Magical Blend* magazine, no. 15, 1985.
22. *I was struck speechless.* Peter Szasz, "Letters," www.sustainedaction.org.
23. *Lightning coming out of my tits!* Bruce Wagner, *Details*, 1994.

Chapter V
Castaneda Reappears

1. *My hands are too tired.* Runyan, pp. 183–84.
2. *C. J. Castaneda. Correspondence.* C. J. his adopted son, gives this account of the meeting: "Walking up to the van, a witch stopped me and said, "You aren't going to

get near him." I asked if she knew who I was. "I know who you are and you aren't going to get near him," she said. Seeing what happened, my father jumped out of the van and yelled, "It's my chocho." We spoke for some time. He asked why I never call or write him. I told him I would always write and call but the witches would say he didn't want to talk with me. "That's absurd," he said. He was always wondering about me and what had happened to me. He asked for my phone number. He said he'd call in a few days and we would go hiking in the mountains once again. After speaking with my mother, he got back into the van. I saw one of the witches get the note with my phone number out of his pocket, wad it up and toss it out the window as the van sped off. I never saw my father alive again."

3. *The sorcerer's idea.* Bruce Wagner, "Interview with Castaneda," *Los Angeles* magazine, May, 1996.
4. *5'2".* Wallace, p. 23. On page 16 of her book, Runyan says Castaneda was 5'5".
5. *I am . . . Carlos Castaneda!* Sunnyvale, CA, seminar, December 3, 1994.
6. *This big lady.* Corey Donovan, *Sunday sessions.* www.sustainedaction.org.
7. *He made a pass at my* culo! Wallace, p. 31.
8. *Once I met a disciple of Gurdjieff.* Graciela Corvalan, "Carlos Castaneda—Evasive Mysteries, Part 2," *Magical Blend,* no. 15. She writes, too, that his friend (Claudio Naranjo) had "insisted that he see the disciple of Gurdjieff because he was convinced that Castaneda needed a teacher more serious than don Juan." Castaneda said "his friend felt full of shame" for what happened.
9. *Sorcerers perceive.* Wallace, pp. 154–55.

10. *Toltec.* Graciela Corvalan, "Carlos Castaneda—Evasive Mysteries, Part 1," *Magical Blend,* no.14, 1985.
11. *I am going to reveal things.* Castaneda, www.sustainedaction.org.
12. *I am the work of the only God, his creation. The Sun Unwound* translated from the Nahuatl by Edward Dorn and Gordon Brotherson (Berkeley, CA: North Atlantic Books, 1999).

Chapter VI
Ideas & Sources

1. *Emanations.* "Six Explanatory Propositions," foreword to the Spanish version of *The Eagle's Gift,* but not published in the English version.
2. *Animate and inanimate energy. The Teachings of Don Juan,* 30th anniversary ed., p. xv. (All citations of this book are from this edition.)
3. *Intent. The Teachings of Don Juan,* p. xvii. *The Power of Silence,* p. 16.
4. *Attention.* "Six Explanatory Propositions."
5. *Cognition. The Teachings of Don Juan,* p. xiii.
6. *Assemblage point. The Art of Dreaming,* pp. 18–19. The *Fire from Within,* pp. 9, 115–17, 225–26. *The Active Side of Infinity,* p. 267.
7. *Description. Journey to Ixtlan,* p. 8.
8. *Human mold. The Second Ring of Power,* pp. 155–56.
9. *Stopping the world. Journey to Ixtlan,* p. 13.
10. *Inner silence. The Active Side of Infinity,* pp. 103–04, 168, 174, 230, 232.
11. *Moving the assemblage point. The Active Side of Infinity,* p. 267. "Six Explanatory Propositions."
12. *Not doing. Journey to Ixtlan,* pp. 226–39.
13. *Gazing. The Second Ring of Power,* pp. 289–96.

14. *Look at the shadow. Journey to Ixtlan,* pp. 234–35.
15. *Testing awareness. The Teachings of Don Juan,* p. xix.
16. *Energy body. The Active Side of Infinity,* p. 216.
17. *Second attention. The Eagle's Gift,* p. 254.
18. *Three attentions.* "Six Explanatory Propositions."
19. *The purposeful guiding of will. The Fire from Within,* p. 173. *The Power of Silence,* pp. 12, 31.
20. *The only way to know it. The Power of Silence,* pp. 30–34.
21. *Power plants cause untold damage. Tales of Power,* pp. 238–40.
22. *Buzzing. The Teachings of Don Juan,* p. 65. *A Separate Reality,* p. 54 (first overt mention of dividing the attention appears here). *The Active Side of Infinity,* pp. 232–33.
23. *Holes between sounds. A Separate Reality,* pp. 223–25.
24. *Bee.* The image of a bee appears on the wall of the Hypostyle Hall at Karnak, the ancient Egyptian temple complex at Thebes. See documentary video *Gurdjieff in Egypt: The Origin of Esoteric Knowledge* (Fairfax, CA: Arete Communications, 2007).
25. *What keeps the assemblage point fixed. The Fire from Within,* p. 137.
26. *Foreign installation. The Active Side of Infinity,* p. 7.
27. *Predator's mind. The Active Side of Infinity,* p. 220.
28. *Depths of the cosmos. The Active Side of Infinity,* pp. 218–21.
29. *Two attentions becoming a single unit. The Second Ring of Power,* p. 283.
30. *Inner silence. The Active Side of Infinity,* pp. 103–05.
31. *Man's battlefield. The Teachings of Don Juan,* p. xi.
32. *Clumps of cohesive energy. The Teachings of Don Juan,* p. xv.
33. *Recapitulation. The Eagle's Gift,* pp. 289–91.
34. *Tonal. Tales of Power,* p. 118.

35. *Nagual. The Power of Silence,* p. 13.
36. *First gate. The Art of Dreaming,* p. 32.
37. *Attention of the Nagual. The Second Ring of Power,* p. 269.
38. *Hands. Journey to Ixtlan,* p. 126.
39. *Tip of tongue. The Art of Dreaming,* p. 95.
40. *Second gate. The Art of Dreaming,* p. 44.
41. *Foreign energy scouts. The Art of Dreaming,* pp. 107, 137.
42. *The danger. The Art of Dreaming,* 178.
43. *Third gate. The Art of Dreaming,* pp. 141–42.
44. *Breakage. The Second Ring of Power,* pp. 269–70.
45. *Completes the energy body. The Art of Dreaming,* p. 142.
46. *Fourth gate. The Art of Dreaming,* p. 200.
47. *A double. Tales of Power,* pp. 51, 268.
48. *Strength the dreaming body develops. The Fire from Within,* p. 183.
49. *The Eagle. The Eagle's Gift,* pp. 176–77.
50. *The Eagle's food. The Fire from Within,* pp. 51, 55.
51. *Selling one's soul. The Art of Dreaming,* p. 173.
52. *Inorganic beings. The Fire from Within,* pp. 188, 110, 99. *The Art of Dreaming,* p. 45.
53. *The word shaman.* Alice Beck Kehoe, *Shamans and Religion* (Long Grove, IL: Waveland Press, Inc., 2000), p. 8.
54. *Manchu word.* M. A. Czaplicka, *Shamanism in Siberia* (Kila, MT: Kessinger Publishing, n.d.), p. 37.
55. *Arctic hysteria.* Czaplicka, p. 4. Shaman's spirits usually appear in the form of animals or birds, p. 16.
56. *Black shaman.* Czaplicka, p. 34.
57. *Indigenous people.* Kehoe, p. 65.
58. *Shamanism in the strict sense.* Mircea Eliade, *Shamanism* (Princeton, NJ: Princeton University Press, 1964), p. 4.
59. *If the word "shaman."* Eliade, p. 3.
60. *To be a sorcerer. The Active Side of Infinity,* p. 69.

61. *In Nahuatl language.* Donald Lee Williams, *Border Crossings* (Toronto: Inner City Books, 1981), p. 90.
62. *There seem to be many parallels.* Sam Keen, "Sorcerer's Apprentice," in Noel, p. 89.
63. *There is an ordinary reality.* Keen, p. 80.
64. *In European membership.* Keen, p. 80.
65. *Western man begins.* Keen, p. 81.
66. *G. I. Gurdjieff.* William Patrick Patterson, *Struggle of the Magicians* (Fairfax, CA: Arete Communications, 1999). Gives an overview of G. I. Gurdjieff. See also the documentary trilogy, *The Life & Significance of G. I. Gurdjieff* composed of *Gurdjieff in Egypt, Gurdjieff's Mission* and *Gurdjieff's Legacy.*
67. *The whole sensation of himself.* Gurdjieff, *Meetings with Remarkable Men* (New York: E. P. Dutton, 1963), p. 205.
68. *What is the sense and significance.* J. G. Bennett, *Making a New World* (London: Turnstone Books, 1973), p. 4.
69. *Only not from the Egypt we know.* Ouspensky, p. 302.
70. *Unless the wisdom of the East.* Fritz Peters, *Gurdjieff Remembered* (New York: Samuel Weiser, 1971), p.122.
71. *The teaching.* Ouspensky, p. 286.
72. *Self-remembering.* G. I. Gurdjieff, *Views from the Real World* (New York: E. P. Dutton, 1973), pp. 79–80.
73. *Stopping thoughts.* Ouspensky, pp. 117–18.
74. *Higher thinking center.* Ouspensky, p. 142.
75. *Nirioonossian-World-Sound.* G. I. Gurdjieff, *All & Everything, First Series* (New York: E. P. Dutton, 1950), p. 489.
76. *Reason of understanding.* Gurdjieff, *All & Everything,* pp. 1166–69.
77. *Formatory mind.* Ouspensky, p. 235.
78. *Kundabuffer.* Gurdjieff, *All & Everything,* pp. 88–89.
79. *The moon.* Ouspensky, p. 85.
80. *Reciprocal maintenance.* Gurdjieff, *All & Everything,*

pp. 1094–95.

81. *Apes.* C. S. Nott, *Teachings of Gurdjieff* (New York: Samuel Weiser, 1962), pp. 96–97.
82. *Self-love and vanity.* Gurdjieff, *All & Everything,* pp. 356, 512, 516, 629, 1059, 1087.
83. *Story of one's life.* Ouspensky, p. 247.
84. *Kesdjan body.* Gurdjieff, *All & Everything,* p. 1106.
85. *Eight-pointed diagram. Tales of Power,* pp. 99, 249. *A Separate Reality,* p. 258. For those inclined, look at the major books as an octave. Doh, *Teachings of Don Juan;* Re, *A Separate Reality;* Mi, *Journey to Ixtlan;* Shock, *Tales of Power;* Fa, *The Second Ring of Power;* Sol, *The Eagle's Gift;* La, *The Fire from Within;* Si, *The Power of Silence;* Shock, *The Art of Dreaming;* Doh, *The Active Side of Infinity,* which begins a new octave. Now, placing the books on the enneagram we see: at point 9, *The Teachings of Don Juan;* point 1, *A Separate Reality;* point 2, *Journey to Ixtlan;* point 3, *Tales of Power;* point 4, *The Second Ring of Power;* point 5, *The Eagle's Gift;* point 6, *The Fire from Within;* point 7, *The Power of Silence;* point 8, *The Art of Dreaming;* and point 9, *The Active Side of Infinity.* Now, by following the lines of the enneagram, the triangle and the period, the inner connection between the books appears. Castaneda's life can also be seen in octaves. The first octave (that we know about) could begin in 1951, when at twenty-six he comes to America; the second octave is 1960 when he meets don Juan; the third octave is in 1973 when he gets his doctorate in anthropology, is feted for his three books, and disappears; the fourth octave occurs in 1985 with the return of Carol Tiggs; and the fifth and last octave is in 1993 when he reappears in public view.
86. *Man without quotation marks.* Gurdjieff, *All & Every-*

thing, p. 1227.

87. *Man is born without a soul.* G. I. Gurdjieff, *Life Is Real Only Then, When "I Am"* (New York: E. P. Dutton, 1975), p. 170. See also, *Views from the Real World*, pp. 87, 191; Fritz Peters, *Boyhood with Gurdjieff* (Fairfax, CA: Arete Communications, 2006), p. 43.
88. *What you are feeling is the flow of energy.* Carlos Castaneda, *A Journal of Applied Hermeneutics*, vol. 1, no. 2.
89. *Think of the owners of a chicken coop.* Wallace, p. 179.
90. *Rich magician hypnotized sheep.* Ouspensky, p. 219.
91. *A weekend at St. Elmo.* Conversation with Don Hoyt, President of the Gurdjieff Foundation of San Francisco, 1984–87. In the summer of 1972 the foundation, under Lord Pentland's direction, published the first issue of *Material for Thought* (San Francisco: Far West Press, 1972), which had a favorable review of *A Separate Reality*, pp. 15–21.
92. *Carol Tiggs.* James Moore, *Gurdjieffian Confessions* (London: Gurdjieff Studies Ltd, 2005), p. 134. "It is known that Carol Tiggs, a pupil of Lord Pentland, became a pupil of Castaneda; it is known that (with Carol as intermediary) Lord Pentland received Castaneda at an open Movements class in San Francisco in 1970."
93. *Carlos, I knew, was acquainted with pupils from Gurdjieff's lineage.* Wallace, p. 53. A key idea of Gurdjieff's is the Ray of Creation which gives numbers to the various levels of vibration. The number of the Earth is forty-eight, and that is the number Castaneda gives man who inhabits the Earth. *Tales of Power*, p. 42.

Chapter VII
Castaneda's Lover

1. *He had one of the most charismatic personalities.* Wallace, p. 366.
2. *I send you to hell!* Wallace, p. 234.
3. *Energetic worms.* Wallace, p. 63.
4. *Husserl didn't live his theories.* Wallace, p. 56.
5. *You can't fuck all the women in the world, but you can try!* Wallace, p. 3.
6. *You should really sleep with Carlos.* Wallace, p. 57.
7. *Tonight Amy Wallace dies.* Wallace, p. 84.
8. *Repeated ejaculations.* Wallace, p. 293.
9. *I piss on you.* Wallace, p. 133.
10. *This is the utmost sorceric importance.* Wallace, p. 217.
11. *Powerful* poto. Wallace, p. 81.
12. *You're my wife now.* Wallace, p. 374.
13. *Prozac.* Wallace, p. 141.
14. *Homosexuality.* Wallace, p. 59. Castaneda's muse, Anaïs Nin, felt the same. "Nin believed homosexuality and the cult of youth had become alarmingly united to the detriment of American literature." What she condemned was "the essential basic problem of homosexuality as a symptom of adolescence, of retarded maturity." Bair, p. 367.
15. *You think you can get our attention.* Wallace, p. 144.
16. *I am very delighted to be here with you, in such holy company. In the Company of a Siddha: Interviews and Conversations with Swami Muktananda* (South Fallsburg, NY: SYDA Foundation, 1978), pp. 147–52.

Chapter VIII
The Nagual's Star

1. *The compound.* Wallace, p. 111.
2. *He had the sickly look.* Gaby Geuter, *Filming Castaneda* (Los Angeles: First Books Library, 2004), p. 192.
3. *Assassin.* Wallace, p. 320.
4. *He can't stand it when I leave.* Wallace, p. 318.
5. *Sorcerer's vocabulary.* Wallace, p. 353.
6. *Twenty-four members of inner circle.* Geuter, p. 119.
7. *The trigger event.* Wallace, p. 332.
8. *Black Nike time.* Wallace, p. 345.
9. *The outward appearance.* Geuter, p. 131.
10. *Like a Renaissance beauty.* Wallace, p. 339.
11. *In the trash.* Geuter, p. 215.
12. *Necklace.* Wallace, p. 342.
13. *My liver's in shreds.* Graciela Corvalan, "A Conversation with Carlos Castaneda," *Seeds of Unfolding,* vol. 1, no. 4, summer 1983.
14. *June 19th.* Geuter, p. 227.
15. *Carlos had begun as a genuine seeker.* Wallace, p. 354.
16. *Famous among us.* Castaneda, *The Art of Dreaming,* p. 192.
17. *The will.* Peter Applebaum, "Carlos Castaneda's Legacy Is in Dispute," *Chicago Tribune,* 2 September 1998.
18. *Usually the Nagual.* Castaneda, *The Fire from Within,* p. 147.
19. *The idea.* Michael Peter Langevin, "Castaneda Casualties: An Interview with Amy Wallace," *Magical Blend,* 2003. Florinda Donner said, "Carol Tiggs, as the Nagual Woman, could very easily be the leader of our group. However, it is a sorcerer's belief that women are universes in themselves. As universes they have no

interest whatsoever in leading other universes! Sorcerers believe that maleness is an extension of femaleness. Therefore it is antithetical to the spirit of womanhood to lead." Ken Eagle Feather and Carol Kramer, "Being-in-Dreaming Interview," *Body, Mind & Spirit*, no. 6, November, 1992.

Chapter IX
The Summing Up

1. *Carlos Castaneda: Enigma of a Sorcerer.* Mick LaSalle, *San Francisco Chronicle*, 7 June 2004, and Dave Kehr, "The Shaman May Have Been Fake, But, Hey the Drugs Were Real," *New York Times*, 2 June 2004.
2. *I had intense experiences.* Douglas Price-Williams. "Silent Strife," an unpublished account of his experiments with Castaneda. Colin Wilson was kind enough to share the basic material which I've condensed and rewritten. "Silent Strife" focuses on experiments in which Price-Williams, his friends and Castaneda engaged in 1974. Castaneda said he had learned how to "raise his ally" and asked Price-Williams to form a group for experimentation with "dream telepathy." At first nothing much happened, but then one member told of a strange dream in which Castaneda stood on a sand dune, a rope round his neck with the end of the rope vertical in space, a swarm of fishes was flying around overhead—"a kind of Hawaiian carp." Then Price-Williams dreamed of being with a woman friend of Castaneda's and two white mice. Price-Williams asked other members of the group if they had dreamed recently. One told of dreaming of two rodent-like fish in a toilet bowl. When she tried to flush them away, the bathroom was flooded with ex-

crement. Price-Williams told her he'd hoped the fish might have been carp. "Sure," she exclaimed, "crap." (Which is a reversal of two of the letters.) Price-Williams wondered if Castaneda's ally might be a fish. Another member of the group dreamed he was being attacked by apes and dogs, including a poodle the size of a mouse. Castaneda was either not consciously responsible for this dream menagerie or was tricking them, because the following weekend, he told Price-Williams he intended to try to "send" something, but everyone slept dreamlessly that weekend.

Later, Castaneda told Price-Williams he had been to Oaxaca, Mexico, and that don Juan had formed a group of seven apprentices, in addition to himself. Together, they formed a symbolic snake. Two, including Castaneda, represented the head, four the body, and one the tail. The following day, Price-Williams heard his dog barking in the "den" outside. He looked and found a small snake trapped under the end of the sliding door. The canyon where Price-Williams lived had many snakes, but this was the first time he had seen one. He tried to release the snake by moving the door, but it only became more entangled. Finally, feeling there was no alternative except to kill it, he hit the snake on the head with a poker. He related the experience to Castaneda, who became upset and told him that he was part of a symbolic snake—its head. Afterward, when his wife saw Price-Williams, he looked shattered. When he told her why, she exclaimed, "My God, you've killed Carlos." Then Price-Williams remembered he had recently awakened from sleep hearing a woman's voice saying: "My God, you've killed Carlos."

Later, Castaneda told Price-Williams he had seen his other seven fellow-apprentices and they were all upset that, having taken the trouble to visit him, Price-Williams attacked them. Price-Williams was inclined to believe that the seven apprentices, like don Juan, did not exist. Now he began to wonder. Castaneda suggested that Price-Williams perhaps possessed paranormal powers, and may himself have induced some of the odd synchronicities and coincidences. By the end of "Silent Strife," the synchronicities ended and telepathic coincidences ceased, and life returned to normal. But Price-Williams was left with the impression of a hidden reality that somehow bound events and people together.

3. *Letters home.* Noel, p. 104.
4. *Missions for U.S. Army Intelligence.* Bruce Bebb, *L.A. Reader*, 17 August 1984.
5. *Carlos told me about the time he was in the Army.* Runyan, pp. 41–42.
6. *Bayonet slicing his groin.* Wallace, p. 213. She says he told her the scar was from a hernia operation.
7. *Wake up.* Langevin, *Magical Blend.*
8. *I killed people.* Wallace, p. 96. It is interesting as well that the subject of murder appears in his first book, *The Teachings of Don Juan*, p. 37, in which don Juan says, " I killed a man with a single blow of my arm."
9. *I think don Juan.* Applebaum, *Chicago Tribune.*
10. *I suspect.* Jay Courtney Fikes, *Carlos Castaneda: Academic Opportunism and the Psychedelic Sixties* (Victoria, BC: Millenia Press, 1993), p. 91.
11. *Don Juan is real.* Runyan, pp. 100–101.
12. *The act of creation.* Nin, *The Novel of the Future*, p. 11.
13. *Fellini.* Wallace, pp. 399–400.

14. *If I had observed Carlos' methods.* Amy Wallace, p. 223.
15. *Die like a dog.* William Patrick Patterson, *Voices in the Dark* (Fairfax, CA: Arete Communications, 2000), p. 176.
16. *Act of unification.* Castaneda, *The Active Side of Infinity,* p. 268.
17. *What happens to sorcerers.* Castaneda, *The Active Side of Infinity,* p. 192.
18. *You will find yourself alive in an unknown land.* Castaneda, *Journey to Ixtlan*, pp. 312–13.
19. *The world of everyday life.* Castaneda, *The Teachings of Don Juan*, p. xi.
20. *A man of knowledge chooses.* Castaneda, *A Separate Reality*, p. 85.
21. *In his day-to-day life.* Castaneda, *A Separate Reality,* pp. 217–18.
22. *Controlled folly.* Castaneda, *A Separate Reality*, p. 77.
23. *Look at every path.* Castaneda, *The Teachings of Don Juan*, pp. 74–75.

Bibliography

Abelar, Taisha

The Sorcerers' Crossing. New York: Arkana, 1992.

Bair, Deirdre

Anaïs Nin: A Biography. New York: G. P. Putnam Sons, 1995.

Bennett, J. G.

Making A New World. London: Turnstone Books, 1973.

Brinton, Daniel G.

Nagualism: A Study in Native American Folklore and

History. Philadelphia, 1894.

Castaneda, Carlos

The Teachings of Don Juan. New York: Simon & Schuster, 1968.

A Separate Reality. New York: Simon & Schuster, 1971.

Journey to Ixtlan. New York: Simon & Schuster, 1972.

Tales of Power. New York: Simon & Schuster, 1974.

The Second Ring of Power. New York: Simon & Schuster, 1977.

The Eagle's Gift. New York: Simon & Schuster, 1981.

The Fire from Within. New York: Simon & Schuster, 1984.

The Power of Silence. New York: Simon & Schuster, 1987.

The Art of Dreaming. New York: HarperCollins, 1993.

The Active Side of Infinity. New York: HarperCollins, 1998.

Magical Passes. New York: HarperCollins, 1998.

Wheel of Time. New York: Washington Square Press, 1998.

Castaneda, Margaret Runyan

A Magical Journey with Carlos Castaneda. Victoria, BC: Millenia Press, 1997.

Czaplicka, M. A.

Shamanism in Siberia. Kilia, MT: Kessinger Publishing, n.d.

De Mille, Richard

Castaneda's Journey. Santa Barbara, CA: Capra Press, 1976.

The Don Juan Papers. Santa Barbara, CA: Ross-Erikson Publishers, 1980.

Donner, Florinda

Shabono. San Francisco: HarperSanFrancisco, 1982.

The Witch's Dream. New York: Simon & Schuster, 1985.

Being-in-Dreaming. San Francisco: HarperSanFrancisco, 1991.

Eliade, Mircea

Shamanism. Princeton, NJ: Princeton University Press, 1964.

Fikes, Jay Courtney

Carlos Castaneda: Academic Opportunism and the Psychedelic Sixties. Victoria, BC: Millenia Press, 1993.

Geuter, Gaby

Filming Castaneda. Los Angeles: First Books Library, 2004.

Gurdjieff, G. I.

All & Everything, First Series. New York: E. P. Dutton, 1950.

Meetings with Remarkable Men. New York: E. P. Dutton, 1963.

Life Is Real Only Then, When "I Am". New York: E. P. Dutton, 1975.

Views from the Real World. New York: E. P. Dutton, 1975.

Heidegger, Martin

Being and Time. New York: Harper & Row, 1962.

Husserl, Edmund

Logical Investigations, Vol. 1 & 2. London: Routledge, 2006.

Kehoe, Alice Beck

Shamans and Religion. Long Grove, IL: Waveland Press, 2000.

Monroe, Robert A.

Journeys Out of the Body. New York: Anchor Books, 1973.

Noel, Daniel

Seeing Castaneda. New York: G. P. Putnam's Sons, 1976.

Nott, C. S.

Teachings of Gurdjieff. New York: Samuel Weiser, 1962.

Parsons, Talcott

The Talcott Parsons Reader. Oxford, England: Blackwell Publishers, 1999.

Patterson, William Patrick

Eating The "I". Fairfax, CA: Arete Communications, 1991

Struggle of the Magicians. Fairfax, CA: Arete Communications, 1996.

Taking with the Left Hand. Fairfax, CA: Arete Communications, 1998.

Ladies of the Rope. Fairfax, CA: Arete Communications, 1999.

Voices in the Dark. Fairfax, CA: Arete Communications, 2000.

The Life & Significance of G. I. Gurdjieff, DVD. Fairfax, CA: Arete Communications, 2007.

Pentland, John

Exchanges Within. New York: Continuum, 1997.

Peters, Fritz

Boyhood with Gurdjieff. Fairfax, CA: Arete Communications, 2006.

Gurdjieff Remembered. New York: Samuel Weiser, 1971.

Ouspensky, P. D.

A New Model of the Universe. New York: Alfred A. Knopf, 1934.

In Search of the Miraculous. New York: Harcourt, Brace & World, Inc., 1949.

Psychology of Man's Possible Evolution. London: Hodder and Stoughton, 1951.
Tertium Organum: A Key to the Enigmas of the World. New York: Alfred A. Knopf, 1933.

Wallace, Amy
Sorcerer's Apprentice: My Life with Carlos Castaneda. Berkeley, CA: Frog, Ltd., 2003.

Williams, Donald Lee
Border Crossings. Toronto, Canada: Inner City Books, 1981.

Castaneda's Reply to R. Gordon Wasson

A gloss is given in brackets and italics.

Dear Mr. Wasson:

It was indeed a great pleasure to receive your letter. I am very familiar with your professional contributions in the field of hallucinogenic mushrooms, thus, I couldn't be more honored with the opportunity of discussing this topic with you. [*As in a chess game, Castaneda's opening is strong and direct, noting his knowledge of Wasson's contributions and his feeling of being honored that Wasson would want to discuss the topic with him; a little like Einstein writ-*

ing a letter to a recent Ph.D. grad in physics asking to discuss relativity theory.] You must bear in mind, however, that I am not an authority, and that my knowledge is limited strictly to the ethnographic data I have collected. [*Castaneda then adroitly limits the field of discussion.*] First of all I should tell you that my field work—and I have already stated this in the introduction of my book—was done under very constricting conditions. It was never an anthropological work proper; my work was rather an inquiry product of my own interest, and since my interest is "content" and "meaning" I became absorbed in the innuendoes that made don Juan's system of beliefs, disregarding to a large extent data which dealt with specific ethnographic details. Since I was dealing with a dramatic and serious system of beliefs I have purposefully blurred in my book more of such pertinent ethnographic details, thus compounding the vagueness in one letter [*Apparently, there was a first letter which Wasson found lacking in detail and so has written a second asking specific questions.*] without going back first to re-establish a better ethnographic context. However, I will try the best way I can to answer your questions in the order in which you have written them. [*Castaneda does not yet have a Ph.D. and so how he responds is crucial.*]

Q: Am I right in concluding from your narrative that you never gathered the mushrooms, nor indeed ever saw a whole specimen?

I have gathered the mushrooms myself. I have held perhaps hundreds of specimens in my hands. Don Juan and I made yearly trips to collect them in the mountains southwest and northwest of Valle Nacional in the state of Oaxaca. I have deleted in my book all specific details about those trips and all the specific details about the collecting process. Don Juan expressed himself very strongly against my desire to include those descriptions as part of my book. He did not object to my revealing specific details about collecting peyote or jimsonweed on the grounds that the deity in peyote was a protector, therefore accessible to every man, and the power in jimsonweed was not his ally *(alidado)*. The power in the mushrooms, however, was his ally and as such it was above everything else. And that entailed a total secrecy about specific processes. [*Here he relies on don Juan to blunt the full thrust of Wasson's question.*]

Q: Did you satisfy yourself that you were dealing with *Psilocybe mexicana*?

No. My botanical identification was a tentative one, and terribly unsophisticated at that. In my book, it appears as though the mushroom was *Psilocybe mexicana*, that is, I am afraid, an editorial error. I should have carried the assertion that it was a tentative classification all the way through, since I have never been completely convinced that it was. [*It is not an "editorial error," it is Castaneda's.*] The particular species used by don Juan looked like the *Psilocybe mexicana* pictures I have seen. A member of the Pharmacology Dept. at UCLA also showed me some specimens that he had, and based on that I concluded I was dealing with that species. However, it never turned into powder upon being handled. Don Juan picked it always with his left hand, transferred it to his right hand and then put it inside a small, narrow gourd. The mushroom would then disintegrate into fine shreds, but never into powder, as it was forced gently inside.

Q: Do you know where your mushrooms grew?

We found them growing on dead trunks of trees, but more often on decomposed remains of dead shrubs.

Q: What is don Juan's cultural provenience? [*This question goes right to the point—who is don Juan?*]

Don Juan is, in my judgment, a marginal man who has been forged by multiple forces outside the purely Yaqui culture. [*Castaneda, too, is just such a "marginal man."*] His name is really Juan. I tried to find a substitute name to use in my book, but I couldn't conceive him in any other way except as don Juan. He is not a pure Yaqui, that is, his mother was a Yuma Indian, and he was born in Arizona. His mixed origin seemed to have rendered him as a marginal man from the beginning.

He lived in Arizona the first years of his life and then moved to Sonora when he was perhaps six or seven years old. He lived there for a while, I am not sure whether with both parents or just with his father. That was the time of the great Yaqui upheavals and don Juan and his family were picked up by the Mexican armed forces and were deported to the state of Veracruz. Don Juan later moved to the area of "el Valle Nacional" where he lived for over thirty years. It is my belief that he moved there with his teacher, who must have been Mazateco. So far I have not been able to determine who his teacher was, nor where he did learn to be a brujo, yet the mere fact that I have to take him every year to Oaxaca to collect mushrooms should be a serious clue as to where he learned, at least, about mushrooms.

As you can see, it is impossible for me at this point to determine with certainty his cultural provenience, except in a guessing manner. However, the subtitle of my book is "A Yaqui Way of Knowledge." This is another mistake [*The first was an "editorial error."*] in which I became involved due to my lack of experience in matters of publications. The Editorial Committee of the University of

California Press suggested upon accepting my manuscript for publication, that the word Yaqui should be included in the title in order to place the book ethnographically. They had not read the manuscript but they concluded that I had said that don Juan was a Yaqui, which was true, but I had never meant that don Juan was a product of the Yaqui culture, as appears to be the case now judging from the title of the book. [*Yes, it does appear so. So don Juan is a Yaqui who is not really a Yaqui, the "marginal man" defense.*] Don Juan considered himself to be a Yaqui and seemed to have deep ties with the Yaquis of Sonora. However, it has become obvious to me now that those ties were only a surface affiliation.

[*Castaneda now returns to Wasson's subject of expertise.*]

I am not familiar with whether or not the hallucinogenic mushrooms grow in the arid regions of Sonora and Chihuahua. Don Juan has never looked for them there to my knowledge. Yet he has asserted repeatedly that once a man learns to command the power in them the mushrooms can grow any place the man wants, that is, they grow by themselves without his direct intervention.

The first time in my life I saw the mushrooms was in Durango. I thought we were going to look for "hongitos" but we wound up collecting peyote in Chihuahua. At that time I saw quite a few, perhaps ten or twelve. Don Juan said they were only a token, and that there were not enough to make use of them. At that time he also told me that we had to make a trip to Oaxaca to find the right number of mushrooms. In 1964 I found one specimen myself in the Santa Monica mountains here in Los Angeles. I took it to the laboratory at UCLA but through carelessness they lost it before identifying it. It was strikingly obvious to me that it was one of the mushrooms used by don Juan; he naturally interpreted the event of finding it as an omen that I was on my way to learning, but my subsequent actions, such as picking it and leaving it with strangers, reassured him, he said, of my utterly fumbling nature. [*How Castaneda depicts himself in the book, in which the reader feels at once superior to him and yet envious of his experience.*]

Q: Have you brought back the powder, or the mixture, in which mushroom powder was an ingredient?

[*Wasson is looking for direct verification.*]

No. However, I am sure I could obtain a very small amount of it, perhaps a dab of it. If that would be enough to examine it under the microscope I can send it to you by the end of this year.

Q: Will there be a Spanish edition of the book?

I hope the University of California Press will consider that possibility. My notes are all in Spanish. In fact this book was almost an English version of a Spanish manuscript.

Q: Did don Juan say "un hombre de conocimiento" or simply "un hombre que sabe?"

You have given me here the most fascinating piece of information. [*A clever rejoinder.*] To define the conditions of being, or the stage of learning of a "man of knowledge," don Juan used the terms "*hombre de conocimiento*" [man of knowledge], "*hombre que sabe*" [man who knows], and "*uno que sabe*" [one who knows]. I have preferred the term "man of knowledge" because it is more concrete than "one who knows."

I have taken some parts of my notes in Spanish dealing with "*el hombre que sabe*" and I have included them here. I hope they are legible. These sheets are a direct transcription of the even more illegible direct notes I took while don Juan talked to me. As a rule I always rewrote my notes immediately so I would not lose the freshness and the flare of don Juan's statements and thoughts.

Q: Was don Juan bilingual, or was he better in Spanish than in Yaqui?

Don Juan speaks Spanish so fluently that I am willing to believe that his command of Spanish is better than any other language he knows. But he speaks also Yaqui, Yuma, and Mazatec. I have reasons to believe that he also speaks English, or at least he understands it perfectly, although I have never heard him using it.

Q: Did you gather in your field notes the Yaqui equivalents of the terms he used?

I have some terms which are not Spanish, but too few to make a serious study. Our conversations were conducted strictly in Spanish and the few foreign terms are not all Yaqui words. [*So, the Yaqui who converses in Spanish, not his mother tongue, and the language of his people's conquerors. But, as Castaneda speaks Spanish and not Yaqui this is understandable, though one would think that the key terms would all be rendered in Yaqui.*]

Q: Do you ever tell your readers whether he could read and write in Spanish?

He reads very well; I have never seen him writing though. [*This blunts the question of whether or not he wrote anything. Hence, a "hombre de conocimiento" who does not write. But this, of course, is a Western idea.*] For a long time I thought he was illiterate, this misjudgment on my part was the result of our differences in emphasis. I stress areas of behavior which are thoroughly irrelevant to him, and vice versa. This cognitive difference between us is the theme I am striving to develop in the biography of don Juan which I am writing now. [*This will be a "biography" like none other. He now gives some information about himself which Wasson would want to know but did not directly ask for.*]

There is not much to tell about myself. My home was in Sao Paulo, Brazil, but I went to school in Buenos Aires, Argentina, before I came to this country. [*As Castaneda says only that his "home" was in Brazil, the question remains open as to whether he is Brazilian or Peruvian by birth, even perhaps Italian.*] My full name is Carlos Aranha. Following the Latin tradition one always adds to one's name the mother's last name, so when I came to the United States I became Carlos A. Castaneda. Then I dropped the A. The name belonged to my grandfather who was from Sicily. I don't know how it was originally, but he himself altered it to Castaneda to suit his fancy.

"On the Study of Dreams" and "Experimental Mysticism"

P. D. Ouspensky, A New Model of the Universe

P. 279, "Dreams change by the fact of their being observed, namely that several times I dreamed that I was observing my dreams. My original aim was to create consciousness in dreams, i.e. to attain the capacity of realizing in sleep that I was sleeping."

P. 282, "Our 'I' feeling is much more obscured in sleep than in a waking state. This is really the chief psychological feature which determines the state of sleep and expresses the whole difference" [between sleep and the waking state].

P. 298, "Passes and strokings of a certain kind, which provoke relaxation of the muscles, a fixed gaze into the eyes, flashing mirrors, sudden impressions, a loud shout, monotonous music: all these are means of hypnotizing. Besides this narcotics are used: first for the weakening of the resistance to hypnotic action, and second for the strengthening of the capacity to hypnotize. . . . The hypnotic state is therefore defined as the state of maximum suggestibility."

P. 300, "All that takes place in the mind of the hypnotizer can be transferred to the person hypnotized by him."

P. 310, "In all descriptions of witchcraft and sorcery in all countries and among all peoples, the use of narcotics is invariably mentioned."

P. 314, "We are accustomed to the constancy of the relation between the subjective and the objective—what is objective is always objective, what is subjective is always subjective. Here I saw that the objective and the subjective could change places. The one becomes the other."

P. 318, "I usually began almost at once to hear 'voices.' The voices spoke to me and often said very strange things which seemed to have a quality of trick in them."

P. 320, "Everything moved, changed, was transformed and became something else. Sometimes I suddenly saw all mathematical relations disappear one after another into infinity. Infinity swallowed everything, filled everything; all distinctions were effaced. And I felt that one moment more and I myself should disappear into infinity. I was overcome with terror at the imminence of this abyss."

P. 334, "The disappearance of the 'I' began to produce in me a feeling of extraordinary calmness and confidence, all the usual troubles, cares and anxieties are connected with the usual sensation of the 'I.'"

P. 342, "The strangest thing in all these experiences was the coming back, the return to the ordinary state, to the state which we call life. This was something very similar to dying or to what I thought dying must be."

Index

W

Nagualism: A Study in Native American Folklore and History

by Daniel G. Brinton, M.D.

Professor of American Archaeology and Linguistics
in the University of Pennsylvania
(Read before the American Philosophical Society,
January 5, 1894)

Contents

1. The words, a *nagual, nagualism*, a *nagualist*, have been current in English prose for more than seventy years; they are found during that time in a variety of books published in England and the United States,* yet are not to be discovered in any dictionary of the English language; nor has *Nagualism* a place in any of the numerous encyclopedias or "Conversation Lexicons," in English, French, German or Spanish.

This is not owing to its lack of importance, since for

* These words occur a number of times in the English translation, published at London in 1822, of Dr. Paul Félix Cabrera's *Teatro Crítico Americano*. The form *nagual* instead of *nahual*, or *naual*, or *nawal* has been generally adopted and should be preferred.

two hundred years past, as I shall show, it has been recognized as a cult, no less powerful than mysterious, which united many and diverse tribes of Mexico and Central America into organized opposition against the government and the religion which had been introduced from Europe; whose members had acquired and were bound together by strange faculties and an occult learning, which placed them on a par with the famed thaumaturgists and theodidacts of the Old World; and which preserved even into our own days the thoughts and forms of a long suppressed ritual.

In several previous publications I have referred briefly to this secret sodality and its aims,* and now believe it worth while to collect my scattered notes and present all that I have found of value about the origin, aims and significance of this Eleusinian Mystery of America. I shall trace its geographical extension and endeavor to discover what its secret influence really was and is.

2. The earliest description I find of its particular rites is that which the historian Herrera gives, as they prevailed in 1530, in the province of Cerquin, in the mountainous parts of Honduras. It is as follows:

> The Devil was accustomed to deceive these natives by appearing to them in the form of a lion, tiger, coyote, lizard, snake, bird, or other animal. To these appearances they apply the name *Naguales,* which is as much as to say, guardians or companions; and when such an animal dies, so does the Indian to whom it was assigned. The way such an alliance was formed was thus: The Indian repaired to some

* For instance, in "The Names of the Gods in the Kiche Myth," pp. 21, 22, in *Proceedings of the American Philosophical Society,* 1881; *Annals of the Cakchiquels,* Introduction, p. 46; *Essays of an Americanist,* p. 170, etc.

> very retired spot and there appealed to the streams, rocks and trees around him, and weeping, implored for himself the favors they had conferred on his ancestors. He then sacrificed a dog or a fowl, and drew blood from his tongue, or his ears, or other parts of his body, and turned to sleep. Either in his dreams or half awake, he would see some one of those animals or birds above mentioned, who would say to him, "On such a day go hunting and the first animal or bird you see will be my form, and I shall remain your companion and *Nagual* for all time." Thus their friendship became so close that when one died so did the other; and without such a *Nagual* the natives believe no one can become rich or powerful.*

This province of Cerquin appears to have been peopled by a tribe which belonged to the great Mayan stock, akin to those which occupied most of the area of what is now Yucatan, Tabasco, Chiapas and Guatemala.† I shall say something later about the legendary enchantress whom their traditions recalled as the teacher of their ancestors and the founder of their nation. What I would now call attention to is the fact that in none of the dialects of the specifically Mexican or Aztecan stock of languages do we find the word *nagual* in the sense in which it is employed in the above extract, and this is strong evidence that the origin of Nagualism is not to be sought in that stock.

3. We do find, however, in the Nahuatl language, which is the proper name of the Aztecan, a number of derivatives from the same root, *na*, among them this very word,

* *Historia de las Indias Occidentales*, Dec. iv, Lib. viii, cap. 4.

† More especially it is the territory of the Chorti dialect, spoken to this day in the vicinity of the famous ancient city of Copan, Honduras. Cerquin lies in the mountains nearly due east of this celebrated site. On the Chorti, see Stoll, *Zur Ethnographie der Republik Guatemala*, pp. 106–9.

Nahuatl, all of them containing the idea "to know," or "knowledge." The early missionaries to New Spain often speak of the *naualli* (plural, *nanahualtin*), masters of mystic knowledge, dealers in the black art, wizards or sorcerers. They were not always evil-minded persons, though they seem to have been generally feared. The earliest source of information about them is Father Sahagún, who, in his invaluable History, has the following paragraph:

> The *naualli*, or magician, is he who frightens men and sucks the blood of children during the night. He is well skilled in the practice of this trade, he knows all the arts of sorcery *(nauallotl)* and employs them with cunning and ability; but for the benefit of men only, not for their injury. Those who have recourse to such arts for evil intents injure the bodies of their victims, cause them to lose their reason and smother them. These are wicked men and necromancers.*

It is evident on examining the later works of the Roman clergy in Mexico that the Church did not look with any such lenient eye on the possibly harmless, or even beneficial, exercise of these magical devices. We find a further explanation of what they were, preserved in a work of instruction to confessors, published by Father Juan Bautista, at Mexico, in the year 1600.

> There are magicians who call themselves *teciuhtlazque*,† and also by the term *nanahualtin*, who conjure the clouds when there is danger of hail, so that the crops may not be injured. They can also make a stick look like a serpent, a mat like a centipede, a piece of stone like a scorpion, and similar deceptions. Others of these *nanahualtin* will transform themselves to all appearances (segun la apariencia), into a tiger, a dog or a weasel. Others again will take the

* Bernardino de Sahagún, *Historia de la Nueva España*, Lib. x, cap. 9.

† Derived from *teciuhtlaza*, to conjure against hail, itself from *teciuh*, hail. Alonso de Molina, *Vocabulario Mexicano*, sub voce.

> form of an owl, a cock, or a weasel; and when one is preparing to seize them, they will appear now as a cock, now as an owl, and again as a weasel. These call themselves *nanahualtin.*[*]

There is an evident attempt in this somewhat confused statement to distinguish between an actual transformation, and one which only appears such to the observer.

In another work of similar character, published at Mexico a few years later, the "Road to Heaven," of Father Nicolas de León, we find a series of questions which a confessor should put to any of his flock suspected of these necromantic practices. They reveal to us quite clearly what these occult practitioners were believed to do. The passage reads as follows, the questions being put in the mouth of the priest:

> Art thou a soothsayer ? Dost thou foretell events by reading signs, or by interpreting dreams, or by water, making circles and figures on its surface? Dost thou sweep and ornament with flower garlands the places where idols are preserved? Dost thou know certain words with which to conjure for success in hunting, or to bring rain?
>
> Dost thou suck the blood of others, or dost thou wander about at night, calling upon the Demon to help thee? Hast thou drunk *peyotl,* or hast thou given it to others to drink, in order to find out secrets, or to discover where stolen or lost articles were? Dost thou know how to speak to vipers in such words that they obey thee?[†]

4. This interesting passage lets in considerable light on the claims and practices of the nagualists. Not the least important item is that of their use of the intoxicant, *peyotl,*

---

* Bautista, *Advertencias para los Confesores*, fol. 112 (México, 1600).

† Nicolas de León, *Camino del Cielo*, fol. 111(México, 1611).

a decoction of which it appears played a prominent part in their ceremonies. This is the native Nahuatl name of a certain plant, having a white, tuberous root, which is the part employed. It is mentioned as "pellote " or "peyote" in the *Farmacopea Mexicana* as a popular remedy, but its botanical name is not added. According to Paso y Troncoso, it is one of the Compositæ, a species of the genus *Cacalia.** It is referred to in several passages by Father Sahagún, who says that it grows in southern Mexico, and that the Aztecs derived their knowledge of it from the older "Chichimecs." It was used as an intoxicant.

> Those who eat or drink of this *peyotl* see visions, which are sometimes frightful and sometimes ludicrous. The intoxication it causes lasts several days. The Chichimecs believed that it gave them courage in time of danger and diminished the pangs of hunger and thirst.†

Its use was continued until a late date, and very probably has not yet died out. Its composition and method of preparation are given in a list of beverages prohibited by the Spanish authorities in the year 1784, as follows:

> *Peyote:* made from a species of vinagrilla, about the size of a billiard ball, which grows in dry and sterile soil. The natives chew it, and throw it into a wooden mortar, where

---

* Paso y Troncoso, in *Anales del Museo Nacional de México*, Tom. iii, p. 180.

† Sahagún, *Historia de Nueva España*, Lib. x, cap. 29, and Lib. xi, cap. 7. Hernández has the following on the mysterious properties of this plant: "Illud ferunt de hac radice mirabile (si modo fides sit vulgatissimæ inter eos rei habendæ), devorantes illam quodlibet præsagire prædicereque; velut an sequenti die hostes sint impetum in eos facturi? Anne illos felicia maneant tempora? Quis supellectilem, aut aliud quidpiam furto subripruerit? Et ad hunc modum alia, quibus Chichimecæ hujusmodi medicamine cognoscendis." Franciscus Hernandus, *Historia Plantarum Novæ Hispaniæ*, Tom. iii, p. 71 (Ed., Madrid, 1790).

> it is left to ferment, some leaves of tobacco being added to give it pungency. They consume it in this form, sometimes with slices of *peyote* itself, in their most solemn festivities, although it dulls the intellect and induces gloomy and hurtful visions (sombras muy funestas).*

The *peyotl* was not the only herb prized as a means of casting the soul into the condition of hypostatic union with divinity. We have abundant evidence that long after the conquest the seeds of the plant called in Nahuatl the *ololiuhqui* were in high esteem for this purpose. In the Confessionary of Father Bartholomé de Alva the priest is supposed to inquire and learn as follows:

> *Question.* Hast thou loved God above all things? Hast thou loved any created thing, adoring it, looking upon it as God, and worshiping it?
>
> *Answer.* I have loved God with all my heart; but sometimes I have believed in dreams, and also I have believed in the sacred herbs, the *peyotl,* and the *ololiuhqui;* and in other such things *(onicneltocac in temictli, in xiuhtzintli, in peyotl, in ololiuhqui, yhuan in occequitlamantli).*†

The seeds of the *ololiuhqui* appear to have been employed externally. They were the efficient element in the mysterious unguent known as "the divine remedy" (*teopatli*), about which we find some information in the works of Father Augustín de Vetancurt, who lived in Mexico in the middle of the seventeenth century. He writes:

> The pagan priests made use of an ointment composed of insects, such as spiders, scorpions, centipedes and the like, which the neophytes in the temples prepared. They burned these insects in a basin, collected the ashes, and rubbed it up with green tobacco leaves, living worms and

* *Diccionario Universal,* Appendice, Tom. i, p. 360 (México, 1856).

† *Confessionario Mayor y Menor en lengua Mexicana,* fol. 8, verso (México, 1634).

> insects, and the powdered seeds of a plant called *ololiuhqui*, which has the power of inducing visions, and the effect of which is to destroy the reasoning powers. Under the influence of this ointment, they conversed with the Devil, and he with them, practicing his deceptions upon them. They also believed that it protected them, so they had no fear of going into the woods at night.
>
> This was also employed by them as a remedy in various diseases, and the soothing influence of the tobacco and the *ololiuhqui* was attributed by them to divine agency. There are some in our own day who make use of this ointment for sorcery, shutting themselves up, and losing their reason under its influence; especially some old men and old women, who are prepared to fall an easy prey to the Devil.*

The botanist Hernández observes that another name for this plant was *coaxihuitl*, "serpent plant," and adds that its seeds contain a narcotic poison, and that it is allied to the genus *Solanum*, of which the deadly night-shade is a familiar species. He speaks of its use in the sacred rites in these words:

> Indorum sacrifici, cum videri volebant versari cum superis, ac responsa accipere ab eis, ea vescebantur planta, ut desiperent, milleque phantasmata et demonum observatium effigies circumspectarent.†

Of the two plants mentioned, the *ololiuhqui* and the *peyotl*, the former was considered the more potent in spiritual virtues. "They hold it in as much veneration as if it were God," says a theologian of the seventeenth century.‡ One who partook of these herbs was called *payni*

---

* Vetancurt, *Teatro Méxicano*, Trat. iii, cap. 9.

† Hernández, *Historia Plantarum Novæ Hispaniæ*, Tom. iii, p. 32.

‡ Dr. Jacinto de la Serna, *Manual de Ministros de Indios para el Conocimiento de sus Idolatrias y Extirpación de Ellas*, p. 163. This

(from the verb *pay*, to take medicine); and more especially *tlachixqui*, a Seer, referring to the mystic "second sight," hence a diviner or prophet (from the verb *tlachia*, to see).

Tobacco also held a prominent, though less important, place in these rites. It was employed in two forms, the one the dried leaf, *picietl*, which for sacred uses must be broken and rubbed up either seven or nine times; and the green leaf mixed with lime, hence called *tenextlecietl* (from *tenextli*, lime).

Allied in effect to these is an intoxicant in use in southern Mexico and Yucatan, prepared from the bark of a tree called by the Mayas *baal-che*. The whites speak of the drink as *pitarilla*. It is quite popular among the natives, and they still attribute to it a sacred character, calling it *yax ha*, the first water, the primal fluid. They say that it was the first liquid created by God, and when He returned to His heavenly home He left this beverage and its production in charge of the gods of the rains, the four Pah-Ahtuns.*

5. Intoxication of some kind was an essential part of many of these secret rites. It was regarded as a method of throwing the individual out of himself and into relation with the supernal powers. What the old historian, Father Joseph de Acosta, tells us about the clairvoyants and telepaths of the aborigines might well stand for a description of their modern representatives:

> Some of these sorcerers take any shape they choose, and fly

---

interesting work was composed about the middle of the seventeenth century by a Rector of the University of Mexico, but was first printed at Madrid, in 1892, from the MS. furnished by Dr. N. León, under the editorship of the Marquis de la Fuensanta del Valle.

* MSS. of the Licentiate Zetina, and *Informe* of Father Baeza in *Registro Yucateco*, Tom. i.

> through the air with wonderful rapidity and for long distances. They will tell what is taking place in remote localities long before the news could possibly arrive. The Spaniards have known them to report mutinies, battles, revolts and deaths, occurring two hundred or three hundred leagues distant, on the very day they took place, or the day after.
>
> To practice this art the sorcerers, usually old women, shut themselves in a house, and intoxicate themselves to the degree of losing their reason. The next day they are ready to reply to questions.*

Plants possessing similar powers to excite vivid visions and distort the imagination, and, therefore, employed in the magical rites, were the *thiuimeezque*, in Michoacán, and the *chacuaco*, in lower California.†

6. In spite of all effort, the various classes of wonderworkers continued to thrive in Mexico. We find in a book of sermons published by the Jesuit Father, Ignacio de Paredes, in the Nahuatl language, in 1757, that he strenuously warns his hearers against invoking, consulting, or calling upon "the devilish spell-binders, the nagualists, and those who conjure with smoke."‡

They have not yet lost their power; we have evidence

* Acosta, *De la Historia Moral de Indias*, Lib. v, cap. 26.

† Of the *thiuimeezque* Hernández writes: "Aiunt radicis cortice unius unciæ pondere tuso, atque devorato, multa ante oculos observare phantasmata, multiplices imagines ac monstrificas rerum figuras, detegique furem, si quidpiam rei familiaris subreptum sit." *Hist. Plant. Nov. Hispan.*, Tom. iii, p. 252. The *chacuaco* and its effects are described by Father Venegas in his *History of California*, etc.

‡ "In Mictlan Tetlachihuique, in Nanahualtin, in Tlahuipuchtin." Paredes, *Promptuario Manual Mexicano*, p. 128 (México, 1757). The *tlahuipuchtin*, "those who work with smoke," were probably diviners who foretold the future from the forms taken by smoke in rising in the air. This class of augurs were also found in Peru, where they were called *Uirapircos* (Balboa, *Hist. du Perou*, p. 28–30).

enough that many children of a larger growth in that land still listen with respect to the recitals of the mysterious faculties attributed to the *nanahualtin*. An observant German traveler, Carlos von Gagern, informs us that they are widely believed to be able to cause sicknesses and other ills, which must be counteracted by appropriate exorcisms, among which the reading aloud certain passages of the Bible is deemed to be one of the most potent.*

The learned historian, Orozco y Berra, speaks of the powers attributed at the present day to the *nahual* in Mexico among the lower classes, in these words:

> The *nahual* is generally an old Indian with red eyes, who knows how to turn himself into a dog, woolly, black and ugly. The female witch can convert herself into a ball of fire; she has the power of flight, and at night will enter the windows and suck the blood of little children. These sorcerers will make little images of rags or of clay, then stick into them the thorn of the maguey and place them in some secret place; you can be sure that the person against whom the conjuration is practiced will feel pain in the part where the thorn is inserted. There still exist among them the medicine-men, who treat the sick by means of strange contortions, call upon the spirits, pronounce magical incantations, blow upon the part where the pain is, and draw forth from the patient thorns, worms, or pieces of stone. They know how to prepare drinks which will bring on sickness, and if the patients are cured by others the convalescents are particular to throw something of their own away, as a lock of hair, or a part of their clothing. Those who possess the evil eye can, by merely looking at children, deprive them of beauty and health, and even cause their death.†

---

* Von Gagern, *Charakteristik der Indianischer Bevölkerung Mexikos*, s. 125.

† *Historia Antigua de México*, Tom.ii, p. 25. Francisco Pimentel, in his thoughtful work, *Memoria sobre las Causas que han originado la Situación Actual de la Raza Indígena de México* (México, 1861),

7. As I have said, nowhere in the records of purely Mexican, that is, Aztecan, Nagualism do we find the word *nagual* employed in the sense given in the passage quoted from Herrera, that is as a personal guardian spirit or tutelary genius. These tribes had, indeed, a belief in some such protecting power, and held that it was connected with the day on which each person is born. They called it the *tonalli* of a person, a word translated to mean that which is peculiar to him, which makes his individuality, his self. The radical from which it is derived is *tona*, to warm, or to be warm, from which are also derived *tonatiuh*, the sun. *Tonalli*, which in composition loses its last syllable, is likewise the word for heat, summer, soul, spirit and day, and also for the share or portion which belongs to one. Thus, *to-tonal* is spirit or soul in general; *no-tonal*, my spirit; *no-tonal in ipan no-tlacat*, "the sign under which I was born," i.e., the astrological day-sign. From this came the verb *tonalpoa*, to count or estimate the signs, that is, to cast the horoscope of a person; and *tonalpouhque*, the diviners whose business it was to practice this art.*

These *tonalpouhque* are referred to at length by Father Sahagún.† He distinguishes them from the *naualli*, though it is clear that they corresponded in functions to the nagualistic priests of the southern tribes. From the number and name of the day of birth they forecast the destiny of the child, and

---

recognizes how almost impossible it is to extirpate their faith in this nagualism. "Conservan los agueros y supersticiones de la antiguedad, siendo cosa de fé para ellos, los *nahaules*," etc., p. 200, and comp. p. 145.

* On these terms consult the extensive *Dictionnaire de la Langue Nahuatl*, by Rémi Simeon, published at Paris, 1887. It is not impossible that *tona* is itself a compound root, including the monosyllabic radical *na*, which is at the basis of *nagual*.

† Sahagún, *Historia de Nueva España*, Lib. iv, *passim*, and Lib. x, cap. 9.

stated the power or spiritual influence which should govern its career.

The *tonal* was by no means an indefeasible possession. It was a sort of independent *mascotte*. So long as it remained with a person he enjoyed health and prosperity; but it could depart, go astray, become lost; and then sickness and misfortune arrived. This is signified in the Nahuatl language by the verbs *tonalcaualtia*, to check, stop or suspend the *tonal*, hence, to shock or frighten one; and *tonalitlacoa*, to hurt or injure the *tonal*, hence, to cast a spell on one, to bewitch him.

This explains the real purpose of the conjuring and incantations which were carried on by the native doctor when visiting the sick. It was to recall the *tonal*, to force or persuade it to return; and, therefore, the ceremony bore the name "the restitution of the *tonal*," and was more than any other deeply imbued with the superstitions of Nagualism. The chief officiant was called the *tetonaltiani*, "he who concerns himself with the *tonal*." On a later page I shall give the formula recited on such an occasion.

8. There is some vague mention in the Aztec records of a semi-priestly order, who bore the name *naualteteuctin*, which may be translated "master magicians." They were also known as *teotlauice*, "sacred companions in arms." As was the case with most classes of the *teteuctin*, or nobles, entrance to the order was by a severe and prolonged ceremony of initiation, the object of which was not merely to test the endurance of pain and the powers of self-denial, but especially to throw the mind into that subjective state in which it is brought into contact with the divine, in which it can "see visions and dream dreams." The order claimed as its patron and founder Quetzalcoatl, "the feathered serpent," who, it will be seen on

another page, was also the patron of the later nagualists.*

The word *naualli* also occurs among the ancient Nahuas in composition as a part of proper names; always with the signification of "magician," as in that of Naualcuauhtla, a chief of the Chalcos, meaning "wizard-stick," referring probably to the rod or wand employed by the magi in conjuration.† So also *Naualac*, the "wizard water," an artificial lake not far from the city of Mexico, surrounded by ruined temples, described by M. Charnay.‡

9. The belief in a personal guardian spirit was one of the fundamental doctrines of Nagualism; but this belief by no means connotes the full import of the term (as Mr. H. H. Bancroft has erroneously stated). The calendar system of Mexico and Central America, which I have shown to be substantially the same throughout many diverse linguistic stocks,§ had as one of its main objects, astrological divination. By consulting it the appropriate nagual was discovered and assigned, and this was certainly a prominent feature in the native cult and has never been abandoned.

In Mexico today, in addition to his special personal guardian, the native will often choose another for a limited time or for a particular purpose, and this is quite consis-

---

* See Ch. de Labarthe, *Revue Américaine*, Série ii, Tom. ii, pp. 222–225. His translation of *naualteteuctin* by "Seigneurs du gènie" must be rejected, as there is absolutely no authority for assigning this meaning to *naualli*.

† *Anales de Cuauhtitlán*, p. 31. The translator renders it "palo brujo."

‡ *Les Anciennes Villes du Nouveau Monde*, pp. 116–143, figured on p. 150. On its significance compare Hamy, *Decades Americanæ*. pp. 74–81.

§ *The Native Calendar of Central America and Mexico* (Philadelphia, 1893).

tent with the form of Christianity he has been taught. For instance, as we are informed by an observant traveler, at New Year or at corn-planting the head of a family will go to the parish church and among the various saints there displayed will select one as his guardian for the year. He will address to him his prayers for rain and sunshine, for an abundant harvest, health and prosperity, and will not neglect to back these supplications by liberal gifts. If times are good and harvests ample the Santo is rewarded with still more gifts, and his aid is sought for another term; but if luck has been bad the Indian repairs to the church at the end of the year, bestows on his holy patron a sound cursing, calls him all the bad names he can think of, and has nothing more to do with him.*

10. A Mexican writer, Andrés Iglesias, who enjoyed more than common opportunities to study these practices as they exist in the present generation, describes them as he saw them in the village of Soteapan, a remote hamlet in the State of Vera Cruz, the population of which speak the Mixe language. This is not related to the Nahuatl tongue, but the terms of their magical rites are drawn from Nahuatl words, showing their origin. Every person at birth has assigned to him both a good and a bad genius, the former aiming at his welfare, the latter at his injury. The good genius is known by the Nahuatl term *tonale*, and it is represented in the first bird or animal of any kind which is seen in or near the house immediately after the birth of the infant.

The most powerful person in the village is the high priest of the native cult. One who died about 1850 was called "the Thunderbolt," and whenever he walked abroad

* Eduard Mühlenpfordt, *Mexico*, Bd. i, s.255.

he was preceded by a group of chosen disciples, called by the Nahuatl name *tlatoques*, speakers or attorneys.* His successor, known as "the Greater Thunder," did not maintain this state, but nevertheless claimed to be able to control the seasons and to send or to mitigate destructive storms—claims which, sad to say, brought him to the stocks, but did not interfere with the regular payment of tribute to him by the villagers. He was also a medicine man and master of ceremonies in certain "scandalous orgies, where immodesty shows herself without a veil."†

11. Turning to the neighboring province of Oaxaca and its inhabitants, we are instructed on the astrological use of the calendar of the Zapotecs by Father Juan de Córdova, whose *Arte* of their language was published at Mexico in 1578. From what he says its principal, if not its only purpose, was astrological. Each day had its number and was called after some animal, as eagle, snake, deer, rabbit, etc. Every child, male or female, received the name of the day, and also its number, as a surname; its personal name being taken from a fixed series, which differed in the masculine and feminine gender, and which seems to have been derived from the names of the fingers.

From this it appears that among the Zapotecs the per-

---

* The word is derived from *tlatoa*, to speak for another, and its usual translation was "chief," as the head man spoke for, and in the name of the gens or tribe.

† The interesting account by Iglesias is printed in the Appendix to the *Diccionario Universal de Geographía y Historia* (México, 1856). Other writers testify to the tenacity with which the Mixes cling to their ancient beliefs. Señor Moro says they continue to be "notorious idolaters," and their actual religion to be "an absurd jumble of their old superstitions with Christian doctrines" (in Orozco y Berra, *Geografía de las Lenguas de México*, p. 176).

sonal spirit or *nagual* was fixed by the date of the birth, and not by some later ceremony, although the latter has been asserted by some writers; who, however, seem to have applied without certain knowledge the rites of the Nahuas and other surrounding tribes to the Zapotecs.*

Next in importance to the assigning of names, according to Father Córdova, was the employment of the calendar in deciding the propriety of marriages. As the recognized object of marriage was to have sons, the couple appealed to the professional augur to decide this question before the marriage was fixed. He selected as many beans as was the sum of the numbers of the two proponents' names, and, counting them by twos, if one remained over, it meant a son; then counting by threes any remainder also meant sons; by fours the remainder meant either sons or daughters; and by five and six the same; and if there was no remainder by any of these five divisors the marriage would result in no sons and was prohibited.

It is obvious that this method of fortunetelling was most auspicious for the lovers; for I doubt if there is any combination of two numbers below fourteen which is divisible by two, three, four, five and six without remainder in any one instance.†

The Zapotecs were one of those nations who voluntarily submitted themselves to the Spaniards, not out of

* For instance, J. B. Carriedo, in his *Estudios Historicos del Estado Oaxaqueño* (Oaxaca, 1949), p. 15, says the *nahualt* was a ceremony performed by the native priest, in which the infant was bled from a vein behind thc car, assigned a name, that of a certain day, and a guardian angel or *tona*. These words are pure Nahuatl, and Carriedo, who does not give his authority, probably had none which referred these rites to the Zapotecs.

† Juan de Córdova, *Arte en Lengua Zapoteca*, pp. 16, 202, 203, 213, 216.

love for the Europeans, but through hatred of the Aztecs, who had conquered them in the preceding century. Their king, Coyopy, and his subjects accepted Christianity, and were generally baptized; but it was the merest formality, and years afterwards Coyopy was detected secretly conducting the heathen ritual of his ancestors with all due pomp. He was arrested, sent to the city of Mexico, deprived of his power and wealth, and soon died; it is charitably supposed, from natural causes. There is no question but that he left successors to the office of pontifex maximus, and that they continued the native religious ceremonies.

12. The sparse notices we have of the astrology of the Mixtecs, neighbors and some think relatives of the Zapotecs, reveal closely similar rites. The name of their king, who opposed Montezuma the First some sixty years before the arrival of Cortéz, proves that they made use of the same or a similar calendar in bestowing personal appellations. It is given as *Tres Micos,* Three Monkeys.

Unfortunately, so far as I know, there has not been published, and perhaps there does not exist, an authentic copy of the Mixtec calendar. It was nevertheless reduced to writing in the native tongue after the conquest, and a copy of it was seen by the historian Burgoa in the Mixtec town of Yanhuitlan.* Each day was named from a tree, a plant or an animal, and from them the individual received his names, as Four Lions, Five Roses, etc. (examples given by Herrera). This latter writer adds that the name was assigned by the priests when the child was seven years old (as among the Tzentals), part of the rite being to conduct it to the temple and bore its ears. He refers also to their

* Quoted in Carriedo, ubi supra, p. 17.

auguries relating to marriage.* These appear to have been different from among the Zapotecs. It was necessary that the youth should have a name bearing a higher number than that of the maiden, and also "that they should be related"; probably this applied only to certain formal marriages of the rulers which were obliged to be within the same *gens.*

13. I have referred in some detail to the rites and superstitions connected with the Calendar because they are all essential parts of Nagualism, carried on far into Christian times by the priests of this secret cult, as was fully recognized by the Catholic clergy. Wherever this calendar was in use, the Freemasonry of Nagualism extended, and its ritual had constant reference to it. Our fullest information about it does not come from central Mexico, but further south, in the region occupied by the various branches of the Mayan stock, by the ancestors of some one of which, perhaps, this singular calendar, and the symbolism connected with it, were invented.

One of the most important older authorities on this subject is Francisco Nuñez de la Vega, a learned Dominican, who was appointed Bishop of Chiapas and Soconusco in 1687, and who published at Rome, in 1702, a stately folio entitled "*Constituciones Dioecesanas del Obispado de Chiappa,*" comprising discussions of the articles of religion and a series of pastoral letters. The subject of Nagualism is referred to in many passages, and the ninth Pastoral Letter is devoted to it. As this book is one of extreme rarity, I shall make rather lengthy extracts from it, taking the liberty of condensing the scholastic prolixity of the author, and omitting his professional admonitions to the wicked.

* *Hist. de las Indias Oc.*, Dec. iii, Lib. iii, cap. 12.

He begins his references to it in several passages of his Introduction or *Preambulo*, in which he makes some interesting statements as to the use to which the natives put their newly-acquired knowledge of writing, while at the same time they had evidently not forgotten the ancient method of recording ideas invented by their ancestors.

The Bishop writes:

> The Indians of New Spain retain all the errors of their time of heathenism preserved in certain writings in their own languages, explaining by abbreviated characters and by figures painted in a secret cypher* the places, provinces and names of their early rulers, the animals, stars and elements which they worshiped, the ceremonies, and sacrifices which they observed, and the years, months and days by which they predicted the fortunes of children at birth, and assign them that which they call the Naguals. These writings are known as Repertories or Calendars, and they are also used to discover articles lost or stolen, and to effect cures of diseases. Some have a wheel painted in them, like that of Pythagoras, described by the Venerable Bede; others portray a lake surrounded by the Naguals in the form of various animals. Some of the Nagualist Masters claim as their patron and ruler Cuchulchan, and they possessed a certain formula of prayer to him, written in the Popoluca tongue (which was called Baha in their time of heathenism), and which has been translated into Mexican.†
>
> Those who are selected to become the masters of these arts are taught from early childhood how to draw and paint these characters, and are obliged to learn by

---

* So I understand the phrase, "figuras pintadas con zifras enigmaticas."

† *Popoluca* was a term applied to various languages. I suspect the one here referred to was the Mixe. See an article by me, entitled "Chontales and Popolucas; a Study in Mexican Ethnography," in the *Compte Rendu* of the Eighth Session of the Congress of Americanists, p. 586, *seq*.

> heart the formulas, and the names of the ancient Nagualists, and whatever else is included in these written documents, many of which we have held in our hands, and have heard them explained by such masters whom we had imprisoned for their guilt, and who had afterwards become converted and acknowledged their sins.*

The Bishop made up his mind that extreme measures should be taken to eradicate these survivals of the ancient paganism in his diocese, and he therefore promulgated the following order in the year 1692:

> And because in the provinces of our diocese those Indians who are Nagualists adore their *naguals,* and look upon them as gods, and by their aid believe that they can foretell the future, discover hidden treasures, and fulfill their dishonest desires: we, therefore, prescribe and command that in every town an ecclesiastical prison shall be constructed at the expense of the church, and that it be provided with fetters and stocks (con grillos y cepos), and we confer authority on every priest and curate of a parish to imprison in these gaols whoever is guilty of disrespect toward our Holy Faith, and we enjoin them to treat with especial severity those who teach the doctrines of Nagualism (y con rigor mayor á los dogmatizantes Nagualistas).†

In spite of these injunctions it is evident that he failed to destroy the seeds of what he esteemed this dangerous heresy in the parishes of his diocese; for his ninth Pastoral Letter, in which he exposes at length the character of Nagualism, is dated from the metropolitan city of Ciudad Real, on May 24, 1698. As much of it is germane to my theme, I translate as follows:

> There are certain bad Christians of both sexes who do not hesitate to follow the school of the Devil, and to occupy themselves with evil arts, divinations, sorceries, conjuring,

---

* *Constit. Diocesan*, p. 19.

† *Constit. Diocesan*, Titulo vii, pp. 47, 48.

enchantments, fortune-telling, and other means to forecast the future.

These are those who in all the provinces of New Spain are known by the name of *Nagualists.* They pretend that the birth of men is regulated by the course and movements of stars and planets, and by observing the time of day and the months in which a child is born, they prognosticate its condition and the events, prosperous or otherwise, of its life; and the worst is that these perverse men have written down their signs and rules, and thus deceive the erring and ignorant.

These Nagualists practice their arts by means of Repertories and superstitious Calendars, where are represented under their proper names all the Naguals of stars, elements, birds, fishes, brute beasts and dumb animals; with a vain note of days and months, so that they can announce which corresponds to the day of birth of the infant. This is preceded by some diabolical ceremonies, after which they designate the field or other spot, where, after seven years shall have elapsed, the Nagual will appear to ratify the bargain. As the time approaches, they instruct the child to deny God and His Blessed Mother, and warn him to have no fear, and not to make the sign of the cross. He is told to embrace his Nagual tenderly, which, by some diabolical art, presents itself in an affectionate manner even though it be a ferocious beast, like a lion or a tiger. Thus, with infernal cunning they persuade him that this Nagual is an angel of God, who will look after him and protect him in his after life.

To such diabolical masters the intelligent Indians apply, to learn from these superstitious Calendars, dictated by the Devil, their own fortunes, and the Naguals which will be assigned to their children, even before they are baptized. In most of the Calendars, the seventh sign is the figure of a man and a snake, which they call Cuchulchan. The masters have explained it as a snake with feathers which moves in the water. This sign corresponds with Mexzichuaut, which means Cloudy Serpent, or, of the clouds.* The people also consult them in order to work injury on their enemies, taking the lives of many through such devilish artifices, and committing unspeakable atrocities.

Worse even than these are those who wander about as physicians or healers; who are none such, but magicians, enchanters, and sorcerers, who, while pretending to cure, kill whom they will. They apply their medicines by blowing on the patient, and by the use of infernal words; learned by heart by those who cannot read or write; and received in writing from their masters by those acquainted with letters. The Master never imparts this instruction to a single disciple, but always to three at a time, so that in the practice of the art it may be difficult to decide which one exerts the magical power. They blow on feathers, or sticks, or plants, and place them in the paths where they may be stepped on by those they wish to injure, thus causing chills, fevers, ugly pustules and other diseases; or they introduce into the body by such arts toads, frogs, snakes, centipedes, etc, causing great torments. And by these same breathings and magic words they can burn down houses, destroy the growing crops and induce sickness. No one of the three disciples is permitted to practice any of these arts without previously informing the other two, and also the Master, by whom the three have been taught.

We have learned by the confession of certain guilty parties how the Master begins to instruct his disciple. First he tells him to abjure God, the saints and the Virgin, not to invoke their names, and to have no fear of them. He then conducts him to the wood, glen, cave or field where the pact with the Devil is concluded, which they call "the agreement" or "the word given" (in Tzental *quiz).* In some provinces the disciple is laid on an ant-hill, and the Master standing above him calls forth a snake, colored with black,

* Rather with the Quetzalcoatl of the Nahuas, and the Gucumatz of the Quiches, both of which names mean "Feathered Serpent." Mixcohuatl, the Cloud Serpent, in Mexican mythology, referred to the Thunder-storm.

white and red, which is known as 'the ant-mother' (in Tzental *zmezquiz).** This comes accompanied by the ants and other small snakes of the same kind, which enter at the joints of the fingers, beginning with the left hand, and coming out at the joints of the right hand, and also by the ears and the nose; while the great snake enters the body with a leap and emerges at its posterior vent. Afterwards the disciple meets a dragon vomiting fire, which swallows him entire and ejects him posteriorly. Then the Master declares he may be admitted, and asks him to select the herbs with which he will conjure; the disciple names them, the Master gathers them and delivers them to him, and then teaches him the sacred words.

These words and ceremonies are substantially the same in all the provinces. The healer enters the house of the invalid, asks about the sickness, lays his hand on the suffering part, and then leaves, promising to return on the day following. At the next visit he brings with him some herbs which he chews or mashes with a little water and applies to the part. Then he repeats the *Pater Noster,* the *Ave,* the *Credo* and the *Salve,* and blows upon the seat of disease, afterwards pronouncing the magical words taught him by his master. He continues blowing in this manner, inhaling and exhaling, repeating under his breath these magical expressions, which are powerful to kill or to cure as he chooses, through the compact he has made with the Devil. Finally, so as to deceive the bystanders, he ends with saying in a loud voice: "God the Father, God the Son, and God the Holy Ghost. Amen."

This physician or healer is called in the towns of some of the provinces *poxta vanegs,* and the medicine *gspoxil;* and everything relating to healing among the Indians to which they apply these terms means also to practice sorcery; and all words derivecl from *pox* allude to the Nagual;

---

* In his Tzental Vocabulary, Father Lara does not give this exact form; but in the neighboring dialect of the Cakchiquel Father Ximenes has *quikeho,* to agree together, to enter into an arrangement; the prefix *zme* is the Tzental word for "mother."

for this in some provinces is called *poxlon,* and in others *patzlan,* and in many *tzihuizin,* which is something very much feared by the Indians. We have ascertained by the confessions of many who have been reconciled that the Devil at times appears to them in the shape of a ball or globe of fire in the air, with a tail like a comet.*

According to the most ancient traditions of these Indians this idol, *poxlon,* was one of the most important and venerated they had in the old times, and the Tzentals revered it so much that they preserved it innumerable years painted on a tablet in the above figure. Even after they were converted to the faith, they hung it behind a beam in the church of the town of Oxchuc, accompanied by an image of their god Hicalahau, having a ferocious black face with the members of a man,† along with five owls and vultures. By divine interposition, we discovered these on our second visit there in 1687, and had no little difficulty in getting

---

* Father Lara, in his *Vocabulario Tzendal MS.* (in my possession), gives for medical (médico), *ghpoxil*; for medicine (medicinal cosa), *pox, xpoxtacoghbil*; for physician (médico), *ghpoxta vinic* (the form *vanegh,* person, is also correct). The Tzendal *pox* (pronounced *posh*) is another form of the Quiche-Cakchiquel *puz,* a word which Father Ximenes, in his *Vocabulario Cakchiquel* MS. (in my possession), gives in the compound *puz-naual,* with the meaning, enchanter, wizard. Both these, I take it, are derived from the Maya *puz,* which means to blow the dust, etc., off of something (soplar el polvo de la ropa ó otra cosa. *Dicc. de la Lengua Maya del Convento de Motul,* MS. The dictionary edited by Pio Pérez does not give this meaning). The act of blowing was the essential feature in the treatment of these medicine men. It symbolized the transfer and exercise of spiritual power. When Votan built his underground shrine he did it *á soplos,* by blowing (Nuñez de la Vega, *Constitut. Diocesan,* p. 10). The natives did not regard the comet's tail as behind it but in front of it, blown from its mouth. The Nahuatl word in the text, *tzihuizin,* is the Pipil form of *xihuitzin,* the reverential of *xihuitl,* which means a leaf, a season, a year, or a comet. Apparently it refers to the Nahuatl divinity *Xiuhtécutli,* described by Sahagún, *Historia de Nueva España,* Lib. i, cap. 13, as god of fire, etc.

† *Hicalahau,* for *ical ahau,* Black King, one of the Tzental divinities, who will be referred to on a later page.

> them down, we reciting the creed, and the Indians constantly spitting as they executed our orders. These objects were publicly burned in the plaza.
>
> In other parts they reverence the bones of the earlier Nagualists, preserving them in caves, where they adorn them with flowers and burn copal before them. We have discovered some of these and burned them, hoping to root out and put a stop to such evil ceremonies of the infernal sect of the Nagualists.
>
> At present, all are not so subject to the promptings of the Devil as formerly, but there are still some so closely allied to him that they transform themselves into tigers, lions, bulls, flashes of light and globes of fire. We can say from the declaration and solemn confession of some penitents that it is proved that the Devil had carnal relations with them, both as incubus and succubus, approaching them in the form of their Nagual; and there was one woman who remained in the forest a week with the demon in the form of her Nagual, acting toward him as does an infatuated woman toward her lover (como pudiera con su proprio amigo una muger amancebada). As a punishment for such horrible crimes our Lord has permitted that they lose their life as soon as their Nagual is killed: and that they bear on their own bodies the wound or mark of the blow which killed it; as the curas of Chamula, Copainala and other places have assured us.
>
> The devilish seed of this Nagualism has rooted itself in the very flesh and blood of these Indans. It perseveres in their hearts through the instructions of the masters of the sect, and there is scarcely a town in these provinces in which it has not been introduced. It is a superstitious idolatry, full of monstrous incests, sodomies and detestable bestialities.

Such are the words of the Bishop of Chiapas. We learn from his thoroughly instructed and unimpeachable testimony that at the beginning of the eighteenth century Nagualism was a widespread and active institution among the Indians of southern Mexico; that it was taught and practiced by professors who were so much feared and respected that, as he tells us in another passage, they were called "masters of the towns;"* that they gave systematic instruction to disciples in classes of three, all of whom were bound together by pledges of mutual information and assistance; that a fundamental principle of the organization and an indispensable step in the initiation into its mysteries was the abjuration of the Christian religion, and an undying hatred to its teachers and all others of the race of the white oppressors; and that when they made use of Christian phrases or ceremonies it was either in derision or out of hypocrisy, the better to conceal their real sentiments.

There are a number of other witnesses from the seventeenth century that may be summoned to strengthen this testimony, if it needs it.

14. In the *History of Guatemala*, written about 1690 by Francisco Antonio Fuentes y Guzman, the author gives some information about a sorcerer of this school, who was arrested in Totonicapan, and with whom the historian had something to do as *corregidor*.

The redoubtable magician was a little old man, *viejezuelo*, and when caught had in his possession a document giving the days of the year according to the European calendar, with the Nagual, which belonged to each one. That for January is alone given by our writer, but it is probable that the other months merely repeated the naguals corresponding to the numbers. It ran as follows:

Nagual Calendar for January.

1. Lion.

17. Arrow.

* "Maestros de los pueblos," *Constitut. Diocesan*, i, p. 106.

2. Snake.
3. Stone.
4. Alligator.
5. Ceiba tree.
6. The quetzal (a bird).
7. A stick.
8. Rabbit.
9. A rope.
10. Leaf.
11. Deer.
12. Guacamayo (parrot).
13. Flower.
14. Toad.
15. Caterpillar.
16. A chip.
18. Broom.
19. Jaguar.
20. Corn-husk.
21. A flute.
22. Green-stone.
23. Crow.
24. Fire.
25. A pheasant.
26. A reed.
27. Opossum.
28. Huracán (the thunder-storm).
29. The vulture.
30. Hawk.
31. Bat.

When the sorcerer was examined as to the manner of assigning the proper nagual to a child he gave the following account:

Having been informed of its day of birth, he in due time called at the residence of the parents, and told the mother to bring the child into the field behind the house. Having there invoked the demon, the *nagual* of the child would appear under the form of the animal or object set opposite its birthday in the calendar, a serpent were it born on the 2d of January, a flower were it on the 13th, fire were it on the 24th, and so on. The sorcerer then addressed certain prayers to the *nagual* to protect the little one, and told the mother to take it daily to the same spot, where its *nagual* would appear to it, and would finally accompany it through all its life. Some, but not all, obtained the power of transforming themselves into the *nagual*, and the author declares that, though he could not cite such a case from his own experience, his father knew of several, and reliable priests, *religiosos de fé,* had told him enough examples to fill volumes.*

The tribes to which this author refers were the Cakchiquels and Quiches, who spoke practically the same tongue. An examination of some of the old dictionaries prepared by the early missionaries furnishes further and interesting information about this obscure subject.

In the Cakchiquel language of Guatemala, the word *naual* was applied both to the magician himself, to his necromantic art, and to the demonic agency which taught and protected him. This is shown by the following explanation, which I quote from Father Coto's *Vocabulario de la Lengua Cakchiquel*, 1651, a manuscript in the library of the American Philosophical Society:

> *Magic* or *Necromancy: puz* or *naual;* and they were accustomed to call their magicians or sorcerers by the same terms. It was a kind of magic which they invoked in order to transform themselves into eagles, lions, tigers, etc. Thus, they said, *ru puz, ru naual, pedro loe cot, balam,* "Peter's power, his *naual,* is a lion, a tiger." They also applied the words *puz* and *naual* to certain trees, rocks and other inanimate objects, whence the Devil used to speak to them, and likewise to the idols which they worshiped, as *gazlic che, gazlic abah, Huyu, k'o ru naual.* "The life of the tree, the life of the stone, of the hill, is its *naual,*" etc.; because they believed there was life in these objects. They used to have armies and soldiery to guard their lands, and the captains, as well as many who were not captains, had their *nauales.* They called the captain *ru g' alache; rohobachi, ti ru gaah, ru pocob, ru gh' amay a ghay ti be chi naualil* [he works magic with his shield, his lance, and his arrows].
>
> To practice such magical arts: *tin naualil* ("I practice magic"), an active verb. They use it, for instance, when a man asks his wife for something to eat or drink, and she

* *Historia de Guatemala, o, Recordación Florida*, Tom. ii, p. 44, *seq.*

> has nothing, owing to his negligence, she will say: "Where do you suppose I can get what you want? Do you expect me to perform miracles—*xa pe ri tin naualih*—that they shall come to my hands?" So when one is asked to lend or give something which he has not, he will exclaim: *Tin naualih pe ri puvak*, etc. ("Can I perform miracles," etc.)
>
> It also signifies to pretend something, concealing the truth, as *xa ru naualim ara neh chu g' ux ri tzih tan tu bijh pedro*, "Peter is feigning this which he is saying." They are also accustomed to apply this word to the power which the priests exert (in the sacraments, etc.).

A long and foolish account of the witchcraft supposed to be practiced among the Pokonchis of Guatemala, also a tribe of Mayan stock, is given by the Englishman, Thomas Gage, who was cura of a parish among them about 1630, and afterwards returned to England and Protestantism. He described, at wearisome length, the supposed metamorphosis of two chiefs of neighboring tribes, the one into a lion, the other into a tiger, and the mortal combat in which they engaged, resulting in the death of one to whom Gage administered absolution. No doubt he had been worsted in a personal encounter with his old enemy, and, being a man of eighty years, had not the vigor to recover. The account is of interest only as proving that the same superstitions at that time prevailed among the Pokonchis as in other portions of Guatemala.*

15. A really mighty nagualist was not confined to a single transformation. He could take on many and varied figures. One such is described in the sacred books of the Quiches of Guatemala, that document known by the name of the Popul Vuh, or National Book. The passage is in reference to one of their great kings and powerful magicians, Gucumatz by name. It says:

* Gage, *A New Survey of the West Indies*, p. 388, *seq*. (4th Ed.).

> Truly he was a wonderful king. Every seven days he ascended to the sky, and every seven days he followed the path to the abode of the dead; every seven days he put on the nature of a serpent, and then he became truly a serpent; every seven days he assumed the nature of an eagle, and then he became truly an eagle; then of a tiger and he became truly a tiger; then of coagulated blood, and he was nothing else than coagulated blood.*

It may be said that such passages refer metaphorically to the versatility of his character, but even if this is so, the metaphors are drawn from the universal belief in Nagualism which then prevailed, and they do not express it too strongly.

16. Among the Maya tribes of Yucatan and Guatemala we have testimony to the continuance to this day of these beliefs. Father Bartolomé de Baeza, cura of Yaxcaba in the first half of this century, reports that an old man, in his dying confession, declared that by diabolical art he had transformed himself into an animal, doubtless his *nagual*; and a young girl of some twelve years confessed that she had been transformed into a bird by the witches, and in one of her nocturnal flights had rested on the roof of the very house in which the good priest resided, which was some two leagues from her home. He wisely suggests that, perhaps, listening to some tale of sorcery, she had had a vivid dream, in which she seemed to take this flight. It is obvious, however, from his account, as well as from other sources, that the belief of the transformation into lower animals was and is one familiar to the superstitions of the

* *Le Popol Vuh, ou Livre Sacré des Quichés*, p. 315 (Ed. Brasseur, Paris, 1861). In the Quiche myths, Gucumatz is the analogue of Quetzalcoatl in Aztec legend. Both names mean the same, "Feathered Serpent."

Mayas.* The natives still continue to propitiate the ancient gods of the harvest, at the beginning of the season assembling at a ceremony called by the Spaniards the *misa milpera*, or "field mass," and by themselves *ti'ch*, "the stretching out of the hands."

The German traveler, Dr. Scherzer, when he visited, in 1854, the remote hamlet of Istlavacan, in Guatemala, peopled by Quiché Indians, discovered that they had preserved in this respect the usages of their ancestors almost wholly unaffected by the teachings of their various Christian curates. The "Master" still assigned the *naguals* to the new-born infants, copal was burned to their ancient gods in remote caves, and formulas of invocation were taught by the veteran nagualists to their neophytes.†

These *Zahoris*,‡ as they are generally called in the Spanish of Central America, possessed many other mysterious arts besides that of such metamorphoses and of

* Baeza's article is printed in the *Registro Yucateco*, Vol. i, p. 165, *seq*.

† "Wird ein Kind im Dorfe geboren, so erhält der heidnische Götzenpriester von diesem Ereignisse viel eher Kunde, als der katholische Pfarrer. Erst wenn dem neuen Weltbürger durch den Aj-quig das Horoskop gestellt, der Name irgend eines Thieres beigelegt, Mi-si-sul (das citronengelbe Harz des Rhus copallinum) verbrannt, ein Lieblingsgötze angerufen, und noche viele andere abergläubische Mysterien verrichtet worden sind, wird das Kind nach dem Pfarrhause zur christlichen Taufe getragen. Das Thier, dessen Name dem Kinde kurz nach seiner Geburt vom Sonnenpriester beigelegt wird, gilt gewöhnlich auch als sein Schutzgeist (*nagual*) fürs ganze Leben." Dr. Karl Scherzer, *Die Indianer von Santa Catalina Istlavacan*, p. 11, Wien, 1856.

‡ The word *zahori*, of Arabic origin, is thus explained in the Spanish and English dictionary of Delpino (London, 1763): "So they call in Spain an impostor who pretends to see into the bowels of the earth, through stone walls, or into a man's body." Dr. Stoll says the Guatemala Indians speak of their diviners, the *Ah Kih*, as *zahorin*. *Guatemala*, s. 229.

forecasting the future. They could make themselves invisible, and walk unseen among their enemies; they could in a moment transport themselves to distant places, and, as quickly returning, report what they had witnessed; they could create before the eyes of the spectator a river, a tree, a house, or an animal, where none such existed; they could cut open their own stomach, or lop a limb from another person, and immediately heal the wound or restore the severed member to its place; they could pierce themselves with knives and not bleed, or handle venomous serpents and not be bitten; they could cause mysterious sounds in the air, and fascinate animals and persons by their steady gaze; they could call visible and invisible spirits, and the spirits would come.

Among the native population of the State of Vera Cruz and elsewhere in southern Mexico these mysterious personages go by the name *padrinos*, godfathers, and are looked upon with a mixture of fear and respect. They are believed by the Indians to be able to cause sickness and domestic calamities, and are pronounced by intelligent whites to present "a combination of rascality, duplicity and trickery."*

17. The details of the ceremonies and doctrines of Nagualism have never been fully revealed; but from isolated occurrences and partial confessions it is clear that its adherents formed a coherent association extending over most of southern Mexico and Guatemala, which everywhere was inspired by two ruling sentiments—detestation of the Spaniards and hatred of the Christian religion.

In their eyes the latter was but a cloak for the exac-

---

* Emetorio Piñeda, *Descriptión Géografica de Chiapas y Soconusco*, p. 22 (México, 1815).

tions, massacres and oppressions exerted by the former. To them the sacraments of the Church were the outward signs of their own subjugation and misery. They revolted against these rites in open hatred, or received them with secret repugnance and contempt. In the Mexican figurative manuscripts composed after the conquest the rite of baptism is constantly depicted as the symbol of religious persecution. Says a sympathetic student of this subject:

> The act of baptism is always inserted in their records of battles and massacres. Everywhere it conveys the same idea,—making evident to the reader that the pretext for all the military expeditions of the Spaniards was the enforced conversion to Christianity of the natives; a pretext on which the Spaniards seized in order to possess themselves of the land and its treasure, to rob the Indians of their wives and daughters, to enslave them, and to spill their blood without remorse or remission. One of these documents, dated in 1526, adds a trait of savage irony. A Spanish soldier is represented dragging a fugitive Indian from a lake by a lasso around his neck; while on the shore stands a monk ready to baptize the recreant on his arrival.*

No wonder that the priests of the dark ritual of Nagualism for centuries after the conquest sought to annul the effects of the hated Christian sacraments by counteracting ceremonies of their own, as we are told they did by the historian Torquemada, writing from his own point of view in these words:

> The Father of Lies had his ministers who aided him, magicians and sorcerers, who went about from town to town, persuading the simple people to that which the Enemy of Light desired. Those who believed their deceits, and had been baptized, were washed on the head and breast by these sorcerers, who assured them that this would re-

---

* Madier de Montjau, "Manuscrits Figuratifs de l'Ancien Mexique," in *Archives de la Sociétè Américaine de France.* 1875, p. 245.

> move the effects of the chrism and the holy oils. I myself knew an instance where a person of prominence, who resided not far from the City of Mexico, was dying, and had received extreme unction; and when the priest had departed one of these diabolical ceremonialists entered, and washed all the parts which had been anointed by the holy oil with the intention to destroy its power.*

Similar instances are recorded by Jacinto de la Serna. He adds that not only did the Masters prescribe sacrifices to the Fire in order to annul the effects of extreme unction, but they delighted to caricature the Eucharist, dividing among their congregation a narcotic yellow mushroom for the bread, and the inebriating pulque for the wine. Sometimes they adroitly concealed in the pyx, alongside the holy wafer, some little idol of their own, so that they really followed their own superstitions while seemingly adoring the Host. They assigned a purely pagan sense to the sacred formula, "Father, Son and Holy Ghost," understanding it to be "Fire, Earth and Air," or the like.†

Whoever or whatever was an enemy to that religion so brutally forced upon these miserable creatures was to them an ally and a friend. Nuñez de la Vega tells us that he found written formulas among them reading: "O Brother Antichrist, Brother Antichrist, Brother Antichrist, come to our aid!"—pathetic and desperate appeal of a wretched race, ground to earth under the iron heels of a religious and military despotism.‡

---

* Torquemada, *Monarquía Indiana*, Lib. xv, cap. 16.

† De la Serna, *Manual de Ministros*, pp. 20, 21, 42,162. The mushroom referred to was the *quauhnanacatl*, probably the same as the *teyhuinti* of Hernández, *Hist. Plant. Nov. Hispan.*, Tom. ii, p. 358, who says that it is not dangerous to life, but disturbs the mind, inciting to laughter and intoxication.

‡ Actual slavery of the Indians in Mexico continued as late as the middle of the seventeenth century. See Cavo, *Tres Siglos de México*, etc., Tom. ii, p. 11.

18. The association embraced various tribes and its members were classified under different degrees. The initiation into these was by solemn and often painful ceremonies. Local sodalities or brotherhoods were organized after the manner of those usual in the Roman Church; but instead of being named after St. John or the Virgin Mary they were dedicated to Judas Iscariot or Pontius Pilate out of derision and hatred of the teachings of the priests; or to the Devil or Antichrist, who were looked upon as powerful divinities in opposition to the Church.*

There were certain recognized centres of the association, near which its most important dignitaries resided, and where their secret councils and most imposing ceremonies were held. One of these was Zamayac, in the province of Suchiltepec; a second near Huehuetan, Soconusco; a third at Totonicapan, Guatemala; a fourth at Cancuc, Chiapas; a fifth at Teozapotlan, Oaxaca; and a few others may be surmised.

The high priest who resided at each of these centres exercised control over all the nagualistic teachers and practitioners in an extensive district. On the occasion of an official inquiry by the Spanish authorities it was ascertained that the high priest of Zamayac included under his rule nearly one thousand sub-priests,† and no doubt others of his rank were not less potent.

The unity between the members of the association over an indefinitely wide area was perfectly well known to the Spanish priests and civil authorities. The ceremonies, formulas and methods of procedure were everywhere

---

* Brasseur, *Hist. des Nations Civilisées de Mexique*, Tom. iv, p. 822.

† *Informe del teniente general, Don Jacobo de Barba Figueroa, corregidor de la Provincia de Suchitepeque*, quoted by Brasseur.

identical or alike. This itself was justly regarded as a proof of the secret intelligence which existed among the members of this cabalistic guild.*

To a certain extent, and at least in some localities, as Chiapas and Guatemala, the priesthood of Nagualism was hereditary in particular families. This is especially stated by the historian Ordoñez y Aguiar, who had exceptional opportunities for acquainting himself with the facts.†

A traveler of the first decade of this century, who has left us a number of curious details of the superstitions of the Christianized Indians in Mexico of that day, Benito Maria de Moxó, informs us that he had discovered the existence of different grades in the native soothsayers and medicine men, and that all in a given locality recognized the supremacy of one whom they referred to as "the little old man," *El Viejito*. But he was unable to ascertain by what superior traits or rights he obtained this distinction.‡

According to some authorities, the highest grade of these native hierophants bore among the Nahuas the symbolic name of "flower weavers," *Xochimilca*, probably from the skill they had to deceive the senses by strange

---

* Jacinto de la Serna says: "Los maestros de estas ceremonias son todos unos, y lo que sucede en esta cordillera en todas sucede." *Manual de Ministros*, p. 52. Speaking of the methods of the nagualists of Chiapas, Bishop Nuñez de la Vega writes: "Concuerdan los més modernos con los más antiguos que se practicaban en México." *Constituciones Diocesanas*, p. 134.

† He observes that there were "familias de los tales sabios en las quales en manera de patrimonio se heredaban, succediendo los hijos a los padres, y principalmente su abominable secta de Nagualismo." *Historia del Cielo y de la Tiera*, MS., p. 7. Ordoñez advances various erudite reasons for believing that Nagualism is a religious belief whose theory and rites were brought from Carthage by Punic navigators in ancient times.

‡ Maria de Moxó, *Cartas Mejicanas*, p. 270, (Genova, n. d.).

and pleasant visions.* In the south they were spoken of as "guardians," which may have been derived from the classes of priests so-called in the Zapotec religion.†

19. It will be seen from the above, that Nagualism, beginning in an ancient superstition dating back to the time of primitive barbarism, became after the Conquest a potent factor in the political and social development of the peoples among whom it existed; that it was the source from which was drawn and the means by which was sustained the race-hatred of the native American towards his foreign conquerors, smouldering for centuries, now and then breaking out in furious revolt and civil war.

There is strong reason to suspect its power where, for obvious reasons, it has not been demonstrated. It has always been a mystery and a matter of surprise to the historians of Yucatan how rapidly spread the plans of the insurrection which secured lasting independence for the natives, after these plans had been agreed upon by the two chiefs, Antonio Ay and Cecilio Chi, at the remote rancho of Xihum, in July, 1847. Such unanimity of action could only have been possible through the aid of a powerful, well-disciplined and widespread secret organization. There can scarcely be a doubt they were the chiefs or masters of the redoubtable order of Nagualism in the Peninsula.‡

---

* *Xochimilca*, que asi llamzvan a los mui sabios encantadores." Torquemada, *Monarquia Indiana*, Lib. xv, cap. 16.

† In Nahuatl, *tlapiani*, a guardian or watchman. The Zapotec priesthood was divided into the *huijatoos*, "greater guardians," and their inferiors, the *copavitoos*, "guardians of the gods." Carriedo, *Estudios Históricos*, p. 9.

‡ See Eligio Ancona. *Historia de Yucatán*, Tom. iv, cap. 1 (Mérida, 1880).

There is no question that such was the case with the brief and bloody revolt of the Mayas in 1761. It suddenly broke out in a number of villages near Valladolid, Yucatán, headed by a full-blood native, Jacinto Can-Ek; but some of the participants afterwards confessed that it was the outcome of a conspiracy which had been preparing for a year.

When the appointed day arrived, Jacinto boldly announced himself as the high priest of the fraternity of sorcerers, a master and teacher of magic, and the lineal successor of the famous ancient prophet, Chilan Balam, "whose words cannot fail." In a stirring appeal he urged his fellow-countrymen to attack the Spaniards without fear of consequences.

> "Be not afraid," he exclaimed, "of their cannons and their forts; for among the many to whom I have taught the arts of magic (el arte de brujeria) there are fifteen chosen ones, marvelous experts, who by their mystic power will enter the fortress, slay the sentinels, and throw open the gates to our warriors. I shall take the leaves of the sacred tree, and folding them into trumpets, I shall call to the four winds of heaven, and a multitude of fighting men will hasten to our aid."*

Saying this, he took a sheet of paper, held it up to show that it was blank, folded it for a moment, and then spread

---

* The mention of the fifteen, 5 x 3, chosen disciples indicates that the same system of initiating by triplets prevailed in Yucatan as in Chiapas (see above, p. 19). The sacred tree is not named, but presumably it was the ceiba to which I refer elsewhere. The address of Jacinto was obtained from those present, and is given at length by the Jesuit Martín del Puerto, in his *Relación hecho al Cabildo Eclesiástico por el preposito de la Compañia de Jesus, acerca de la muerte de Jacinto Can-Ek y socios*, Dec. 26, 1761. It is published, with other documents relating to this revolt, in the Appendix to the *Diccionario Universal*, edited by Orozco y Berra, México, 1866. On the prophecies of Chilan Balam, see my *Essays of an Americanist*, pp. 255–273 (Philadelphia, 1890).

it out covered with writing! This deft trick convinced his simple-minded hearers of the truth of his claims and they rushed to arms. He led them, clothed in the robe of the Virgin and with her crown on his head. But neither their enthusiasm nor their leader's art magic availed, and soon Jacinto and his followers fell victims to the stake and the gallows. After their death the dance of "the tiger," or of Chac-Mool—the "ghost dance" of the Mayas—was prohibited; and the use of the sacred drum—the favorite instrument of the native priests—was forbidden.*

In fact, wherever we have any full accounts of the revolts against the Spanish domination during the three centuries of its existence in New Spain, we can manifestly trace the guiding fingers of the powerful though hidden hand of Nagualism. An earlier revolt of the Mayas in Yucatán occurred in 1585. It was led by Andrés Chi, a full-blood Indian, and a descendant of the ancient royal house of the Cocomes. He also announced himself as a priest of the ancient faith, a prophet and a worker of miracles, sent to instruct his own people in a new religion and to give them an independent political existence. Seized by the Spaniards, he was charged with idolatry, sorcery and disturbing the peace, and was ignominiously hanged.†

Not less definitely inspired by the same ideas was the Mixe Indian, known as "Don Pascual," who led the revolt of the Tehuantepec tribes in 1661. He sent out his summons to the "thirteen governors of the Zapotecs and Chontales" to come to his aid, and the insurrection threatened to assume formidable proportions, prevented only

---

* Eligio Ancona, *Hist. de Yucatan*, Tom. ii, p. 152.

† See Pedro Sánchez de Aguilar, *Informe contra Idolum Cultores en Yucatán* (Madrid, 1639); Eligio Ancona, *Historia de Yucatán*, Tom. ii, pp. 128, 129.

by bringing to bear upon the natives the whole power of the Roman Church through the Bishop of Oaxaca, Cuevas Davalos.*

Nearly the same locality had been the scene of the revolt of the Zapotecs in 1550, when they were led by a native priest who claimed to be an incarnation of the old god Quetzalcoatl, the patron deity of the nagualists.†

In the city of Mexico itself, in the year 1692, there was a violent outbreak of the natives, when they destroyed three million dollars worth of property. Doubtless this was partly attributable to the scarcity of food which prevailed; but that the authorities traced it also to some secret ceremonials is evident from the law which was immediately passed forbidding the Indians to wear the *piochtli*, or scalp-lock, a portion of the hair preserved from birth as part of the genethliac rituals,‡ and the especial enactments against the *octli*.

As for the revolt of the Tzentals of Chiapas, in 1712, it was clearly and confessedly under the leadership of the nagualistic priesthood, as I shall indicate on a later page.

---

* The chief authority on this revolt is Juan de Torres Castillo, *Relacion de lo Sucedido en las Provincias de Nexapa, Iztepex y Villa Alta* (México, 1662). See also Cavo, *Los Tres Siglos de México durante el Gobierno Español*, Tom. ii, p. 41, and a pamphlet by Christoval Manso de Contreras, *Relacion cierta y verdadera de lo que sucedio en esta Provincia de Tehuantepec, etc.* (printed at México, 1661), which I know only through the notes of Dr. Berendt. Mr. H. H. Bancroft, in his very meagre account of this event, mistakenly insists that it took place in 1660. *History of Mexico*, Vol. iii, p. 164.

† See Brasseur de Bourbourg, *Histoire des Nations Civilisées de la Mexique*, Tom iv, 824.

‡ Cavo, *Los Tres Siglos*, etc., Tom. ii, p. 82. On the use and significance of the *piochtli* we have some information in Vetancurt, *Teatro Mexicano*, Tom. ii, p. 464, and de la Serna, *Manual de Ministros*, pp. 166, 167. It was the badge of a certain order of the native priesthood.

The history of the native American race under the Spanish power in North America has never yet been written with the slightest approach to thoroughness. He who properly qualifies himself for that task will certainly reach the conclusion expressed a number of years ago by the eminent American antiquary and historian, Mr. E. G. Squier, in these words:

> Among the ruling and priestly classes of the semi-civilized nations of America, there has always existed a mysterious bond, a secret organization, which all the disasters to which they have been subjected have not destroyed. It is to its present existence that we may attribute those simultaneous movements of the aborigines of Mexico and Central America, which have more than once threatened the complete subversion of the Spanish power.*

That mysterious bond, that secret organization, is Nagualism.

20. A remarkable feature in this mysterious society was the exalted position it assigned to Women. Not only were they admitted to the most esoteric degrees, but in repeated instances they occupied the very highest posts in the organization. According to the traditions of the Tzentals and Pipils of Chiapas, when their national hero, Votan, constructed by the breath of his mouth his darkened shrine at Tlazoaloyan, in Soconusco, he deposited in it the sacred books and holy relics, and constituted a college of venerable sages to be its guardians; but placed them all in subjection to a high priestess, whose powers were absolute.†

---

* *Adventures on the Musquito Shore*, by S. A. Ward, pseudonym of Mr. Squier, p. 258 (New York, 1855).

† Nuñez de la Vega, *Constituciones Diocesanas*, p. 10, and comp. Brasseur de Bourbourg, *Hist. des Nat. Civ. de Mexique*, Tom. i, p. 74.

The veracious Pascual de Andagoya asserts from his own knowledge that some of these female adepts had attained the rare and peculiar power of being in two places at once, as much as a league and a half apart;* and the repeated references to them in the Spanish writings of the sixteenth and seventeenth centuries confirm the dread in which they were held and the extensive influence they were known to control. In the sacraments of Nagualism, Woman was the primate and hierophant.

21. This was a lineal inheritance from pre-Columbian times. In many native American legends, as in others from the old world, some powerful enchantress is remembered as the founder of the State, mistress of men through the potency of her magic powers.

Such, among the Aztecs, was the sorceress who built the city of Mallinalco, on the road from Mexico to Michoacán, famous even after the conquest for the skill of its magicians, who claimed descent from her.† Such, in Honduras, was Coamizagual, queen of Cerquin, versed in all occult science, who died not, but at the close of her earthly career rose to heaven in the form of a beautiful bird, amid the roll of thunder and the flash of lightning.‡

According to an author intimately familiar with the Mexican nagualists, the art they claimed to possess of transforming themselves into the lower animals was taught their predecessors by a woman, a native Circe, a mighty enchantress, whose usual name was Quilaztli (the

---

* Herrera, *Hist. de las Indias Occidentales*, Dec. ii, Lib. iii, cap. 5.

† Acosta, *Hist. Nat. y Moral de las Indias*, Lib. vii, cap. 5.

‡ The story is given in Herrera, *Hist. de las Indias*, Dec. iv, Lib. viii, cap. 4. The name Coamizagual is translated in the account as "Flying Tigress." I cannot assign it this sense in any dialect.

etymology of which is unknown), but who bore also four others, representing her four metamorphoses, Cohuacihuatl, the Serpent Woman; Quauhcihuatl, the Eagle Woman; Yaocihuatl, the Warrior Woman; and Tzitzimecihuatl, the Specter Woman.*

The powers of these queens of magic extended widely among their sex. We read in the chronicles of ancient Mexico that when Nezahualpilli, the king, oppressed the tribes of the coast, the *tierra caliente,* they sent against him, not their warriors, but their witches. These cast upon him their fatal spells, so that when he walked forth from his palace, blood burst from his mouth, and he fell prone and dead.†

In Guatemala, as in ancient Delphos, the gods were believed to speak through the mouths of these inspired seeresses, and at the celebration of victories they enjoyed a privilege so strange and horrible that I quote it from the old manuscript before me without venturing a translation:

> ...Despues de sacrificar los antiguos algun hombre, despedacandolo, si era de los que avian cogido en guerra, dicen que guardaban el miembro genital y los testiculos del tal sacrificado, y se los daban a una vieja que tenian por profeta, para que los comiese, y le pedian rogasse a su idolo les diesse mas captivos.‡

---

* Jacinto de la Serna, *Manual de Ministros*, p. 138. Sahagún identifies Quilaztli with Tonantzin, the common mother of mankind and goddess of childbirth (*Hist. de Nueva España*, Lib. i, cap. 6, Lib. vi, cap. 27). Further particulars of her are related by Torquemada, *Monarquia Indiana*, Lib. ii, cap 2. The *tzitzime* were mysterious elemental powers, who, the Nahuas believed, were destined finally to destroy the present world (Sahagún,1. c., Lib. vi, cap. 8). The word means "flying haired" (Serna).

† Torquemada, *Monarquia Indiana*, Lib. ii, cap. 62.

‡ Fr. Tomas Coto, *Diccionario de la Lengua Cakchiquel*; MS., s.

When Captain Pedro de Alvarado, in the year 1524, was marching upon Quetzaltanango, in Guatemala, just such a fearful old witch took her stand at the summit of the pass, with her familiar in the shape of a dog, and "by spells and nagualistic incantations" undertook to prevent his approach.*

As in the earliest, so in the latest accounts. The last revolt of the Indians of Chiapas occurred among the Zotzils in 1869. The cause of it was the seizure and imprisonment by the Spanish authorities of a "mystical woman," known to the whites as Santa Rosa, who, together with one of their *ahaus* or chieftains, had been suspected of fomenting sedition. The natives marched thousands strong against the city of San Cristobal, where the prisoners were, and secured their liberation; but their leader, Ignacio Galindo, was entrapped and shot by the Spaniards, and the mutiny was soon quelled.†

22. But perhaps the most striking instance is that recorded in the history of the insurrection of the Tzentals of Chiapas, in 1713. They were led by an Indian girl, a native Joan of Arc, fired by like enthusiasm to drive from her country the hated foreign oppressors, and to destroy

---

v. *Sacrificar*: in the Library of the American Philosophical Society at Philadelphia.

* "Trataron de valerse del arte de los encantos y *naguales*" are the words of the author, Fuentes y Guzmán, in his *Recordación, Florida*, Tom. i, p. 60. In the account of Bernal Diaz, it reads as if this witch and her dog had both been sacrificed; but Fuentes is clear in his statement, and had other documents at hand.

† Teobert Maler, "Mémoire sur l'État de Chiapas," in the *Revue d' Ethnographie*, Tom. iii, pp. 309-311. This writer also gives some valuable facts about the Indian insurrection in the Sierra de Alicia, in 1873.

every vestige of their presence. She was scarcely twenty years old, and was known to the Spaniards as Maria Candelaria. She was the leader of what most historians call a religious sect, but what Ordoñez y Aguiar, himself a native of Chiapas, recognizes as the powerful secret association of Nagualism, determined on the extirpation of the white race. He estimates that in Chiapas alone there were nearly seventy thousand natives under her orders—doubtless an exaggeration—and asserts that the conspiracy extended far into the neighboring tribes, who had been ordered to await the result of the effort in Chiapas.

Her authority was absolute, and she was merciless in requiring obedience to it. The disobedient were flayed alive or roasted over a slow fire. She and all her followers took particular pleasure in manifesting their hatred and contempt for the religion of their oppressors. They defiled the sacred vessels of the churches, imitated with buffoonery the ceremonies of the mass, which she herself performed, and stoned to death the priests whom they caught.

Of course, her attempt against the power of Spain was hopeless. It failed after a bitter and protracted conquest, characterized by the utmost inhumanity on both sides. But when her followers were scattered and killed, when the victorious whites had again in their hands all the power and resources of the country, not their most diligent search, nor the temptation of any reward, enabled them to capture Maria Candelaria, the heroine of the bloody drama. With a few trusty followers she escaped to the forest, and was never again heard of.*

* The long account given by Mr. H. H. Bancroft of this insurrection is a travesty of the situation drawn from bitterly prejudiced Spanish sources, of course, utterly out of sympathy with the motives which prompted the native actors. See his *History of the Pacific States*, Vol. ii,

More unfortunate were her friends and lieutenants, the priestesses of Guistiupan and Yajalon, who had valiantly seconded Maria in her patriotic endeavors. Seized by the Spaniards, they met the fate which we can easily imagine, though the historian has mercifully thrown a veil on its details.*

23. Of just such a youthful prophetess did Mr. B. G. Squier hear during his travels in Central America, a "*sukia* woman," as she was called by the coast Indians, one who lived alone mid the ruins of an old Maya temple, a sorceress of twenty years, loved and feared, holding death and life in her hands.† Perhaps his account is somewhat fanciful; it is so, indeed; but it is grounded on the unshaken beliefs and ancient traditions of the natives of those climes, and on customs well known to those who reside there.

The late distinguished Americanist, the Abbé Brasseur de Bourbourg, during his long travels in Mexico and Central America, had occasion more than once to come in contact with this trait of the ancient faith of the Na-

---

p. 696, *seq*. Ordoñez y Aguiar, who lived on the spot within a generation of the occurrences, recognizes in Maria Candelaria (whose true name Bancroft does not give) the real head of the rebellion, "quien ordenaba los ardides del motin; ...de lo que principalmente trataban las leyes fundamentales de su secta, era de que no quedase rastro alguno de que los Europeos havian pisado este suelo." His account is in his unpublished work, *Historia del Cielo y de la Tierra*, written at Guatemala about 1780. Juarros, speaking of their rites, says of them: "Apostando de la fé, profanando los vasos sagrados, y ofreciendo sacrilegos cultos a una indizuela." *Historia de la Ciudad de Guatemala*, Tom. i, p. 17.

* Bancroft, ubi supra, p. 705, note. One was hanged, whom Garcia Pelaez calls "una india bruja." *Memorias para la Historia de Guatemala*, Tom. ii, p. 153.

† Squier, ubi supra, passim.

gualists, still alive in their descendants. Among the Zapotecs of the Isthmus of Tehuantepec he saw one of the queens of the mystic fraternity, and he describes her with a warmth which proves that he had not lost his eye for the beautiful.

> She wore a piece of light-green stuff loosely folded around her form at the hips, and falling to a little distance above the ankle; a jacket of red silk gauze with short sleeves and embroidered with gold, clothed the upper part of her person, veiling her bosom, upon which lay a chain of heavy gold pieces, pierced and strung on a cord. Her rich black hair was divided on the forehead, and drawn back in two splendid tresses fastened with blue ribbons, while a white muslin kerchief encircled her head like the calantica of the ancient Egyptians. Never in my life have I seen a more striking figure of an Isis or a Cleopatra.
>
> There was something strange in her expression. Her eyes were the blackest and the brightest in the world; but there were moments when she suddenly paused, leaned against the billiard table or the wall, and they became fixed and dead like those of a corpse. Then a fiery glance would shoot from beneath her dark lashes, sending a chill to the heart of the one to whom it was directed. Was it madness, or was it, as those around her believed, a momentary absence of soul, an absorption of her spirit into its *nagual,* a transportation into an unknown world? Who shall decide?*

24. It would be a mistake to suppose that Nagualism was an incoherent medley of superstitions, a mass of jumbled fragments derived from the ancient paganism. My study of it has led me to a widely different conclusion. It was a perpetuation of a well-defined portion of the native cult, whose sources we are able to trace long anterior to the

---

* *Voyage á l'Isthmus de Tehuantepec,* p. 164. He adds a number of particulars of the power she was supposed to exercise.

period of the conquest, and which had no connection with the elaborate and bloody ritual of the Aztecs. The evidence to this effect is cogent.

Wherever in later days the Catholic priests found out the holy places and sacred objects of the nagualists, they were in caves or deep rock-recesses, not in artificial structures. The myths they gleaned, and the names of the gods they heard, also point to this as a distinguishing peculiarity. An early instance is recorded among the Nahuas of Mexico. In 1537 Father Perea discovered a cavern in a deep ravine at Chalma, near Mallinalco (a town famous for its magicians), which was the sanctuary of the deity called *Oztoteotl*, the Cave God (*oztotl*, cave; *teotl*, god), "venerated throughout the whole empire of Montezuma."* He destroyed the image of the god, and converted the cavern into a chapel.

We cannot err in regarding Oztoteotl as merely another name of the Nahuatl divinity, Tepeyollotl, the Heart, or Inside, of the Mountain, who in the Codex Borgia and the Codex Vaticanus is represented seated upon or in a cavern. His name may equally well be translated "the Heart of the Place," or "of the Town."

Dr. Eduard Seler has shown beyond reasonable question that this divinity did not originally belong to the Aztec Pantheon, but was introduced from the South, either from the Zapotecs, the Mixtecs, or the Mayan tribes, beyond these.† The Cave God of the Aztecs is identical with

* "Que era venerado en todo el imperio de Montezuma." See *Diccionario Universal*, Appendice, s. v. (México, 1856).

† "Dass der Gott Tepeyollotl im Zapotekenlande und weiter südwärts seine Wurzeln hat, und dem eigentlichen Aztekischen Olymp fremd ist, darüber kann kein Zweifel mehr obwalten." See Dr. Seler's able discussion of the subject in the *Compte-Rendu* of the Seventh International Congress of Americanists, p. 559, *seq*. The adoption of

the Votan of the Tzentals of Chiapas, and with the U-q'ux Uleuh of the Quiches of Guatemala, and probably with the Cozaana of the Zapotecs.

The rites of all of these were conducted in caverns, and there have been preserved several interesting descriptions of the contents of these sacred places. That relating to the "dark house of Votan" is given thus in the work of the Bishop of Chiapas:

> Votan is the third hero who is named in the calendar, and some of his descendants still reside in the town of Teopisca, where they are known as Votans. He is sometimes referred to as Lord of the Sacred Drum, and he is said to have seen the great wall (which must have been the Tower of Babel), and to have divided this land among the Indians, and given to each tribe its language.
>
> They say further that he once dwelt in Huehuetan, a town in the province of Soconusco. Near there, at the place called Tlazoaloyan, he constructed, by blowing with his breath, a dark house, and put tapirs in the river, and in the house a great treasure, and left all in charge of a noble lady, assisted by guardians *(tlapiane)* to preserve. This treasure consisted of earthenware vases with covers of the same material; a stone, on which were inscribed the figures of the ancient native heroes as found in the calendar; *chalchiuites,* which are green stones and other superstitious objects.
>
> All of these were taken from the cave, and publicly burned in the plaza of Huehuetan on the occasion of our first diocesan visit there in 1691, having been delivered to us by the lady in charge and the guardians. All the Indians have great respect for this Votan, and in some places they call him "the Heart of the Towns."*

---

subterranean temples was peculiarly a Zapotecan trait. "Notandose principalmente en muchos adoratorios de los Zapotecos, estan los mas de ellos cubiertos, o en subterraneos espaciosos y lóbregos." Carriedo, *Estudios Historicos*, Tom. i, p. 26.

* *Constituciones Diocesanas*, pp. 9, 10.

The English priest, Thomas Gage, who was curate of a parish among the Pokonchi Indians of Guatemala about 1630, relates his discovery of such a cave, in which the idol was preserved, and gives this description of it:

> We found the Idol standing upon a low stool covered with a linen cloth. The substance of it was wood, black shining like jet, as if it had been painted or smoked; the form was of a man's head unto the shoulders, without either Beard or mustachoes; his look was grim, with a wrinkled forehead, and broad staring eyes.
>
> They boasted of this their god, saying that he had plainly told them they should not believe anything I preached of Christ, but follow the old ways of their forefathers.*

The black color here mentioned was a relic of ancient symbolism, referring to the night, darkness: and the obscurity of the holy cavern. Vetancurt informs us that the priests of the ancient paganism were accustomed to rub their faces and bodies with an ointment of fat and pine soot when they went to sacrifice in the forests, so that they looked as black as negroes.† In the extract from Nuñez de la Vega already given, *Ical Ahau,* the "Black King," is named as one of the divinities of the nagualists.

In some parts the principal idol found in the caves was the mummied or exsiccated body of some former distinguished priest or chieftain. One such is recorded by Bartholomé de Pisa, which was found among the Zapotecs of Coatlan. It bore a name taken from the calendar, that of the tenth day, and was alleged to be the preserved ca-

---

* Gage, *A New Survey of the West Indies*, pp. 389, 393.

† *Teatro Mexicano*, Tratado iii, cap. 11. Mr. Baudelier has called attention to the naming of one of the principal chiefs among the Aztecs, *Tlilancalqui*, "Man of the Dark House," and thinks it related to the Votan myth. *Twelfth Annual Report of the Peabody Museum*, p. 888.

daver of a celebrated ruler.* Another interesting example is narrated by Villa Señor y Sánchez,† who describes it as an eyewitness. It was discovered in a spacious cave located some distance to the west of the city of Mexico, in Nahuatl territory, on the side of what was known as "the Sun mountain—*la Mesa de Tonati.*" He speaks of it as remarkably well preserved, "both the muscles and the bones."

> It was seated in an armchair which served for a throne, and was clothed in a mantle, which fell from the shoulders to the feet. This was richly adorned with precious stones, which, according to the native custom, were sewed into the texture of the cloth. The figure also wore shoulder straps, collars, bracelets and fastenings of silver. From its forehead rose a crown of beautiful feathers of different colors arranged so that one color should alternate with another. The left hand was resting on the arm of the chair, while in the right was a sharp cutlass with silver mountings. At its feet were several vases of fine stone, as marble and alabaster, in which were offerings of blood and meat, obtained from the sacrifices.

The same writer refers to other examples of these sacred caves which he had seen in his journeys. One was near the town of Teremendo, where the sides and roof had been artificially dressed into the shape of huge arches. A natural altar had been provided in a similar manner, and on it, at the time of his visit, were numerous idols in the figures of men and animals, and before them fresh offerings of copal and food. Elsewhere he refers to many such caverns still in use as places resorted to by the natives in *la*

---

* Herrera, *Historia de las Indias Occidentales,* Dec. iii, Lib. iii, cap. 14.

† Villa Señor, *Teatro Americano,* Lib. v, cap. 38 (México, 1747). Father Cavo adds that there were signs of human sacrifices present, but of this I can find no evidence in the earlier reports. Comp. Cavo, *Los Tres Siglos de México durante el Gobierno Españal,* Tom. ii, p. 128.

gran Sierra de Tlascala.[*]

These extracts prove the extent of this peculiar worship and the number of these subterranean temples in recent generations. The fame of some of the greater ones of the past still survives, as the vast grotto of Chalcatongo, near Achiutla, which was the sepulchral vault of its ancient kings; that of Totomachiapa, a solemn scene of sacrifice for the ancient priests; that of Justlahuaca, near Sola (Oaxaca), which was a place of worship of the Zapotecs long after the Conquest; and that in the Cerro de Monopostiac, near San Francisco del Mar.[†]

The intimate meaning of this cave-cult was the worship of the Earth. The Cave God, the Heart of the Hills, really typified the Earth, the Soil, from whose dark recesses flow the limpid streams and spring the tender shoots of the food-plants, as well as the great trees. To the native Mexican, the Earth was the provider of food and drink, the common Father of All; so that to this day, when he would take a solemn oath, he stoops to the earth, touches it with his hand, and repeats the solemn formula: *Cuix amo nechitla in toteotzin?* "Does not our Great God see me?"

25. The identity of the Tepeyollotl of the Nahuas and the Votan of the Tzentals is shown not only in the oneness of meaning of the names, but in the fact that both represent the *third* day in the ritual calendar. For this reason I take it, we find the number *three* so generally a sacred number in the symbolism of the nagualists. We have already learned

---

* *Teatro Americano*, Lib. ii, cap. 11; Lib. iii, cap. 13.

† See Mühlenpfordt, *Mexico*, Bd. ii, pp. 200–66; Brasseur, *Hist. des Nations Civ. de la Mexique*, Vol. iv, p. 821; Herrera, *Historia de las Indias*, Dec. iii, Lib. iii, cap. 12, etc.

in the extract from Nuñez de la Vega that the neophytes were instructed in classes of three. To this day in Soteapan the fasts and festivals appointed by the native ministrants are three days in duration.* The semi-Christianized inhabitants of the Sierra of Nayerit, the Nahuatl-speaking Chotas, continued in the last century to venerate three divinities, the Dawn, the Stone and the Serpent;† analogous to a similar "trinity" noted by Father Duran among the ancient Aztecs.‡

The number *nine*, that is, 3 x 3, recurs so frequently in the conjuration formulas of the Mexican sorcerers that de la Serna exclaims: "It was the Devil himself who inculcated into them this superstition about the number nine."§

The other number sacred to the nagualists was *seven.* I have, in a former essay, given various reasons for believing that this was not derived from the seven days of the Christian week, but directly from the native calendar.¶ Nuñez de la Vega tells us that the patron of the seventh day was *Cuculcan*, "the Feathered Serpent," and that many nagualists chose him as their special protector. As already seen, in Guatemala the child finally accepted its *naual* when seven years old; and among some of the Nahuatl tribes of Mexico the *tonal* and the calendar name was formally assigned

* *Diccionario Universal*, Appendice, s. v.

† Their names were Ta Yoapa, Father Dawn; Ta Te, Father Stone; Coanamoa, the Serpent which Seizes. *Dicc. Univ.*, App., Tom. iii, p. 11.

‡ Duran, *Historia de los Indios*, Tom. ii, p. 140. They were Tota, Our Father; Yollometli, the Heart of the *Maguey* (probably pulque); and Topiltzin, Our Noble One (probably Quetzalcoatl, to whom this epithet was often applied).

§ "Fue el Demonio que les dió la superstición del numero nueve." *Manual de Ministros*, p. 197.

¶ *The Native Calendar of Central America and Mexico*, p. 12.

on the seventh day after birth.* From similar impressions the Cakchiquels of Guatemala maintained that when the lightning strikes the earth the "thunder stone" sinks into the soil, but rises to the surface after seven years.†

The three and the seven were the ruling numbers in the genealogical trees of the Pipiles of San Salvador. The "tree" was painted with *seven* branches representing degrees of relationship within which marriage was forbidden unless a man had performed some distinguished exploit in war, when he could marry beyond the nearest *three* degrees of relationship.‡ Another combination of 3 and 7, by multiplication, explains the customs among the Mixes of deserting for 21 days a house in which a death has occurred.§

The indications are that the nagualists derived these numbers from the third and seventh days of the calendar "month" of twenty days. Tepeololtec, the Cave God, was patron of the third day and also "Lord of Animals," the transformation into which was the test of nagualistic power.¶ Tlaloc, god of the mountains and the rains, to whom the seventh day was hallowed, was represented by the nagualistic symbol of a snake doubled and twisted on itself, and was generally portrayed in connection with the "Feathered Serpent" (Quetzalcoatl, Cuculchan, Guku-

---

* Motolinia, *Ritos Antiguos, Sacrificios e Idolatrias de los Indios de la Nueva España*, p. 340 (in *Colección de Documentos ineditos para la Historia de España*).

† Thomas Coto, *Vocabulario de la lengua Cakchiquel*, MS., sub voce, *Rayo*.

‡ Herrera, *Historia de las Indias*, Dec. iv, Lib. viii, cap. 10.

§ *Diccionario Universal*, Appendice, ubi supra.

¶ "Señor de los Animales." *Codex Telleriano-Remensis*, Parte ii, Lam. iv.

matz, all names meaning this), represented as carrying his medicine bag, *xiquipilli*, and incensory, the apparatus of the native illuminati, his robe marked with the sign of the cross to show that he was Lord of the Four Winds and of Life.*

26. The nagualistic rites were highly symbolic, and the symbols used had clearly defined meanings, which enable us to analyze the religious ideas underlying this mysterious cult.

The most important symbol was Fire. It was regarded as the primal element and the immediate source of life. Father Nicolas de León has the following suggestive passage in this connection:

> If any of their old superstitions has remained more deeply rooted than another in the hearts of these Indians, both men and women, it is this about fire and its worship, and about making new fire and preserving it for a year in secret places. We should be on the watch for this, and when in their confessions they speak of what the Fire said and how the Fire wept, expressions which we are apt to pass by as unintelligible, we must lay our hands on them for reprehension. We should also be on the watch for their baptism by Fire, a ceremony called the *yiahuiltoca*,† shortly after the

---

* See Dr. Seler's minute description in the *Compte Rendu* of the Eighth Section of the Congrés International des Américanistes, pp. 688, 589. In one of the conjuration formulas given by de la Serna (*Manual de Ministros*, p. 212) the priest says: "Yo soy el sacerdote, el dios *Quetzalcoatl*, que se bajará al infierno, y subiré a lo superior, y hasta los nueve infiernos." This writer, who was very competent in the Nahuatl, translates the name Quetzalcoatl by "culebra con cresta" (*id.*, p. 171), an unusual, but perhaps a correct rendering.

† His words here are somewhat obscure. They are, "El baptismo de fuego, en donde las ponen los sobre nombres que llaman *yahuiltoca*, quando nacen." This may be translated, "The baptism of fire in which they confer the names which they call *yahuiltoca*." The ob-

> birth of a child when they bestow on it the surnames; nor must the lying-in women and their assistants be permitted to speak of Fire as the father and mother of all things and the author of nature; because it is a common saying with them that Fire is present at the birth and death of every creature.

This curious ceremony derived its name from the *yiahuitli,* a plant not unlike the absinthe, the powdered leaves of which, according to Father Sahagún, the natives were accustomed to throw into the flames as an offering to the fire.* Long after the conquest, and probably to this day, the same custom prevails in Mexico, the fumes and odor of the burning leaves being considered very salubrious and purifying to the air of the sick room.†

The word *yiahuiltoca* means "the throwing of the *yiauhtli*" (from *toca*, to throw upon with the hands). Another name for the ceremony, according to Father Vetancurt, who wrote a century later than León, was *apehualco*, which has substantially the same meaning, "a throwing upon" or

---

scurity is in the Nahuatl, as the word *toca* may be a plural of *tocaitl*, name, as well as the verb *toca*, to throw upon. The passage is from the *Camino del Cielo*, fol. 100, verso.

* Sahagún, *Historia de la Nueva España*, Lib. iv, cap. 25.

† It is mentioned as useful for this purpose by the early physicians, Francisco Ximenes, *Cuatro Libros de la Naturaleza*, p. 144; Hernández, *Hist. Plant. Novæ Hispaniæ*, Tom. ii, p. 200. Capt. Bourke, in his recent article on "The Medicine Men of the Apaches" (in *Ninth Annual Report of the Bureau of Ethnology*, p. 521), suggests that the *yiahuitli* of the Aztecs is the same as the "hoddentin," the pollen of a variety of cat-tail rush which the Apaches in a similar manner throw into the fire as an offering. Hernández, however, describes the *yiahuitli* as a plant with red flowers, growing on mountains and hillsides—no species of rush, therefore. De la Serna says it is the anise plant, and that with it the natives perform the conjuration of the "yellow spirit" (conjuro de amarillo espiritado), that is, of the Fire (*Manual de Ministros*, p. 1957).

"a throwing away."* He adds the interesting particulars that it was celebrated on the fourth day after the birth of the child, during which time it was deemed essential to keep the fire burning in the house, but not to permit any of it to be carried out, as that would bring bad luck to the child.

Jacinto de la Serna also describes this ceremony, to which he gives the name *tlecuixtliliztli*, "which means that they pass the infant over the fire"; and elsewhere he adds: "the worship of fire is the greatest stumbling-block to these wretched idolaters."†

27. Other ceremonies connected with fire worship took place in connection with the manufacture of the pulque, or *octli*, the fermented liquor obtained from the sap of the maguey plant. The writer just quoted, de Vetancurt, states that the natives in his day, when they had brewed the new pulque and it was ready to be drunk, first built a fire, walked in procession around it and threw some of the new liquor into the flames, chanting the while an invocation to the god of inebriation, Tezcatzoncatl, to descend and be present with them.

This was distinctly a survival of an ancient doctrine which connected the God of Fire with the Gods of Drunkenness, as we may gather from the following quotation from the history composed by Father Diego Duran:

> The *octli* was a favorite offering to the gods, and especially to the God of Fire. Sometimes it was placed before

* From the *verb apeua*. Vetancurt's description is in his *Teatro Mexicano*, Tom. i, pp. 462, 463 (Ed. México, 1870).

† His frequent references to it show this. See his *Manual de Ministros*, pp. 16, 20, 22, 24, 36, 40, 66, 174, 217, etc. The word *tlecuixtliliztli* is compounded of *tlecuilli*, the hearth or fireplace, and *ixtliluia*, to darken with smoke.

> a fire in vases, sometimes it was scattered upon the flames with a brush, at other times it was poured out around the fireplace.*

28. The high importance of the fire ceremonies in the secret rituals of the modern Mayas is plainly evident from the native Calendars, although their signification has eluded the researches of students, even of the laborious Pio Perez, who was so intimately acquainted with their language and customs. In these Calendars the fire-priest is constantly referred to as *ah-toc,* literally the fire-master. The rites he celebrates recur at regular intervals of twenty days (the length of one native month) apart. They are four in number. On the first he takes the fire; on the second he kindles the fire; on the third he gives it free play, and on the fourth he extinguishes it. A period of five days is then allowed to elapse, when these ceremonies are recommenced in the same order. Whatever their meaning, they are so important that in the *Buk Xoc,* or General Computation of the Calendar, preserved in the mystic "Books of Chilan Balam," there are special directions for these fire-masters to reckon the proper periods for the exercise of their strange functions.†

---

* Duran, *Historia de los Indios de la Nueva España,* Tom. ii, p. 210. Sahagún adds that the *octli* was poured on the hearth at four separate points, doubtless the four cardinal points. *Historia de Nueva España,* Lib. i, cap. 13. De la Serna describes the same ceremony as current in his day, *Manual de Ministros,* p. 35. The invocation ran:—"Shining Rose, light-giving Rose, receive and rejoice my heart before the God."

† A copy of these strange "Books of Chilan Balam" is in my possession. I have described them in my *Essays of an Americanist* (Philadelphia, 1890).

29. What, now, was the sentiment which underlay this worship of fire? I think that the facts quoted, and especially the words of Father de León, leave no doubt about it. Fire was worshiped as the life-giver, the active generator, of animate existence. This idea was by no means peculiar to them. It repeatedly recurs in Sanskrit, in Greek and in Teutonic mythology, as has been ably pointed out by Dr. Hermann Cohen.* The fire-god Agni *(ignis)* is in the Vedas the Maker of men; Prometheus steals the fire from heaven that he may with it animate the human forms he has moulded of clay; even the connection of the pulque with the fire is paralleled in Greek mythos, where Dionysos is called *Pyrigenes*, the "fire-born."

Among the ancient Aztecs the god of fire was called the oldest of gods, *Huehueteotl*, and also "Our Father," *Tota*, as it was believed from him all things were derived.† Both among them and the Mayas, as I have pointed out in a previous work, he was supposed to govern the generative proclivities and the sexual relations.‡ Another of his names was *Xiuhtecutli*, which can be translated "God of the Green Leaf," that is, of vegetable fecundity and productiveness.§

To transform themselves into a globe or ball of fire was, as we have seen (ante, p. 21), a power claimed by expert nagualists, and to handle it with impunity, or to blow it from the mouth, was one of their commonest exhibi-

---

* See his remarks on "Apperception der Menschenzeugung als Feuerbereitung," in the *Zeitschrift fur Völkerpsychologie*, Bd. vi, s. 113, *seq.*

† Sahagún, *Historia de Nueva España*, Lib. i, cap. 13. The Nahuatl text is more definite than the Spanish translation.

‡ See my *Myths of the New World*, p. 154, seq.

§ In the Nahuatl language the word *xihuitl* (*xiuitl*) has four meanings: a plant, a turquoise, a year, and a comet.

tions. Nothing so much proved their superiority as thus to master this potent element.

30. The same name above referred to "the Heart of the Town," or "of the Hills," was that which at a comparatively late date was applied to an idol of green stone preserved with religious care in a cavern in the Cerro de Monopostiac, not far from San Francisco del Mar. The spot is still believed by the natives to be enchanted ground and protected by superhuman powers.*

These green stones, called *chalchiuitl*, of jadeite, nephrite, green quartz, or the like, were accounted of peculiar religious significance throughout southern Mexico, and probably to this day many are preserved among the indigenous population as amulets and charms. They were often carved into images, either in human form or representing a frog, the latter apparently the symbol of the waters and of fertility. Bartholomé de Alva refers to them in a passage of his Confessionary. The priest asks the penitent:

> Dost thou possess at this very time little idols of green stone, or frogs made of it (*in chalchiuh coconeme, chalchiuh tamazoltin*)?
>
> Dost thou put them out in the sun to be warmed? Didst thou keep them wrapped in cotton coverings, with great respect and veneration?
>
> Dost thou believe, and hold for very truth, that these green stones give thee food and drink, even as thy ancestors believed, who died in their idolatry? Dost thou believe that they give thee success and prosperity and good things, and all that thou hast or wishest? Because we know very well that many of you so believe at this very time.†

* J. B. Carriello, *Estudios Históricos del Estado Oaxaqueño*, Tom. i, p. 82, etc.

† Alva, *Confessionario en Lengua Mexicana*, fol. 9.

Down to quite a recent date, and perhaps still, these green stones are employed in certain ceremonies in vogue among the Indians of Oaxaca in order to ensure a plenteous maize harvest. The largest ear of corn in the field is selected and wrapped up in a cloth with some of these chalchiuite. At the next corn-planting it is taken to the field and buried in the soil. This is believed to be a relic of the worship of the ancient Zapotec divinity, Quiegolani, who presided over cultivated fields.*

They are still in use among the natives as lucky stones or amulets. In the Zotzil insurrection of 1869, already referred to, one was found suspended to the neck of one of the slain Indians. It came into the possession of M. Maler, who has described and figured it.† It represents a human head with a curious expression and a singular headdress.

From specimens of these amulets preserved in museums it is seen that any greenish stone was selected, preferably those yielding a high, vitreous polish, as jadeite, turquoise, emerald, chlormelanite or precious serpentine. The color gave the sacred character, and this, it seems to me, was distinctly meant to be symbolic of water and its effects, the green of growing plants, and hence of fertility, abundance and prosperity.

31. There is another symbol, still venerated among the present indigenous population, which belongs to Nagualism, and is a survival from the ancient cult; this is the Tree. The species held in especial respect is the ceiba, the silk-

---

* Carriedo, *Estudios Historicos*, pp. 6, 7.

† In the *Revue d' Ethnographie*, Tom. iii, p. 313. Some very fine objects of this class are described by E. G. Squier, in his "Observations on the Chalchihuitl," in the *Annals of the Lyceum of Natural History*, Vol. i (New York, 1869).

cotton tree, the *ytzamatl* (knife-leaved paper tree) of the Nahuas, the *yax che* (green, or first tree) of the Mayas, the *Bombax ceiba* of the botanists. It is of great size and rapid growth. In Southern Mexico and Central America one is to be seen near many of the native villages, and is regarded as in some way the protecting genius of the town.

Sacred trees were familiar to the old Mexican cult, and, what is curious, the same name was applied to such as to the fire, *Tota*, Our Father. They are said to have represented the gods of woods and waters.* In the ancient mythology we often hear of the "tree of life," represented to have four branches, each sacred to one of the four cardinal points and the divinities associated therewith.

The conventionalized form of this tree in the Mexican figurative paintings strongly resembles a cross. Examples of it are numerous and unmistakable, as, for instance, the cruciform tree of life rising from a head with a protruding tongue, in the Vienna Codex.†

32. Thus, the sign of the cross, either the form with equal arms known as the cross of St. Andrew, which is the oldest Christian form, or the Latin cross, with its arms of unequal length, came to be the ideogram for "life" in the Mexican hieroglyphic writing; and as such, with more or less variants, was employed to signify the *tonalli* or *nagual*, the sign of nativity, the natal day, the personal spirit.‡

---

* Diego Duran, *Historia de los Indios de Nueva España*, Tom. ii, p 140.

† In Kingsborough, *Antiquities of Mexico*, Vol. ii, Pl. 180. On the cross as a form derived from a tree see the observations of W. H. Holmes, in the *Second Annual Report of the Bureau of Ethnology*, pp. 270, 271.

‡ "Au Mexique, le cadre croisé, la croix en sautoir, comme celle

The ancient document called the Mappe Quinatzin offers examples, and its meaning is explained by various early writers. The peculiar character of the Mexican ritual calendar, by which nativities were calculated, favored a plan of representing them in the shape of a cross; as we see in the singular *Codex Cruciformis* of the Boturini-Goupil collection.

33. But the doctrines of Nagualism had a phase even more detestable to the missionaries than any of these, an esoteric phase, which brought it into relation to the libidinous cults of Babylon and the orgies of the "Witches' Sabbaths" of the Dark Ages. Of these occult practices we of course have no detailed descriptions, but there are hints and half-glances which leave us in no doubt.

When the mysterious metamorphosis of the individual into his or her *nagual* was about to take place, the person must strip to absolute nudity;* and the lascivious fury of bands of naked Nagualists, meeting in remote glades by starlight or in the dark recesses of caves, dancing before the statues of the ancient gods, were scenes that stirred the fanaticism of the Spanish missionaries to its highest pitch. Bishop Landa informs us that in Yucatan the dance there known as the *naual* was one of the few in which both men and women took part, and that it "was not very decent." It was afterwards prohibited by the priests. We have excellent authority that such wild rites continued well into the

de St. André, avec quelques variantes, representait le signe de nativité, *tonalli*, la fête, le jour natal." M. Aubin, in Boban, *Catalogue Raisonnée de la Collection Goupil*, Tom. i, p. 227. Both Gomara and Herrera may be quoted to this effect.

* See a curious story from native sources in my *Essays of an Americanist*, pp. 171, 172. It adds that this change can be prevented by casting salt upon the person.

present century, close to the leading cities of the State,* and it is highly likely that they are not unknown today.

34. Moreover, it is certain that among the Nagualists, one of their most revered symbols was the *serpent;* in Chiapas, one of their highest orders of the initiated was that of the *chanes,* or serpents. Not only is this in Christian symbolism the form and sign of the Prince of Evil and the enemy of God, but the missionaries were aware that in the astrological symbols of ancient Mexico the serpent represented the *phallus;* that it was regarded as the most potent of all the signs;† and modern research has shown, contrary to the opinion long held, that there was among these nations an extraordinary and extensive worship of the reciprocal principle of nature, associated with numerous phallic emblems.‡

Huge phalli of stone have been discovered, one, for

---

* Benito Maria de Moxó, *Cartas Mejicanas*, p. 257; Landa, *Cosas de Yucatán*, p. 193.

† Pedro de los Rios, in his notes to the Codex Vaticanus, published in Kingsborough's great work, assigns the sign, *cohautl*, the serpent, to "il membro virile, il maggio augurio di tutti gli altri." It is distinctly so shown on the 75th plate of the Codex. De la Serna states that in his day some of the Mexican conjurors used a wand, around which was fastened a living serpent. *Manual de Ministros*, p. 37.

‡ There is abundant evidence of this in certain plates of the Codex Troano, and there is also alleged to be much in the Codex Mexicanus of the Palais Bourbon. Writing about the latter, M. Aubin said as far back as 1841—"le culte du lingam ou du phallus n'était pas étranger aux Mexicains, ce qu'établissent plusieurs documents peu connus et des sculptures découvertes depuis un petit nombre d'années." His letter is in Boban, *Catalogue Raisonné de la Collection Goupil*, Tom. ii, p. 207. On the frequent identification of the serpent symbol with the phallus in classical art, consult Dr. Anton Nagele's article, "Der Schlangen-Cultus," in the *Zeitschrift für Völkerpsychologie*, Band xvii, p. 285, *seq*.

instance, on the Cerro de las Navajas, not far from the city of Mexico, and another in the State of Hidalgo.* Probably they were used in some such ceremonies as Oviedo describes among the Nahuas of Nicaragua, where the same symbol was represented by conical mounds of earth, around which at certain seasons the women danced with libidinous actions. Although as a general rule the pottery of ancient Mexico avoids obscenity, Brasseur stated that he had seen many specimens of a contrary character from certain regions,† and Dr. Berendt has copied several striking examples, showing curious *yoni* symbols, which are now in my possession.

We may explain these as in some way connected with the worship of Pantecatl, the male divinity who presided over profligate love, and of Tlazolteotl, the *Venus Impudica* of the Aztec pantheon; and it is not without significance that the cave-temple of Votan, whose contents were destroyed by the Bishop of Chiapas, in 1691 (see above, p. 39), was located at *Tlazoaloyan*, both names being derived from a root signifying sexual action.‡ The other name of the divinity, called "the Heart of the Hills," is in Quiche, *Alom*, "he who begets," and the Zapotec *Cozaana*, another analogue of the same deity, is translated by Seler, "the Begetter." Such facts indicate how intimately the esoteric doctrines of Nagualism were related to the worship of the reproductive powers of nature.

---

* Cf. G. Tarayre, *Exploration Minéralogique des Régions Mexicaines*, p. 233 (Paris, 1869), and *Bulletin de la Sociétè d'Anthropologie de Paris*, Juin, 1893.

† *Sources de l'Histoire Primitive de Mexique*, p. 81.

‡ From *zo*, to join together. Compare my *Essays of an Americanist*, p. 417 (Philadelphia, 1890).

35. It will readily be understood from what has been said that Nagualism was neither a pure descendant of the ancient cults, nor yet a derivative from Christian doctrines and European superstitions. It was a strange commingling of both, often in grotesque and absurd forms. In fact, the pretended Christianity of the native population of Mexico today is little more than a figment, according to the testimony of the most competent observers.*

The rituals and prayers of the nagualists bear witness to this. It is very visible in those I have quoted from Nuñez de la Vega, and I can add an interesting example of it which has not heretofore been published. I take it from the MSS. of Father Vicente Hernández Spina, cura of Ixtlavacan, in Guatemala, a remote village of the Quiches. He wrote it down in the native tongue about forty years ago, as recited by an *ah-kih*, "reader of days," a native master of the genethliac art, who had composed it in favor of a client who had asked his intercession.

Prayer of an Ah-Kih.

> O Jesus Christ my God: thou God the Son, with the Father and the Holy Spirit, art my only God. Today, on this day, at this hour, on this day Tihax, I call upon the holy souls which accompany the sun-rising and the sun-setting of the day: with these holy souls I call upon thee, O chief of the genii, thou who dwellest in this mountain of Siba Raxquin: come, ye holy spirits of Juan Vachiac, of Don Domingo Vachiac, of Juan Ixquiaptap, the holy souls of Francisco Excoquieh, of Diego Soom, of Juan Fay, of Alonzo Tzep; I call the holy souls of Diego Tziquin and of Don Pedro Noh: you, O priests, to whom all things are revealed, and thou, chief of the genii, you, lords of the mountains, lords of the plains, thou, Don Purupeto

* "El indio Mexicano es todavia idolatra." F. Pimentel, *La Situacion actual de la Raza Indígena de México*, p. 197.

Martin, come, accept this incense, accept to-day this candle.*

Come also, my mother Holy Mary, the Lord of Esquipulas, the Lord of Capetagua, the beloved Mary of Chiantla, with her who dwells at San Lorenzo, and also Mary of Sorrows, Mary Saint Anna, Mary Tibureia, Mary of Carmen with Saint Michael the Archangel, the captain St. James, St. Christoval, St. Sebastian, St. Nicolas, St. Bonaventura, St. Bernardin, St. Andrew, St. Thomas, St. Bartholomew, and thou my beloved mother St. Catherine, thou beloved Mary of the Conception, Mary of the Rosary, thou lord and king Pascual, be here present.

And thou, Frost, and thou, excellent Wind, thou, God of the plain, thou, God of Quiac-Basulup, thou, God of Retal-Uleu, thou, lord of San Gregorio, thou, lord of Chii-Masa. [These are mountains and localities, and in the original there follow the names of more than a hundred others. The prayer concludes as follows:]

. . . I who appoint myself godfather and godmother, I who ask, I the witness and brother of this man who asks, of this man who makes himself your son, O holy souls, I ask, do not let any evil happen unto him, nor let him be unhappy for any cause.

I the priest, I who speak, I who burn this incense, I who light this candle, I who pray for him, I who take him under my protection, I ask you that he may obtain his subsistence with facility. Thou, God, canst provide him with money; let him not fall ill of fever; I ask that he shall not become paralytic; that he may not choke with severe coughing; that he be not bitten by a serpent; that he become neither bloated nor asthmatic; that he do not go mad; that he be not bitten by a dog; that he be not struck by lightning; that he be not choked with brandy; that he be not killed with iron, nor by a stick, and that he be not carried off by an eagle; guard him, O clouds; aid him, O lightning; aid him, O thunder; aid him, St. Peter; aid him,

* The "holy souls" who are here appealed to by name are those of deceased *ah-kih*, or priests of the native cult.

St. Paul; aid him, eternal Father.

And I who up to this time have spoken for him to you, I ask you that sickness may visit his enemies. So order it, that when his enemies go forth from their houses, they may meet sickness; order it, that wherever they go, they may meet troubles; do your offices of injury to them, wheresoever they are met; do this that I pray, O holy souls. God be with you; God the Father, God the Son, God the Holy Spirit: Amen, Jesus.

Most of such invocations are expressed in terms far more recondite and symbolic than the above. We have many such preserved in the work of Jacinto de la Serna, which supply ample material to acquaint us with the peculiarities of the sacred and secret language of the nagualists. I shall quote but one, that employed in the curious ceremony of "calling back the *tonal*," referred to on a previous page. I append an explanation of its obscure metaphors.

Invocation for the Restitution of the Tonal.

Ho there! Come to my aid, mother mine of the skirt of precious stones![1] What keeps thee away, gray ghost, white ghost?[2] Is the obstacle white, or is it yellow? See, I place here the yellow enchantment and the white enchantment.[3]

I, the Master of the Masters of enchantments, have come, I, who formed thee and gave thee life.[4] Thou, mother mine of the starry skirt, thou, goddess of the stars, who givest life, why hast thou turned against this one?[5]

Adverse spirit and darkened star, I shall sink thee in the breadth and depth of the waters.[6] I, master of spells, speak to thee. Ho there! Mother mine, whose skirt is made of gems, come, seek with me the shining spirit who dwells in the house of light,[7] that we may know what god or mighty power thus destroys and crushes to earth this unfortunate one. Green and black spirit of sickness, leave him and seek thy prey elsewhere.

Green and yellow ghost, who art wandering, as if lost, over mountains and plains, I seek thee, I desire thee; return to him whom thou hast abandoned. Thou, the nine times beaten, the nine times smitten, see that thou fail me not.[8] Come hither, mother mine, whose robe is of precious gems; one water, two waters; one rabbit, two rabbits; one deer, two deers; one alligator, two alligators.[9]

Lo! I myself am here; I am most furious; I make the loudest noise of all; I respect no one; even sticks and stones tremble before me. What god or mighty power dare face me, me, a child of gods and goddesses?[10] I have come to seek and call back the tonal of this sick one, wherever it is, whithersoever it has wandered, be it nine times wandered, even unto the nine junctures and the nine unions.[11] Wherever it is, I summon it to return, I order it to return, and to heal and clean this heart and this head."

Explanations.

1. The appeal is to Water, regarded as the universal Mother. The "skirt of precious stones" refers to the green of the precious green stones, a color sacred to water.

2. The question is addressed to the *tonal.*

3. The yellow enchantment is tobacco; the white, a cup of water.

4. That is, assigned the form of the nagual belonging to the sick man.

5. This appeal is directed to the Milky Way.

6. The threat is addressed to the *tonal*, to frighten it into returning.

7. The "shining spirit" is the Fire-god.

8. The yellow tobacco, prepared ceremonially in the manner indicated.

9. These are names of days in the native calendar which are invoked.

10. The priest speaks in the person of his god.

11. Referring to the Nahuatl belief that there are nine upper and nine under worlds.

From the same work of de la Serna I collect the following list of symbolic expressions. It might easily be extended, but these will be sufficient to show the figurative obscurities which they threw around their formulas of conjuration, but which were by no means devoid of coherence and instruction to those who could understand them.

Symbolic Expressions of the Nagualists.

Blood.—"The red woman with snakes on her gown" (referring to the veins).

Copal Gum.—"The white woman" (from the whitish color of the fresh gum).

Cords (for carrying burdens).—"The snake that does woman's work" (because women sit still to knit, and the cord works while itself is carried).

Drunkenness.—"My resting time," or "when I am getting my breath."

The Earth.—"The mirror that smokes" (because of the mists that rise from it); "the rabbit with its mouth upward" (the rabbit, in opposition to the one they see in the moon; with its mouth upward, because of the mists which rise from it like the breath exhaled from the mouth); "the flower which contains everything" (as all fruit proceeds from flowers, so does all vegetable life proceed from the earth, which is therefore spoken of as a flower); "the flower which bites the mouths" (a flower, for the reason given; it eats the mouths, because all things necessarily return to it, and are swallowed by it).

Fingers.—"The five fates," or "the five works," or "the five fields" (because by the use of his fingers man works out his own destiny. Hence also the worship of the Hand among the Nahuas as the god Maitl, and among the Mayas as the god Kab, both which words mean "hand").

Fire.—"Our Father of the Four Reeds" (because the

ceremony of making the new fire was held on the day Four Reeds, 4 Acatl); "the shining rose;" " the yellow flyer"; "the red-haired one;" "the yellow spirit."

A Knife of Copper.—"The yellow Chichimec" (because the Chichimecs were alleged to tear out the bowels of their enemies).

The Maguey Plant.—"My sister, the eight in a row" (because it was planted in this manner).

A Road.—"That which is divided in two, and yet has neither beginning, middle nor end" (because it always lies in two directions from a person, and yet all roads lead into others and thus never end).

Sickness.—"The red woman"; "the breath of the flame;" "our mother the comet " (all referring to the fever); "the Chichimec" (because it aims to destroy life, like these savage warriors); "the spider" (because of its venomous nature).

Smoke.—"The old wife" (i.e., of the fire).

The Sun.—"Our holy and pockified Uncle" (referring to the myth of Nanahuatl, who was syphilitic, and leaping into the flames of a fire rose as the sun).

Tobacco.—"The nine (or seven) times beaten" (because for sacred purposes it was rubbed up this number of times); "the enchanted gray one" (from its color and use in conjuring).

Water.—"The Green Woman" (from the greenness which follows moisture); "our Mother, whose robe is of precious stones" (from the green or vegetable life resembling the turquoise, emerald, jade, etc.).

36. It might be asked how the dark arts and secret ceremonies of the Nagualists escaped the prying eyes of the officers of the Holy Inquisition, which was established in Mexico in 1571. The answer is that the inquisitors were instructed by Cardinal Diego de Espinosa, who at that time was Inquisitor General and President of the Council of the Indies, "to abstain from proceedings against Indians,

because of their stupidity and incapacity, as well as scant instruction in the Holy Catholic faith, for the crimes of heresy, apostasy, heretical blasphemy, sorcery, incantations, superstitions," etc.

Energetic inquisitors, however, conceded very grudgingly this exemption. In the imposing *auto de fé* celebrated in the city of Mexico, in 1659, a half-breed, Bernardo del Carpio by name, son of a full-blood Indian mother, accused of blasphemy, etc., endeavored to escape the Holy Office by pleading his Indian blood; but his appeal was disallowed, and the precedent established that any admixture whatever of European blood brought the accused within the jurisdiction of the Inquisition.* Even this seems to have been a concession, for we find the record of an *auto da fé* held in 1609, in the province of Tehuantepec, in which eight full-blood natives were punished for worshiping the goddess Pinopiaa.† Mr. David Ferguson, however, who has studied extensively the records of the inquisition in Mexico, informs me that in none of the trials read by him has he observed any charges of Nagualism, although many white persons were accused, and some tried, for consulting Indian sorcerers.

37. It will be seen from what I have said, that the rites of Nagualism extended as widely as did the term over Mexico and Central America. It becomes, therefore, of importance to discover from what linguistic stock this term

* See the *Relacion del Auto celebrado en México, año de oficio 1659* (México, En la Imprenta del Santo Officio, 1659).

† J. B. Carriedo, *Estudios Históricos del Estado Oaxaqueño*, Tom. i, pp 8, 9 (Oaxaca, 1849). About 1640 a number of Indians in the province of Acapulco were put to death for having buried enchanted ashes beneath the floor of a chapel! (Serna, *Manual de Ministros*, p. 52.)

and its associated words are derived. From that source it is reasonable to suppose the rites of this superstition also had their origin.

The opinions on this subject have been diverse and positive. Most writers have assumed that it is a Nahuatl, or pure Mexican, word; while an eminent authority, Dr. Stoll, is not less certain that it is from a radical belonging to the neighboring great stock of the Mayan dialects, and especially the Quiche, of Guatemala.* Perhaps both these positions are erroneous, and we must look elsewhere for the true etymology of these expressions. Unquestionably they had become domesticated in both Maya and Nahuatl; but there is some reason to think they were loan-words, belonging to another, and perhaps more venerable, civilization than either of these nations could claim.

To illustrate this I shall subjoin several series of words derived from the same radical which is at the basis of the word nagual, the series, three in number, being taken from the three radically diverse, though geographically contiguous, linguistic stocks, the Maya, the Zapotec and the Nahuatl.

From the Maya, of Yucatan.

Naual, or *nautal,* a native dance, forbidden by the missionaries.

Naatil, talent, skill, ability.

Naat, intelligence, wisdom.

Naatah, to understand, to divine.

---

* "Nagual ist in seiner correcten Form *naoal* ein echtes Quiché-Wort, ein Substantivum instrumentale, vom Stamme naó, wissen, erkennen. *Naoal* ist dasjenige, womit oder woran etwas, in diesem Falle das Schiksal des Kindes, erkaunt wird, und hat mit dem mexikanischen *nahualli* (Hexe), mit dem man es vielleicht in Verbindung bringen möchte, nichts zu schaffen." *Guatemala*, s. 238.

Nanaol, to consider, to contemplate, to meditate, to commune with one-self, to enter into oneself.

Noh, great, skillful; as *noh ahceh,* a skillful hunter.

From Maya Dialects.

QUICHE-CAKCHIQUEL

Naual, a witch or sorcerer.

Naualin, to tell fortunes, to predict the future.

Qui naualin, to sacrifice, to offer sacrifices.

Na, to feel, to suspect, to divine, to think in one's heart.

Nao, to know, to be alert or expert in something.

Naol, a skillful person, a rhetorician.

Naotizan, to make another intelligent or astute.

Natal, the memory.

Natub, the soul or shadow of a man.

Noh, the god of reason ("Genius der Vernunft," Scherzer).

Noh, to fecundate, to impregnate *(Popol Vuh).*

TZENTAL

X-qna, to know.

X-qnaulai, to know often or thoroughly (frequentative).

Naom, wise, astute *(naom vinic,* hombre sabio).

Naoghi, art, science.

Naoghibal, memory.

Ghnaoghel, a wise man.

Alaghom naom, the Goddess of Wisdom.

From the Zapotec, of Oaxaca.

Nana, gana, góna, to know.

Nona, to know thoroughly, to retain in the memory.

Nana ticha, or *nona lii,* a wise man.

Guela nana, or *guela nona,* wisdom, knowledge.

Hue gona, or *ro gona,* a teacher, a master.

Nu lii, truth; *ni na lii,* that which is true.

Naciña, or *naciina,* skill, dexterity.

Hui naa, a medicine man, a "nagualist."

Nahaa, to speak pleasantly or agreeably.

Nayaa, or *nayapi,* to speak easily or fluently.

Rigoo gona, to sacrifice, to offer sacrifice.

Ni nana, the understanding, the intelligence, generally.

Nayanii, the superior reason of man.

Nayaa, Naguii, superiority, a superior man (gentileza, gentil hombre).

From the Nahuatl, of Mexico.

Naua, to dance, holding each other by the hands.

Naualli, a sorcerer, magician, enchanter.

Navallotl, magic, enchantment, witchcraft.

Nauatl, or *nahuatl,* skillful, astute, smart; hence, superior; applied to language, clear, well-sounding, whence (perhaps) the name of the tongue.

Nauati, to speak clearly and distinctly.

Nauatlato, an interpreter.

38. I believe that no one can carefully examine these lists of words, all taken from authorities well acquainted with the several tongues, and writing when they still retained their original purity, without acknowledging that the same radical or syllable underlies them all; and further, that from the primitive form and rich development of

this radical in the Zapotec, it looks as if we must turn to it to recognize the origin of all these expressions, both in the Nahuatl and the Maya linguistic stocks.

The root *na*, to know, is the primitive monosyllabic stem to which we trace all of them. *Nahual* means knowledge, especially mystic knowledge, the Gnosis, the knowledge of the hidden and secret things of nature; easily enough confounded in uncultivated minds with sorcery and magic.*

It is very significant that neither the radical *na* nor any of its derivatives are found in the Huasteca dialect of the Mayan tongue, which was spoken about Tampico, far removed from other members of the stock. The inference is that in the southern dialects it was a borrowed stem.

Nor in the Nahuatl language—although its very name is derived from it†—does the radical *na* appear in its simplicity and true significance. To the Nahuas, also, it must have been a loan.

It is true that de la Serna derives the Mexican *naualli*, a sorcerer, from the verb *nahualtia*, to mask or disguise oneself, "because a *naualli* is one who masks or disguises himself under the form of some lower animal, which is his *nagual*";‡ but it is altogether likely that *nahualtia* derived its meaning from the custom of the medicine men to wear masks during their ceremonies.

---

* The Abbé Brasseur observes: "Le mot *nahaul*, qui veut dire toute science, ou science de tout, est fréquemment employé pour exprimer la sorcellerie chez ces populations." *Bulletin de la Societé de Géographie*, 1857, p. 290. In another passage of his works the speculative Abbé translates *naual* by the English "know all," and is not averse to believing that the latter is but a slight variant of the former.

† See an article by me, entitled "On the Words 'Anahuac' and 'Nahuatl,'" in the *American Antiquarian*, for November, 1893.

‡ *Manual de Ministros*, p. 50.

Therefore, if the term *nagual*, and many of its associates and derivatives, were at first borrowed from the Zapotec language, a necessary corollary of this conclusion is, that along with these terms came most of the superstitions, rites and beliefs to which they allude; which thus became grafted on the general tendency to such superstitions existing everywhere and at all times in the human mind.

Along with the names of the days and the hieroglyphs which mark them, and the complicated arithmetical methods by means of which they were employed, were carried most of the doctrines of the Nagualists, and the name by which they in time became known from central Mexico quite to Nicaragua and beyond.

The mysterious words have now, indeed, lost much of their ancient significance. In a recent dictionary of the Spanish of Mexico *nagual* is defined as "a witch; a word used to frighten children and make them behave,"* while in Nicaragua, where the former Nahuatl population has left so many traces of its presence in the language of today, the word *nagual* no longer means an actor in the black art, or a knowledge of it, but his or her armamentarium, or the box, jar or case in which are kept the professional apparatus, the talismans and charms, which constitute the stock in trade or outfit of the necromancer.†

Among the Lacandons, of Mayan stock, who inhabit the forests on the upper waters of the Usumacinta river, at the present day the term *naguate* or *nagutlat* is said to be applied to any one "who is entitled to respect and obedi-

---

* Jesús Sánchez, *Glosario de Voces Castellanas derivadas del Idioma Nahuatl*, sub voce.

† "*Nagual*—el lugar, rincón, cajon, nambira, etc., donde guarda sus talismanes y trajes de encanta la bruja." Berendt, *La Lengua Castellana de Nicaragua*, MS.

ence by age and merit;"* but in all probability he is also believed to possess superior and occult knowledge.

39. All who have any acquaintance with the folklore of the world are aware that the notion of men and women having the power to change themselves into beasts is as wide as superstition itself and older than history. It is mentioned in the pages of Herodotus and in the myths of ancient Assyria. It is the property of African negroes, and the peasantry of Europe still hold to their faith in the reality of the were-wolf of Germany, the *loup-garou* of France and the *lupo mannaro* of Italy. Dr. Richard Andrée well says in his interesting study of the subject: "He who would explain the origin of this strange superstition must not approach it as a national or local manifestation, but as one universal in its nature; not as the property of one race or family, but of the species and its psychology at large."†

Even in such a detail as the direct connection of the name of the person with his power of change do we find extraordinary parallelisms between the superstition of the red man of America and the peasant of Germany. As in Mexico the *nagual* was assigned to the infant by a form of baptism, so in Europe the peasants of east Prussia hold that if the godparent at the time of naming and baptism thinks of a wolf, the infant will acquire the power of becoming one; and in Hesse to pronounce the name of the person in the presence of the animal into which he has been changed will restore him to human shape.‡

---

* Emetorio Pineda, *Descripcion Geográfica de Chiapas y Soconusco*, p. 23 (México, 1845).

† See his article "Wer-wolf," in his *Ethnographische Parallelen und Vergleiche*, p. 62, seq.

‡ Richard Andrée, *ibid.*, ss. 63, 64.

40. I need not say that the doctrine of personal spirits is not especially Mexican, nor yet American; it belongs to man in general, and can be recognized in most religions and many philosophies. In ancient Greece both the Platonicians and later the Neo-Platonicians thought that each individual has a particular spirit, or *daimon*, in whom is enshrined his or her moral personality. To this *daimon* he should address his prayers, and should listen heedfully to those interior promptings which seem to arise in the mind from some unseen silent monitor.*

Many a member of the Church of Rome substitutes for the *daimon* of the Platonists the patron saint after whom he is named, or whom he has chosen from the calendar, the hagiology, of his Church. This analogy did not fail to strike the early missionaries, and they saw in the Indian priest selecting the *nagual* of the child a hideous and diabolical caricature of the holy rites.

But what was their horror when they found that the similarity proceeded so far that the pagan priest also performed a kind of baptismal sacrament with water; and that in the Mexican picture writing the sign which represents the natal day, the *tonal*, by which the individual demon is denoted, was none other than the sign of the cross, as we have seen. This left no doubt as to the devilish origin of the whole business, which was further supported by the wondrous thaumaturgic powers of its professors.

41. How are we to explain these marvelous statements? It will not do to take the short and easy road of saying they are all lies and frauds. The evidence is too abundant for us to doubt that there was skillful jugglery among the proficients in the occult arts among those nations. They

* See Alfred Maury, *La Magie et l'Astrologie*, pp. 88, 89, 267, etc.

could rival their colleagues in the East Indies and Europe, if not surpass them.

Moreover, is there anything incredible in the reports of the spectators? Are we not familiar with the hypnotic or mesmeric conditions in which the subject sees, hears and feels just what the master tells him to feel and see? The tricks of cutting oneself or others, of swallowing broken glass, of handling venomous reptiles, are well-known performances of the sect of the Aissaoua in northern Africa, and nowadays one does not have to go off the boulevards of Paris to see them repeated. The phenomena of thought transference, of telepathy, of clairvoyance, of spiritual rappings, do but reiterate under the clear light of the close of the nineteenth century the mystical thaumaturgy with which these children of nature were familiar centuries ago in the New World, and which are recorded of the theosophists and magicians of Egypt, Greece and Rome.* So long as many intelligent and sensible people among ourselves find all explanations of these modern phenomena inadequate and unsatisfactory, we may patiently wait for a complete solution of those of a greater antiquity.

42. The conclusion to which this study of Nagualism lends is, that it was not merely the belief in a personal guardian spirit, as some have asserted; not merely a survival of fragments of the ancient heathenism, more or less diluted by Christian teachings, as others have maintained; but that above and beyond these, it was a powerful secret organi-

* In the *Notice Préliminaire* to the second part of his work, *La Magie et l'Astrologie dans l'Antiquité et au Moyen Age*, Mr. Alfred Maury admirably sums up the scientific resources at our command for explaining the mystical phenomena of experience, without denying their reality as actual occurrences.

zation, extending over a wide area, including members of different languages and varying culture, bound together by mystic rites, by necromantic powers and occult doctrines; but, more than all, by one intense emotion—hatred of the whites—and by one unalterable purpose—that of their destruction, and with them the annihilation of the government and religion which they had introduced.

Arete Communications

Publishers of Self-Transformation books and videos

Books and videos are available at all serious bookstores or from
Arete Communications by mail or on our website.
When ordering by mail, add $5.00 for postage within the U.S.
Outside the U.S., add $14 for air mail.
Add $1.00 for each additional book, music CD or video.

773 Center Boulevard #58
Fairfax, CA 94978-0058

Distributors

In North America:

DeVorss
(800) 843-5743 • Camarillo, California

New Leaf
(800) 326-2665 • Lithia Springs, Georgia

Baker & Taylor
(800) 775-1800 • Charlotte, North Carolina

For a full selection of books, videos and music, see
www.Gurdjieff-Legacy.Org

The First Video Trilogy of The Fourth Way

The Life & Significance of George Ivanovitch Gurdjieff

Each Video a Gold Award Winner for Biography at Worldfest, One of the Oldest & Most Prestigious International Film & Video Festivals

---

Gurdjieff's Legacy Part III

Establishing The Teaching in the West 1924–49

$29.95 • Color video • 1 hr. 26 min.
DVD ISBN 978-1-879514-72-0

Monte Carlo, London, Lyne Place, New York and Mendham. Gurdjieff's life is traced from his near-fatal car crash in 1924 and the closing of the Institute at the Prieuré, to the writing of his Legominism, *All and Everything*, his work with the Rope, the meetings he held during the Nazi occupation of Paris, the return of his students after the war and his death in 1949.

Gurdjieff's Mission Part II

Introducing The Teaching to the West

$29.95 • Color video • 1 hr. 10 min.
DVD ISBN 978-1-879514-71-3

Based on William Patrick Patterson's *Struggle of the Magicians*, shot on-site in St. Petersburg, Moscow, Constantinople, London, Paris and New York, the video follows Gurdjieff from his arrival in Russia in 1912 through to 1924. Having finally established his Institute for the Harmonious Development of Man in France, he risked all in a make-or-break gamble to take the teaching to America.

Gurdjieff in Egypt Part I

The Origin of Esoteric Knowledge

$29.95 • Color video • 60 min.
DVD ISBN 978-1-879514-51-5

Exploration, discovery, struggle and adversity, all occurring amidst continual geopolitical upheaval—this was the outer life of George Ivanovitch Gurdjieff. Shot on-site at the Giza Plateau, Thebes, Temple of Man, Karnak Temple complex, Valley of the Kings, Tomb of Tuthmoses III and the Temple of Edfu, this documentary follows Gurdjieff's search for—and discovery of—the origin of esoteric knowledge.

$19.95 • 416 pp. • 6 X 9
New Revised Edition
Color Gallery of Author Paintings
ISBN 978-1-879514-77-5

Eating The "I"

A Direct Account of The Fourth Way—The Way of Using Ordinary Life to Come to Real Life

by William Patrick Patterson

"*Eating The 'I'* is about as good as it gets. Patterson is an excellent writer, with a gifted novelist's ability to capture a character through a few lines of dialogue or seemingly casual notes on expression or dress. Patterson's work is in a class with Christopher Isherwood's devastatingly frank, and brilliant, story of his spiritual quest, *My Guru and His Disciple.*

"The author was a member of a New York Gurdjieff group under the direction of the legendary Lord John Pentland, the British aristocrat appointed by Gurdjieff himself to head the Work in America. Pentland fulfilled this task consummately until his death in 1984, and *Eating the 'I'* culminates with an account of Lord Pentland's funeral."

—Robert S. Ellwood, Chairman
Department of Religion, USC

"Patterson has two fine Irish gifts: a vivid memory and a storyteller's ear. Paced like a novel, this spiritual autobiography is certain to appeal to those who want a rare and engaging inside glimpse of the Gurdjieff Work."

—Stephan Bodian, Editor, *Yoga Journal*

"*Eating The 'I'* gives as full a picture of the Work as it may be possible to get without joining it. It comes from a great depth and carries much conviction. Readers will taste this teaching in action and will also get an extraordinary glimpse of an extraordinary teacher—Lord John Pentland, the British businessman who as president of the Gurdjieff Foundation brought the Gurdjieff Work to life for so many people."

—Richard Smoley, Editor, *Gnosis*

"I am sure Eating The 'I' will be one of the more important writings on the Gurdjieff Work, after Ouspensky's In Search of the Miraculous."

—Miguel Serrano, Author, *Serpent in Paradise*

$19.95 • 354 pp. • 5.5 x 8.5
Second Edition, References, Notes, Bibliography, Index
ISBN 978-1-879514-02-7

Struggle of the Magicians
Exploring the Teacher-Student Relationship
by William Patrick Patterson

"Yes, what an excellent book—full of things I didn't know. A real contribution to our understanding of Gurdjieff and Ouspensky."
—Colin Wilson, author
The Strange Life of P. D. Ouspensky

"The central focus of the book is the sacred, archetypal relationship of the Master and disciple. This revealing look at the roles of Guru and disciple in the compelling work of self-transformation makes the book of special interest and value to those on any path."
—*Light of Consciousness*

"One of the most exhilarating accounts of the history of the Fourth Way. Ouspensky, Orage and Bennett were exceptional men, possessed of genius, but men nevertheless, with weaknesses and flaws."
—*Gnosis*

$14.95 • 176 pp. • 5.5 x 8.5
References, Notes, Bibliography, Appendices, Index
ISBN 978-1-879514-10-2

Taking with the Left Hand
Origin of the Enneagram, Fellowship of Friends & Spiritual Theft
by William Patrick Patterson

"A lucid and compelling account of conflict and charlatanism surrounding one of the most important spiritual movements of our day. A 'white paper' for those concerned about the fate of the Gurdjieff movement, and a case study of contemporary spiritual movements."
—Robert S. Ellwood, Chairman
Department of Religion, USC

"In this collection of three essays about various aspects of the legacy of the influential spiritual teachings of G. I. Gurdjieff, the author tackles the enneagram craze, the teachings of Boris Mouravieff and a Gurdjieff splinter group, expanding his discussion of these relatively parochial issues to raise more universal questions about the nature and transmission of spiritual truth."
—*Publishers Weekly*

$27.95 • 248 pp. • 5.5 x 8.5 • Hardcover
(No softcover printing.)
Photos, Notes, Index
ISBN 978-1-879514-05-8

BOYHOOD WITH GURDJIEFF

by Fritz Peters
With an introduction
by William Patrick Patterson

We are pleased to announce the quality hardcover reissue of the classic account of a youngboy'slifeinthe1920swithG.I.Gurdjieff, one of the seminal spiritual teachers of the last century. Long out of print, this account of a young boy's five-year relationship with G. I. Gurdjieff at the Prieuré (1924–29) is now reissued in a special hardcover edition which includes an introduction by William Patrick Patterson, photos and notes.

"Fritz Peters portrays his vivid impressions of life at the Prieuré, that 'small world that would reproduce the conditions of the larger, outside world,' with the same artistry and awareness of the inner life of the young that he showed in his exceptional first novel *Finistère*. The expansive range and interplay of human feelings and relationships that emerge out of the many amusing, sometimes sorrowful events that Peters reports, evoke a sense of community life at the Prieuré that pulsates with intelligence. *Boyhood with Gurdjieff* remains a unique account of Gurdjieff's knowledge of life and people, and how he used this knowledge to create a house for 'work.' Each of the book's brief chapters is a gem in itself."

—*Material for Thought*

September 2009

GURDJIEFF REMEMBERED

by Fritz Peters
With an introduction
by William Patrick Patterson
Photos, Notes, Index

ISBN 978-1-879514-03-4

October 2008

A Woman's Work

with Gurdjieff, Ramana Maharshi, Krishnamurti & Anandamayi Ma

The Spiritual Life Story of Ethel Merston

by Mary Ellen Korman

ISBN 978-1-879514-07-2

Spring 2008

Conscious Survival

In a Radically Changing World Time

by William Patrick Patterson

Hardcover • $24.95

ISBN 978-1-879514-87-4

2009

The Rise & Fall of the New Age

by William Patrick Patterson

ISBN 978-1-879514-98-0